J.S. Bach's Sacred Cantatas:
A Cultural Christian's Companion

Volume 1: Advent to Easter

J.S. Bach's Sacred Cantatas:
A Cultural Christian's Companion

Volume 1: Advent to Easter

Thelma Lovell

Da Capo Books

Copyright © Thelma Lovell 2025

Thelma Lovell has asserted her moral right to be identified as the author of this Work in accordance with the Copyright, Designs and Patents Act 1988

First published in 2025 by Da Capo Books, an imprint of Lulu.com

Set in 12/12.5/14 Georgia

ISBN 978-1-300-61803-4

To Julia and Rob

The fact is that people can only react to the emotions expressed in a work of art according to their own capacity to feel those emotions...Music is no more incapable of being emotionally intelligible because it is bound by the laws of musical construction, than poetry is because it is bound by the laws of verbal grammatical construction. In fact, in both cases, it should be a truism to say that that the construction of a work of art is guided both by the feelings and the intellect: the intellect brings craftsmanship to bear on realising the overall shape which is *felt* before it is intellectually apprehended.

Deryck Cooke: *The Language of Music*

Contents

Preface	1
Introduction	5
Brief Glossary of Musical Terms	37
A Note on Performance	39
December: Prefatory Note	40
BWV 61	42
BWV 62	49
BWV 36	54
BWV 132	59
BWV 63	65
BWV 91	72
BWV 110	78
BWV 40	84
BWV 121	91
BWV 57	97
BWV 64	105
BWV 133	111
BWV 151	116
BWV 152	121
BWV 28	128
BWV 122	134
January: Prefatory Note	140
BWV 190	141
BWV 41	148
BWV 16	154
BWV 171	160
BWV 153	166
BWV 58	173
BWV 65	178
BWV 123	185

BWV 154	191
BWV 124	198
BWV 32	203
BWV 155	209
BWV 3	214
BWV 13	220
BWV 73	226
BWV 111	232
BWV 72	237
BWV 156	243
BWV 81	250
BWV 14	255
February: Prefatory Note	261
BWV 83	262
BWV 125	267
BWV 82	273
BWV 71	280
BWV 144	287
BWV 92	292
BWV 84	300
BWV 18	305
BWV 126	311
BWV 181	317
BWV 22	322
BWV 23	328
BWV 127	334
BWV 159	340
March: Prefatory Note	346
BWV 182	347
BWV 1	354
BWV 4	361
BWV 31	368
A Note on Translations	375

Sources and Select Bibliography   376

Acknowledgements   384

Index of Cantatas (BWV Number)   385

Preface

Let us (since life can little more supply
Than just to look about us and to die)
Expatiate free o'er all this scene of man;
A mighty maze! but not without a plan

                    Alexander Pope: *An Essay on Man*

The purpose of this book – the first of three volumes – is to present a new guide to J.S. Bach's sacred cantatas. Who is it intended for, and why might it be useful?

    To begin with, it fills a gap, as there is no recent comprehensive guide intended for the intellectually curious but non-specialist reader. Writing about music both accurately and clearly is always a challenge, especially when, as in this case, the whole project has to be related to a great hinterland of religious beliefs and assumptions whose contours have shifted over the centuries. Whether familiar or alien to the present-day listener, they were undeniably the background and motive force for the music of Bach's sacred cantatas.

    Reflecting both the man and his time, these works contain music that continues to inspire and console, even though their original function is remote from the world of today. Composed in the first half of the eighteenth century, they were settings of Lutheran religious texts – sermons in music, in fact, inserted into weekly church services – and their expressive power was dedicated to a particular set of values and view of life's purpose.

    While the overriding aim of this guide is to give the reader a closer understanding and appreciation of Bach's music – suggesting how and why it achieves its effects – it invites the cantatas into a wider space. To make complete sense of them calls for a sympathetic, though not uncritical, historical imagination and cultural perspective. Above all, we need to recognise that embedded in the cantata texts are certain universal fears and hopes, especially regarding mortality and the incurable human need to find meaning in life.

Hence the reference to the "cultural Christian" – not a precise term, but one that includes those who, while disinclined (reasonably enough) to believe in miracles, find themselves in sympathy with certain aspects of Christian belief. These may be ethical, socially pragmatic, or philosophical, in the sense that humans have forever leaned toward the idea of something universal and unchanging behind the shifts of time and circumstances. If religions have failed to identify this elusive factor, it has not been for want of trying.

As in its progression through the ages the Christian narrative has inspired countless products of the artistic imagination, here too it may attract fellow travellers through its potent iconography of life and death – of idealised motherhood, the suffering of an innocent man, the shameful brutality of the crucifixion. Bach's sacred cantatas are themselves part of this heritage, with their delights accessible to all who care to listen. But the words also count and are incontrovertibly religious; the present book engages with them – as it must – but tries to show how the music lifted them into a further, less bounded, dimension of meaning.

As each cantata account stands by itself, the reader may dip in and out as required. The sections are organised according to the Church calendar, following its week-by-week trajectory. After supplying the basic information about the date of composition and the librettist (if known), I explain the sweep of the narrative, integrating the text into a description of the form and style of each movement. There is some technical analysis, not as an end in itself but rather to give some idea of the means by which Bach interpreted verbal concepts in the language of music.

In a fundamental sense, this book is also a work of translation, suggesting possibilities of exchange between today's conceptual vocabulary and that of another time and place. My intention is to look at the larger picture, without which it is impossible to understand the framing of the cantatas: the theological certainties, the intimate knowledge of scripture, the actual physical precariousness of life, the historical experience of war and plague that informed the outlook of the writers of the texts, and the long memory of defiance that was embedded in the Lutheran imagination.

Such factors shape the psychological parameters of the world of Bach's sacred cantatas, with their sense of human frailty, and humility in the face of an imagined higher power. The dark side of this was an inclination to self-disgust and a fear of not passing muster with God in the afterlife. One's own self became the battle ground on which the forces of evil struggled with the faltering aspiration toward the divine ideal.

I have attempted to give a sense of each work as a unique artistic statement – although of course there are many shared stylistic features and expressive tropes that are the trademarks of the composer and the common musical vocabulary of his time. While the guide consists of many separate units, the whole can be thought of as a mosaic which builds up, piece by piece, some idea of an orientation that helped people navigate the pain and randomness of life. True, the librettists were all distinct personalities (though Bach worked with some of them multiple times), but we should not be distracted by the narcissism of small differences. The essential picture hardly changes: that this life brings inevitable suffering, and those who hold fast to the vision of a better world after death will gain their everlasting reward.

The beliefs that permeate the cantatas are ingrained in many people's cultural history. We may or may not have consciously discarded them, but we need to understand them if we are to have full access to the musical glories that Bach produced in their honour; he placed all his creative powers at the service of his faith. There were of course many other composers who produced sacred cantatas. Bach, though, has global reach as one of the giants of the artistic universe.

Though settling for a fairly modest status in his lifetime (1685–1750), he emerged as one of those towering figures whose creative imagination transcends boundaries of time and place. As a master manipulator of sound in his interplay of pattern, style, textures, and rhythms, expressive melodies and sheer energy of invention, he is peerless – enticing the listener with vivid and fascinating details, yet fusing the sensuous appeal of music with supreme command of form.

To call Bach "mathematical" (as some occasionally do) is to forget that his control of structure is an integral part of a highly charged emotionalism. The result is a kind of brinkmanship: a permanent tension between musical hints of wildness and dissolution and the composer's focused gaze on the greater whole. Imagination and security find a way to coexist. This is the great secret of an aesthetic appeal that continues to the present day; to listen with pleasure to Bach is to absorb unwittingly a view of the universe in which all, in the end, will be well.

Introduction

Without Bach, God would be an entirely second-rate figure.

Emil Cioran: *Newsweek*

A classic is a work which persists as background noise even when a present that is totally incompatible with it holds sway.

Italo Calvino: *Why Read the Classics?* trans. Martin McLaughlin

The subject of this book is the sacred cantatas of J.S. Bach, arranged according to the calendar of the Church year. Taking their place in Lutheran worship, they were psychodramas of faith, acting out and resolving the mental conflicts caused by the struggle to believe in a divinely ordained and ultimately benevolent order. Numerous writers of a theological and literary disposition supplied the texts, which in Bach's hands were allied to – one might almost say transformed into – music of extraordinary vitality and expressive range.

The cantatas reflect an entire philosophy of life, seen through the lens of the Christian belief of that time and place. This holds (among other things) that the human individual is weak but may lean on a power beyond the self. Life is bound to be tough; there are moments of despair but not resentment, for hope of another, better world in the hereafter sustains the mortal journey. For such a hope to be realised, the precondition is faith: God will take care of his own.

The general format of the cantatas is a succession of movements varying in style and texture. Each of them has its own story to tell. Solo arias expressing a particular emotional state are usually melodic, in contrast with the more speech-like character of recitative. There are vocal duets and trios, and richly imaginative choruses that often set the scene at the beginning of a cantata. A four-part harmonisation of a traditional hymn is virtually always the conclusion. The congregation probably joined in, for such chorales were the shared property of the entire community: a means of bonding with fellow believers, past and present.

These works of Bach are one example among many of the close partnership of art with religious belief. Here, while the words may point the mind in a certain direction, it is the music that gives them new life by awakening a powerful and irresistible emotional response. When the two elements – the verbal and the musical – are in lockstep we might wonder to what extent the pleasure given by the music implies at least some sympathy with the message of the text. That was certainly Bach's purpose, which was, by means of his creative skill, to support and strengthen the religious convictions of his audience.

~

Born into a long-established musical family in 1685, Johann Sebastian Bach was a product of the Lutheran heartland of central Germany. In his early youth he began learning the craft of a working musician; his gifts were soon recognised and he was appointed at the age of eighteen to his first post as organist at Arnstadt. A few years later, in 1707, he moved to a similar position in Mühlhausen, and after spells of working at the princely courts of Weimar and Köthen he became, in 1723, director of church music for the city of Leipzig. Here he stayed until his death in 1750. Although he had been composing church cantatas at least as early as his time in Mühlhausen (secular works are not included in this book), the majority were produced, one per week, in five yearly cycles, in Leipzig; many have been lost. There Bach had particular responsibilities for the churches of St. Nicholas and St. Thomas, of which he was appointed Cantor.

With its long history as a trading centre, Leipzig was a prosperous city with a population of about 30,000. As with all societies, it contained a number of strata, from the élite merchants and professionals to artisans, shopkeepers and servants. The Sunday services were important events. About a third of the citizens attended at one church or another, and the buildings were packed: St. Nicholas's contained around 2,500 pews, each with its own designated occupant, and with standing room for another 500 people. The bells pealed their summons at 7.00 am and the citizens made their way to worship, either in carriages or on foot, according to wealth and position. The interior of the church was in Bach's time visually sumptuous, full of Baroque colour and splendour to impress the senses. This was the house of God, furnished according to the tastes of the time and place (though some co-religionists favoured plainer surroundings).

As the services lasted for three hours or more, it was usual, especially for the richer members of the congregation, to arrive after the beginning. What mattered was to hear (and later to discuss) the sermon which lasted an hour, occupying a central place in the proceedings and followed by the taking of communion. The cantata was performed before the sermon, and sometimes there was another one later. While, as in opera houses of the period, there was always a certain amount of distraction and coming-and-going, the sale of cantata libretti beforehand suggests that the congregation included attentive listeners to the music.

~

Though originally part of a ceremony whose necessity was taken for granted by its participants, Bach's sacred cantatas are today likely to be presented in a different context. As any work surviving from the past is distanced from the setting of its age, the questions to be considered in this book include: How might the cantatas speak to us now? How do we approach the relationship between the aesthetic and the religious elements? What might we have lost, in terms of the full imaginative possibilities of the whole, when we try to separate them? The aim is to set the two side by side, considering each in the light of the other. Even if it is the music that draws us to the cantatas, it does not follow that the texts are an optional extra. It is precisely because the music matters so much that we need to examine the end that it was meant to serve. This, after all, brings us closer to the original, authentic experience, when the listeners understood and cared about the words.

In his cantatas, Bach transmutes a certain type of Christian doctrine into musical splendour. He projects a vision of life within a cosmic framework, much as Greek drama called on a shared heritage of myth to locate the individual within the bounds of a common human destiny. Despite three centuries of cultural and technological change, the music has not lost its power to move us, though it is unlikely that Bach would have imagined himself composing for posterity. Musicians were employees, respected – and often sought after – for their professional skills, but the nineteenth-century veneration for the status of the artist was yet to come.

The texts are in a different category. Their conceptual language (in which Bach himself was unselfconsciously fluent) has largely fallen into disuse. Despite the close bond between the two, must the mind that now happily consumes the music discard the associated texts like unwanted cherry stones? Or is there a way to see them as an expression of anxieties and self-healing consolations that are endemic to the human condition? If the latter, we have a better chance of appreciating the cathartic effect of Bach's settings.

Because the Christian narrative in one form or another has influenced much of the world's (especially, but not exclusively, the Western world's) imagination for two millennia, we need to stand back and consider it as objectively as possible. This can be difficult in an era whose culture, though largely secular, still frames its ethical outlook in terms of long-established Christian values – even though the original formulation can seem like an elderly relative whose precepts one has unconsciously absorbed, though it is annoying to be reminded of it.

~

To become widely accepted, any major religion must answer a number of psychological and social needs – and for many people that remains the case. Christianity, for instance, has been endlessly adaptable. It is a great portmanteau of creation story, the unfolding of human destiny, the promise of immortality, and an ethical guide to living. Each of the cantata scripts explores an aspect of this complex package, working from the Lutheran perspective that shaped Bach's world. This, as we shall see, included attitudes of awe, humility and a stoic determination to endure the trials of life, but also gratitude and rejoicing. It emphasized above all how to conquer the fear of death through faith in divine power to confer immortality.

Taken by themselves, the libretti that Bach set to music are now perhaps mostly of interest to historians of religious culture and of the development of a German literary language. They were supplied by numerous writers, mostly men and often with an administrative, legal or theological background; we know some, but not all, of their identities. To engage with their mental picture, we must first look at the essentials of the Christian story and then consider what were the chief preoccupations of the cantatas. The Christian religion places its construction on life within a poetic and mythological framework – by which no disrespect is intended. Some take delight in allegory, others do not. The difference between philosophical and mythological narratives is arguably in the presentation, whether in abstract or human terms. There is an affinity between poetry and religion, for both hint at what is not fully graspable. In so doing, they call attention to the limits of human understanding – a thought both mind-expanding and humbling.

The entire armoury of faith in the cantatas was forged from an amalgam of ancient Hebrew writings (the Old Testament) with a centuries-later account (the New Testament) of the life of a messianic figure. In brief: the apparent confusion of the material world is held to be under the control of a supernatural being, i.e. God. He created Adam and Eve: a first, perfect couple who allowed themselves to be corrupted by the force of evil (the devil). This led to disobedience towards God and left all subsequent humans with a permanent moral taint, doomed to bodily death. But God eventually took pity and returned to earth in mortal form as the historical person of a Jewish preacher, known as Jesus Christ. His mission was to reconcile sinful humans with their creator, indicating through parables and pronouncements how to live with the mind oriented towards celestial rather than earthly values.

Christ was considered by his followers to be the physical embodiment of the deity – and hence was called the Son of God. Though blameless, he allowed himself to be tortured to death by crucifixion; the event was both a demonstration of the human capacity for wickedness and a model of transcending it. Subsequently Christ proved his divinity to his disciples by returning to life and appearing in their midst, until at last he disappeared on high to be united in perpetuity with his divine Father. According to Christian dogma, those who sincerely believe that Christ was God and that he did indeed achieve resurrection will also enjoy a life of everlasting blessings with him in the next world. It is believed that God also exists in a third, immaterial form as the Holy Spirit that communicates between the divine and the human.

~

The fundamental message is that humanity can transcend its flaws: the guiding principle of life should be a constant striving to imitate the revealed model of virtue and to rise above the seductions and pains of bodily existence. As Lin Yutang observes: "You can't make a man a Christian unless you first make him believe he is a sinner". Faith in the possibility of personal transfiguration is the cornerstone of the Lutheran belief structure, and the fear of it becoming dislodged is the single most important feature of the cantata texts. Anxiety is never far away, followed by the intense joy of overcoming it, so that Bach's music, amongst its many other features, constantly paints a turbulent inner picture. It is intensely dramatic, reflecting (one could even say normalising) the changes of mood that constantly flit through most people's minds. Above all, the cantatas give an unflinching portrait of doubt and how to resolve it.

Creation myths are as old as recorded time: projections of that search for meaning that haunts the curious human mind and becomes the motive force of art – itself an attempt to corral the unknowable wildness in which we all flail about. The Luba – one of the Bantu people of Africa – imagined the creator god (Kabezya-Mpungu) as withdrawing after he had made the world and the first people. But he sent in return a heart: Mutshima. This yearned always for the absent god and entered into the human, which henceforth became the vessel of longing for the divine.

Similarly, the quest for salvation also appears in other religions, for example the popular and ritual form of Daoism that flourished in China at a similar time to the establishment of early Christianity. This included the idea of the "seed citizens": the select righteous few who would enjoy the grace of Heaven and populate the world after the end-time calamity. The parallels with the Christian notion of the Day of Judgement are obvious. This is always part of the mental scenery of the cantatas, sometimes coming to the fore, as in BWV 70: "Watch! Pray! Pray! Watch!" and BWV 90: "A frightful end is coming upon you". Faith is to be rewarded at last with eternal life, while the reprobates are cast into hell.

~

The effectiveness of an artistic narrative – i.e. its ability to keep someone's attention engaged – depends on a well-paced rhythm of tension and release. Though Bach's writers are minor figures in literary history, each cantata libretto finds a way to re-tell the old story of lost and then recovered mental security, of unworthiness and the possibility of redemption. By so doing, his versified scripts gave Bach the opportunity to create the maximum contrast of mood. The jittering and the serene, the jagged and the smooth, the harsh and the healing are all at the disposal of his versatility and skilful suggestion through the play of sound.

This is the operative phrase, for making patterns in sound was – as with any musician – Bach's lifelong passion and purpose. The productive paradox of the cantatas is that the music's vitality partners the anti-hedonism of the texts, which insist on the superiority of a spiritualised existence. But the music, even as it responds to the sense of the words, has ideas of its own. It counters the ferocious gloom of the Augustinian strictures that left Christianity with a lingering unease about the body. The texts gesture to death; Bach insists on life. His illustration of the words is rarely less than highly coloured and there is a rhythmic energy that time and again overflows into dance. Cosmopolitan in taste, he drew equally on Italianate brilliance, French pomp and grace, and German expertise in part-writing (counterpoint).

One of the details – there are not so very many – that we have about Bach's personal life is that he was a twice-married (his first wife died with shocking suddenness) and devoted husband with a large family. His portraits reveal the kind of heavy-set face that fits with a powerful physique – certainly not an etiolated ascetic. He was a man of immense vigour, judging by his demanding life as teacher and musician and his vast compositional output. Perhaps he sensed that the impermanence of existence sharpens our need to make the most of it; on the other hand he needed his salary. As it happens, Martin Luther himself enjoyed food and drink; he married an ex-nun after he left the monastery and regarded music as the most important adjunct to the life of the spirit. It seems that in the hierarchy of the senses, the ear is regarded as less earthbound than taste and touch.

~

If we look beyond (but do not discount) the mental barriers created by the conviction in the texts of the literal truth of scripture, we can still find common ground in the outlook of the cantatas. We should, for instance, remember that the vulnerability they often express reflects a time in which war and ill health were far more of an immediate threat than in the securer parts of the world today. There was a more urgent need for the consolations of faith; wealth and status were no defence when medicine had such limited resources. Perhaps we too easily forget that we are the same creatures of flesh and blood, subject to the same instinctual needs and governed by the same constraints of time and mortality. Changes in material circumstances can disguise how much we may be unconsciously anchored to ways of thinking familiar to those writers of three centuries ago. We merely speak a dialect version of their conceptual language.

The belief in a power beyond the self, the promise of a better world to come, the striving for perfection, guilt at falling short, the value attached to self-sacrifice, the dream of universal brotherhood, the leaning on idealised role models, the tendency to split the world into good and evil agents, the sacralisation of the victim: these are some of the pervasive mental dispositions of our time that might be considered Christianity's legacy and that feature in the cantatas. No doubt they were – still are – aspirations rather than common attributes; no one would need to preach such things if they were already reflected in behaviour. In any case, whether or not they are desirable is a matter of judgement; Nietzsche, for one, railed against them.

But there are aspects of the mentality of the cantatas that are thoroughly out of fashion amidst today's prosperity, chief of which is a lack of resentment against the hardships of life. There would have been many of those in a world made fragile by disease, early death and war. Yet a sense of entitlement is not part of the programme: the believer was told not to protest against the ordinances of God. Quite the contrary: suffering was no more than the faulty human deserved and was to be welcomed as the path to heaven. BWV 144 ("Take what is yours and go away") rejects all resistance to divine justice. Again, whatever one's view of this attitude, it is likely always to have been honoured more in the breach than the observance.

Even so, there is a sublime yet deeply human heroism in these psychological strategies for embracing the inevitable. The ultimate case is of course death, which can be considered the central point of the cantatas. They may be thought of collectively as an elegy on the mortal condition, in one sense tragic, and yet encouraging in their hope of a renewed and perfect existence. For example, BWV 125 ("With peace and joy I journey there") is an exceptionally moving account of the elderly Simeon as, having glimpsed the infant Christ, he reaches out to death as life's fulfilment. There is also an admirable humility in the acknowledgement that utopia is not achievable by humans. That requires the power of the divine.

~

The Church year had its own contours, with prescribed readings from the Bible on each Sunday. The texts of the cantatas were a reflection on these, and the variety of register and mood is fascinating. Writing for the same point in the Church year, individual librettists might deliver fist-banging threats or propose a more resigned and tender hope. What they all had in common, however, was their German identity, with its roots in Luther's revolutionary translation of Hebrew and Greek scripture into the vernacular. This might seem too obvious to be worth mentioning, but it is striking how much their cultural consciousness is contained within a biblical perspective. The stories and characters of the Old and New Testaments are their familiar companions, just as the tales of the Greek gods lingered in the literary imagination of so many other writers from the Renaissance onwards.

It was as if Bach's librettists saw themselves as the descendants of the historically and geographically distant Hebrews. They owned the same God (who now of course spoke their language, just as other nations made their God in their own linguistic image), with all the moral advantages that this brought. Pastor Erdmann Neumeister's text of BWV 24 makes its claim at the outset: "A sincere spirit of German loyalty and goodness makes us beautiful before God and people". The Bible represented the world: a complete resource of history, fable and philosophy. Every part of it was considered to be full of symbolic meaning, and the writers of the cantata texts were steeped in its colour and drama. There was so much material for the multiple allusions that enriched the literary style and linked past to present in the manner of flashbacks. All of this contributed to expanding the time consciousness of the listener, which is one of the great purposes of religious belief: though creatures of now, we are part of the great flow of existence, linked in sympathy to those who have been, and in a sense – the Christian promise – will never actually die.

This is the central issue of the cantatas: the relationship of the individual to his or her mortality. Although one could accuse the texts of self-obsession, this would perhaps be unfair because they were, after all, offered at a point in the week especially devoted to concerns above and beyond the everyday. Sexual love is referenced, but only as a metaphor for the union of the human with the divine spirit, as in BWV 49 ("I go and search with longing"); similarly, family relationships are only hinted at in a sacred context, such as the search by his parents for the young Christ in BWV 154 ("My dearest Jesus is lost"). There is often joy and musical wit, but irony and humour are not part of the scheme. There is instead a pared-down essentialism in the cantatas, a worrying away at what might be the purpose and value of life. The Advent cantata BWV 132 contains a bass aria that opens with a challenge: "Who are you? Ask your conscience, then you will hear the proper judgement over whether you are true or false".

What characterises the pressures of the cantata texts is that they are internalised. Their tensions do not take physical shape in terms of oppression by fellow humans but belong to the private conversation between the believer and God about one's intrinsic worth. Others may not take on the role of inquisitor, because they too are flawed. Policing thought, though it has been the self-appointed task of all manner of tyrants (allegedly religious or not), cannot be delegated to fellow sinners. It is of course impossible to enter the mind of Bach's contemporaries (and no doubt they included a spectrum of attitudes to faith); but what we can do is to consider what the joint conceptual and artistic value of the sacred cantatas might be today, bearing in mind their place in our cultural heritage.

~

Which brings us to the nature of the music: its underlying mechanisms and structures, how Bach used his craft to promote the view of life contained in the words, and what sort of reasons there might be for this music's continuing power to move us. In the afterword to his book *What Good are the Arts?* John Carey asks: "How could an artist acquire global fame if his or her work did not enshrine some sort of universal value, even though we may be unable to identify exactly what it is?" Despite the impossibility of giving a definitive answer, this has not deterred many (Carey included) from addressing the question. Interpretative and analytical criticism is a kind of conversation: part of an ongoing dialogue which responds to the creative impulse that produced the artwork in the first place. It is proof of its continuing presence – its inherent usefulness – even after a great lapse of time and fashions.

Broadly speaking, the artistic drive is an aspect of the human need to play. Art cannot feed or clothe us, but once the conditions for physical survival are met the human brain is predisposed to imagine, explore and invent. These are fundamental impulses and to satisfy them is intrinsically pleasurable, whether it is a child engrossed in making a plasticine model or Michelangelo at work on a sculpture. The first brings brief – though none the less meaningful – enjoyment to the creator and possibly an onlooker; the second fascinates and delights countless numbers over centuries.

The chief reason for the difference is an enhanced complexity of imaginative vision and the requisite level of skill to convey it in whatever medium is used. There are endless ways of perceiving beauty, but the art whose satisfactions endure over time hints at multiple possibilities of meaning; its surface is chameleon-like, evoking and responding to a spectrum of moods and associations. As a paradigm of life, the identity of a memorable artwork is recognisable but never entirely fixed. Bach's music fulfils these conditions. What is perhaps especially remarkable in the sacred cantatas is that their variety of styles, textures and tone colours is always anchored in the same message: that of the need to live in the present in the context of eternity. A serious subject, of course, but one that generates all sorts of reactions, from terror to hope and from wretchedness to ecstasy. Embracing these contrasts is a notable aspect of Bach's genius. Even as the last aria of BWV 57 ("Blessed is the man") ends in a question about what is to come after death, the solo violin part shimmers with life. Music brings the answer.

Like many types of play – including sport and board games – art also compels our attention because it challenges itself to work within certain parameters: it has its rules. It does not matter what these are, as long as the terms are understood. Limits bring tightness, tension and excitement. Without them there can be no productive struggle between the ingenuity of the creator and established boundaries. While forms are needed, creativity does not entail the invention of new ones; it is more often a case of seeing previously undiscovered patterns after shaking the kaleidoscope of the familiar. As it happens, Bach's early musical training and his own diligent curiosity provided him with an encyclopedic range of possibilities inherited from the past. He was able to draw on these, for instance calling at will on his command of part-writing for his magnificent choruses that showcase the dignity of an ancient hymn. But he was equally at home with the high emotion of a theatricalised aria and the grace and energy of the dance. He was heard to remark: "I have had to work hard; anyone who works just as hard will get just as far".

~

But before looking further at his repertoire of forms and structures, we need to take into account a particular innovation which was integral to Bach's artistic development and upon which he, though not the only musician involved, had an enormous influence. This development concerned a new approach to the tuning of the scale. It had not merely theoretical but also practical consequences, and to put it in context requires a brief technical and historical digression.

When a note is sounded, it produces a ripple of vibrations. The wavelength of the first and largest of these creates the fundamental impression of pitch. But overlaying this, though barely apparent to the senses, is a further sequence of smaller and smaller wavelengths that decrease in mathematical succession – 1/2, 1/4, 1/3 etc. – in proportion to the original: these constitute the harmonic series, fixed by the principles of acoustics. The first harmonic is the most prominent and is what we call the octave above the fundamental: to put it another way, the octave refers to our physiological response to two notes whose speed of vibration differs by a ratio of 1:2. Their close affinity is easily recognised, and a listener may even have difficulty telling them apart.

Across cultures and epochs the octave represents an unalterable relationship of pitch. Its boundaries act as the top and bottom rungs of a sound-ladder, and we describe the sequence of pitches between them as a scale. But while the outer limits of the octave are fixed, the spacing of those inner rungs varies according to musical tradition, giving each its recognisable character. Before Bach's time – roughly speaking, before the beginning of the seventeenth century – composers worked with a number of different scales, known as modes, and supposedly based on ancient Greek models; each of them carried certain emotional associations. This practice, however, was gradually supplanted (the composer Monteverdi, whose life spanned the sixteenth and seventeenth centuries, was a crucial figure) by the favouring of only two scale variants: those we now refer to as major and minor. The main difference between them is in the lowered pitch of two of the notes of the minor scale, the effect of which is to cast an emotional cloud: of seriousness at the very least, but often of grief and anxiety.

If the reduced number of scale types counted as a loss, there was a potential compensatory gain in new approaches to musical design. The emphasis now was on devising a narrative that could journey through a number of key centres. A piece rooted in one keynote and the scale that it generated (whether major or minor) might unfold (modulate) through further keys before returning to its starting point. There was a problem, though: tuning systems in general use in Bach's youth limited the options for this kind of adventurousness, the reason being that the precise pitch of the individual notes of a scale (a fixed sequence of tones and semitones) was calibrated according to the harmonic series. As a result, not all the tones were the same exact aural distance apart, and neither were the semitones. Because of this intrinsic unevenness, if an instrument was tuned to work perfectly in one key, it would begin to sound jarring if it moved to another.

~

The solution favoured by Bach was a standardised tuning of twelve more or less identical semitone steps within the octave. As the semitones were exactly the same as each other, so too were the tones. With this compromise – so-called equal temperament – music was able to escape the exactitude of physics. As we listen, we make instinctive inner adjustments for the slight loss of the sweetness produced by chords tuned to the harmonic series. The artifice of equal temperament was in a sense an Enlightenment project, for it was a rational solution devised by a practical mind to the awkward imperatives of nature. The forty-eight preludes and fugues of Bach's Well-Tempered Clavier are a manifesto and advertisement for the new system, demonstrating with their extraordinary variety what an instrument prepared in this way could do. In fact, this method of tuning has shaped our musical consciousness ever since – up to and including the present.

Thanks largely to Bach's pioneering efforts, composers now had complete freedom to hint at multiple tonal distractions and destinations to enhance the psychological pleasure of returning to the home key of a piece of music. It was a development for artistic purposes but it coincided rather well with the omnipresent subject of the cantatas: the struggle to conquer the torments of doubt with a renewed faith in God's plan. The underlying key centre can be regarded as a symbol of security and belonging. It also represents the boundaries that harmonic exploration, as a metaphor of straying into new territories, must test. Bach sometimes teeters on the edge of dissolution. The opening chorus of BWV 101, "Take from us, Lord and faithful God, severe punishment and great distress", shows him at his most unflinching. Dissonance pushed to the limit becomes the agony of the human, cowering before disease and war.

Despite being in the forefront of new concepts of tonality, Bach still delighted in his fluency in the older language of the modes. The patina of age made them appropriate signallers of timeless authority, the impenetrable and yet authentic voice of truth. For instance, BWV 38 ("In deep distress I cry to you, O Lord"), is based on Luther's own hymn of 1524. The words are a translation of the Old Testament Psalm 130 and the melody is in the Phrygian mode (in modern terms this spans the white keys on a keyboard from E to E). The setting shows us a composer not merely respectful of an antique legacy but completely at one with its style and spirit. He sets before us a world in which time is no longer linear: the ancient is always with us as an intimation of our place in eternity. Bach's education began by the thorough assimilation, through copying, of the masters who preceded him. His wide reading, so to speak, gave him a large stylistic vocabulary that he could draw on and recombine throughout his life. Though a citizen of his own time and, as it turned out, of the future, he was the prisoner of neither.

~

There is abundant evidence of Bach's integration of old and new in his treatment of the traditional chorales. These were a shared resource of the religious community: well-known hymns that confirmed a mutual identity of belief. If the nearest analogy is with football chants and national anthems, the great difference is that the chorales turn inward towards the believer's relationship with God; if there is an enemy, it is more likely to be identified as the self's weakness and faltering faith – though the responsibility for failings is often outsourced to the malign schemes of the Devil. The chorales were expressions of simple fervour, set to melodies that demanded no musical expertise to sing.

While virtually all the cantatas end with one verse of a hymn set in four-part harmony, many of them are closely tied throughout to an entire chorale, either quoted verbatim or paraphrased by a librettist. In the case of these so-called chorale cantatas, the opening movement is usually a creative fusion of old and new in which the ornate and the simple elevate each other. The plain hymn tune is set in an elaborate context of voices and instruments; in turn, their display of colour and movement takes on greater depth and resonance because it serves a purpose beyond the pleasure of the here and now. In general, Bach's choruses are one of the great glories of the cantatas; their splendour, skill and variety impress on their own terms even when the listener does not know the text.

A particularly appealing example is the opening movement of BWV 26 ("Ah how fleeting, ah how worthless"). Though the hymn on which the cantata is based points to the transitoriness of life, Bach's setting abounds with in-the-moment vigour. An instrumental band of strings, flute, three oboes and continuo dashes through an Italian-style concerto, in which the participants converse with each other in groups. The predominant musical motto flies away like a puff of smoke, anticipating the verbal message. This emerges phrase by phrase in the slow-moving soprano line (a melody singled out in such a manner is known as the *cantus firmus*) while the other voices reiterate the words in their own way. The modern (the concerto style) and the old (the hymn) complement each other within the united design of the whole.

While a chorale chorus frequently gives the hymn tune to one of the voices, there was no rigid template. Bach varied his practice according to his artistic judgement. BWV 14 ("If God were not with us at this time") gains enormously in dramatic impact by the contrast between the huddled and desperate humans and the trumpet proclamation of the hymn that, wordlessly, soars above their fear. The hymn tune, as so often, is modal in character: not an abandoned relic of former times (though it dated back to Luther) but a living connection between what was and is. Composed in 1735, BWV 14 is a relatively late cantata and the part writing in this chorus – the voices moving constantly in opposite directions – marries technical virtuosity with expressive power. It shows Bach's grounding in the disciplines of counterpoint, together with his use of the new freedom to glide between semitones – the kind of chromatic colouring that greatly enhanced his expressive palette. Here, as often, it paints gloom and fearfulness.

~

The music of the cantatas is alive with contrasts of texture, colour and pace, but always contained within structure of one type or another. While a small number of these works are for a solo voice, the more characteristic practice is for an alternation between the group and the individual. Typically, a cantata begins and ends with a four-part chorus (the number of singers on each part being a matter for the discretion of the performers): the opening movement is extended and elaborate, and the final one a plainly sung hymn. Within this framework is an exploration of personal feeling expressed through the deliberations of recitative and expanded in the solo arias. These too were predicated on contrast, especially in the standard three-part *da capo* design favoured in the musical Baroque era.

This was the vehicle for depicting the fluctuating state of mind of characters on the operatic stage, and Bach's librettists provided him with texts suited to a similar dramatisation of feeling. The words were relatively brief: a first sentence or two indicated a certain emotional attitude, and this was followed by another, either opposing or complementary. When both in turn had been explored in the language of music, the instruction *da capo* required a repeat of the entire first section to complete an ABA pattern. The whole design allowed both for the contrast beloved of the Baroque and formal symmetry. Might there be also a hint of something indeterminate? In theory, the sections – and the feelings they represent – could repeat on an endless loop, but this would contradict the demands of drama, whether secular or religious, which must move to a resolution.

There is no question that in such arias – short in text but musically substantial – the poetic function, which is to say the ability to arouse a response that disturbs but eludes definition, becomes the responsibility and property of the composer. Where, then, is the boundary between the musical and the verbal? The question is particularly relevant to the cantatas, as Christianity – especially in its Lutheran version – gives supreme status to the written word: God's message revealed in scripture. Next in importance are preaching and commentary through which a priestly and learned class use yet more words to expound the sacred texts to others. It is this (so to speak) second tier that supplied the libretti for the cantatas. But however earnest and sincerely felt these scripts may be, conveying the rapture of the religious impulse is beyond them. This is the gap filled by music.

~

The balance between music and words is a little different, however, when the setting is in the less melodic style of recitative. Here the preacher comes to the fore, sometimes as an external, finger-wagging critic or alternatively as the internal voice of self-reproach or deep meditation. Words, as the means of reasoning and discussion, then take precedence. The composer's task in recitative is to give them as much impact as possible by exaggerating the natural pitch contours of speech; meanwhile, underlying harmonic progressions – again the eloquence of key shifts – urge on changes of mood. What is always evident is Bach's alertness to the sense of the text. The recitatives are essential to the argument of any cantata; knowing the words really counts.

The leanest type of recitative – so-called *secco* (dry) – relies only on a continuo instrument to support the voice. At other times there is a fuller instrumental backing – *stromentato* – generally sustained string chords. Two rather fierce recitatives, each aimed at denouncing human inadequacy, demonstrate the difference. BWV 25 ("There is nothing healthy in my body") was composed to a text by Johann Jacob Rambach, a younger contemporary of Bach and evidently a theologian of an uncompromising disposition. A tenor recitative, accompanied by chords on the organ, begins by announcing that "The whole world is just a hospital". The wildness of the vocal line matches the melodramatic excess of the preacher as he thunders out his homily (even the children in their cradle are sick with sin). The other example is from BWV 47 ("Whoever exalts himself shall be humbled"); the librettist here was Johann Friedrich Helbig, just five years older than Bach. A bass recitative enjoins humility, reminding the listener that "Mankind is muck"; violins and viola hover thoughtfully above.

Though one can identify all manner of recurring stylistic habits, the cataloguing of which is not the primary purpose of this book, there is enormous variety in the cantatas. All sorts of combinations and permutations were possible: choruses, duets, arias and recitatives (some interpersed with melodic episodes), along with numerous solo instruments, such as violin, cello, trumpet, flute and oboe, to add colour and character. The timbre and style of the instrumental solos are often integral to the drama as a reflection of the singer's state of mind: whining, grumbling, grieving, pleading, complaining, raging or rejoicing – as the case may be. The plangent sound of the oboe and its softer and deeper version, the oboe d'amore, suits moments of sorrow and remorse but can equally well suggest rusticity. The flute and recorder can either dazzle or mourn, the trumpet is all power, splendour and triumph; the violin is both brilliant and ethereal, and Bach's choice for an intimation of the Holy Spirit.

~

Each cantata has something to say, a drama to enact, that is meant to be of the greatest personal importance to the listener. There are many different ways to do this; boredom is not an option. For instance, BWV 178 ("If God the Lord was not at our side") takes an exceptionally inventive approach to a libretto based on a hymn by Luther's fellow theologian, Justus Jonas (1493–1555). The words are a rendering in German of Psalm 124 and are full of an Old Testament sense of persecution from which only God can save his people. An unknown writer has made additions to include the plight of Christians. Dating from 1524, the melody is modal in character: Dorian, as it happens, which is a good fit with the minor scale.

A chorale chorus, with the first verse of the old hymn inserted into a choppy and agitated orchestral texture, is followed by an imaginative treatment of the second verse. Each line of the chorale is interspersed with recitative commentary, expressing confidence in God's protection. The third movement is a surging bass aria, with unison strings above and the continuo below evoking the waves that threaten the little Christian boat. The real point arrives in the sixth movement: a tenor aria that reveals what is truly at stake. The Satan that is so greatly feared is within one's own mind, disrupting the faith in eternity that makes life endurable. The vocal line cries out to suppress what it calls the unsteadiness of reason – translated into dizzy musical contours. Security returns with the final two verses of the chorale. God is sure to assist in the struggle against doubt.

~

Music apart, there is a larger question here, connected with the earlier suggestion of the affinity between religion and poetry. The dismissal of reason, as in the text of BWV 178, seems at the very least absurd, if not dangerous, but it needs to be placed in context. Luther himself was a fierce defender of the mystery of faith, which he regarded as a qualitatively different kind of knowledge from human reason. For him, nothing could override the conviction of closeness to God. Yet at least since Thomas Aquinas in the thirteenth century, there have been many attempts to reconcile reason with faith. One approach is represented by the biologist Stephen Jay Gould, who proposed separate but equal domains, while the contemporary thinker Iain McGilchrist has recast the Gradgrindian opposition of fact and fancy in terms of the different functions of the left and right cerebral hemispheres.

Art may be the best solution to the dilemma. Bach's fusion of emotionalism and technique in the cantatas is exceptionally convincing. Each feeds off and intensifies the other. His conjuror's dexterity within the constraints of form brings its own excitement, but there is another tributary of feeling, which originates in the need to make sense of the individual's life and death. This desire is the fundamental driver of religion, and possibly few minds are without it. As there can never be empirical evidence for a transcendental reality, faith is the only recourse. It is the poetic fiction that, for better or for worse, sustains the self. The emotional intensity of Bach's settings in the cantatas is perhaps his way of reaching toward the ideal – both far off and yet near, because it is present in the imagination.

Accounting for the quality of a work of art is a complex task. It has to begin with looking at the conventions – again, the rules of the game. Bach inhabited a particular epoch with its own musical vocabulary. Setting aside the question of certain structural norms, such as the *da capo* aria and the principle of *ritornello*, which simply meant the multiple recurrence of a section of music within the same piece, there were standard moves and habits of repetition, such as the sequential passages that enabled one key to slip into another. There was necessarily a limited number of arrangements of notes that could be devised from within the scale. There were, too, standard chord progressions, and imitative counterpoint was another shared discipline. Fugue, for instance, required a number of parts to follow each other at settled intervals of pitch (the fifth and the octave).

Given such a wealth of common denominators, the questions are: what makes one composer more memorable than another? How is it that an individual voice is recognisable? A combination of factors is involved. Part of the answer lies in the handling of repetition, i.e. redundancy. Like most types of music, the Baroque – Bach's music – was strongly patterned. Recurring motifs offer the comfort of familiarity, acting as a reference point to the listener and a foil to set off the unexpected. Few of these motifs were remarkable in themselves, for they were part of the stock in trade of the time; what mattered was how to use them without being hidebound and predictable. The formulaic is the enemy of the unique.

~

An exceptional artist such as Bach keeps one foot in the familiar and the other in a place of invention. Mastery of all manner of compositional techniques was for him endlessly absorbing, but beyond all else a means to a creative end. He knows when and how to avoid the saturation point of a repeated motto, so that while glad to hear it again, we are not bored by it; his sequences, for instance, are not allowed to outstay their welcome. Bach was not intentionally avant-garde in terms of devising new forms or a radically different language, yet he did increase his inherited vocabulary. His originality lay in seeing, in a way that others did not, how to push boundaries without destroying them. In this respect, his sacred cantatas can be seen as a paradigm of the free possibilities of life within divinely ordained limits.

He was a constructive revolutionary whose daring still surprises; to create challenging dissonances and then pull back from the brink of chaos to a secure resolution was a mark of his confidence and an imagination that saw infinite possibilities in the legacy of the past. In the case of the cantatas we must always remember that his deepest desire was to compose for the greater glory of God. Working at his craft – his art – he was a seeker: what impelled him was not ego (although he was much respected as a virtuoso performer, composer and teacher) but a sense of music as a conduit to a world of unfathomable perfection. If the mark of the romantic is a yearning for the ideal, was Bach in spirit a citizen of the nineteenth century? Perhaps that is to put the cart before the horse, because Romanticism itself arguably borrows much from the Christian dream of paradise.

Bach's energy abounds in the cantatas: it features psychologically in his vivid response to whatever the librettist of the day had put before him, and in a dramatic instinct that turned every movement into an impassioned personal statement. Sometimes an entire work is for one singer alone, as with the cantata for alto voice, BWV 170 ("Happy rest, beloved joy of the soul"), which is a deep meditation on the blessing of faith. There are also dialogues, as for example the split-personality format of BWV 60 ("O eternity, word of thunder"). A great conflict is taking place, between terror at what lies beyond the moment of death and trust in Christ's promise of immortality. Two actors – alto and tenor – take on the roles of Fear and Hope respectively. The music characterises their opposition, beginning with the jittering rhythms of Fear and the soaring response of Hope.

They argue with each other in the recitative that follows – each in a different key. Yet these two keys (B minor and D major) are in a tonal sense closely related, as if to signal that Fear and Hope are both aspects of the same mind. Towards the end of the cantata, the voice of Christ himself appears, sung by the bass, as if his presence has at last entered the trembling human. His music is calm, slow, beautiful, with a steady pulse that communicates the physiological benefit of faith. Without sharing the religious beliefs of the cantatas, it is not so difficult to empathise with the universal anxiety about death and – for the moment – to be carried along by a musical rhetoric that promises deliverance.

~

In responding to the pictorial, Bach did not invent the practice of using sound as a synaesthetic metaphor for what we see – the music of his time was fond of such effects – but as with so much else, he did it with especial verve. The idea of water – flowing, swirling, storming – is a gift to the sensuously inclined composer, as in a typical example from BWV 81 ("Jesus sleeps, what hope do I have?"). The biblical reference is to a storm on the sea of Galilee: the first movement evokes the ominous swell of the waves. In a subsequent tenor aria the violin part dashes about to mimic their fury, until finally the figure of Christ appears to calm the water and the turbulence of doubt.

There are many examples of sheer physicality, as with the musical writhings in the bass aria from BWV 40 ("This is why the Son of God appeared"), which depict the devilish serpent that Christ has come to wrestle down. There are, too, resplendent ceremonies and celebrations, heralded by the trumpet. Perfect kingship is the model for divinity, perceived as the grand and just lawgiver, stern, gracious and merciful as required. Nature is frequently referenced, as for instance when four violas and bassoon suggest the gentle fall of rain in the lovely instrumental prelude to BWV 18 ("Just as the rain and snow fall from heaven"). Then BWV 181 ("Shallow minded fickle souls"), linked to the parable of the sower, begins with a bass aria about the lightweights who ignore the divinely inspired message; jerky little movements in the accompaniment suggest a kind of bird-brained pecking.

While the life-and-death importance of their subject matter brings an underlying fervour to the cantatas, there are many moments of intense happiness – a superabundant joy that is all the greater for the underlying anxiety that it conquers. Perhaps one of the best clues to intrinsic musical meaning can be found when Bach fits part of a pre-existing composition into one of the cantatas. For example, the overture to the Orchestral Suite in D becomes, with the extra glamour of trumpets and drums, the start of the Christmas Day cantata, BWV 110 ("May our mouths be full of laughter and our tongues full of praise").

The ceremonious beginning of the French-style overture becomes the preamble to a great flow of triplet rhythms. We do not need the words to tell us that the message is of boundless rejoicing: tempo and style speak for themselves. Though the accompanying text cannot alter our immediate response to the music, it does have a purpose, which is to give definition to that response. As a sort of hermit crab, emotion has no fixed abode until encased by words. Yet the pleasure gained from the vitality of the music is not the exclusive property of a devout believer thinking of God's presence on earth. What really counts is that for Bach there was no distinction between his creative life and his apparent philosophy of being – his sense of the fullness of things.

~

Bach's distinctive energy shows itself in the cantatas in his tireless attention to detail, command of form and passionate emotionalism. But there is also the question of pulse. Music, like the heart, has a continuous beat; its pace, whether fast or slow, has a bodily effect. Everywhere in Bach there is a forward impetus that communicates itself as life's urgency. It is obvious in the vigour of – to pick one at random – the opening chorus of BWV 72 ("Everything according to God's will") but is equally apparent in the steady rocking motion of the opening of BWV 125 ("With peace and joy I go there"), mentioned earlier: Simeon looks to death not as ending but as continuation. The entirety of BWV 125, poignant in its serenity, exemplifies one of the most universal aspects of the cantatas. Irrespective of one's attitude to religious belief (of any persuasion or none), an acceptance of the interrelationship of life and death is surely both desirable and consoling.

Which is to say: the mystery of mortality and the fear of it that has always haunted the human imagination are not denied or hidden away but regularly confronted and placed in a context of hope. All artistic form represents a triumph of order over disorder – all the more when the signs of disorder are allowed maximum freedom before being reined in. Baroque music had its own ways of managing this productive tension, and Bach was a master of them all. In the theology of the cantatas, evil, death and chaos are interchangeable. The musical symbol of this is the potential destabilising of key centre, rhythm and structure. In this respect, Bach's ability to play with danger and then resist it becomes a token of faith's miraculous power to conquer despair. We do not have to share this faith to be dazzled, consoled and satisfied by his skill and positive vision.

Committed to his role as intermediary between the listener and the sacred mysteries that his librettists strained towards, Bach found a way for music to wipe away humanity's grubby tears over its fate. In so doing, he left his personal, inimitable fingerprint as composer, believer and human. If, to adapt Zola's dictum, art is reality viewed through a temperament, there is plenty of evidence in his works that this particular individual – J.S. Bach – was there to respond to life to the fullest extent, as long as his God granted.

~

In the end, the texts do matter. For the theological programme of the cantatas can only be explained in words: it is not political, but it concerns the organisation of the mind in a way that makes it as independent as possible both from the shocks of life and the pressures of the consensus – for human opinions are fallible. The focus is on the mental space inhabited by the private self. The paradox is that concentrating on salvation in a world to come can also provide the psychological tools for making the most of life in the present. The dream of a celestial future lends brightness to an existence that is otherwise merely drab and painful.

In the austere Christian belief of the cantatas, everyone becomes their own vigilante, guarding against the tendency to please oneself, which risks a dangerous loss of contact with the divine ideal. The inner realm is shared only with God; moral responsibility cannot be outsourced to others; conscience is king. But music is waved through as a sweetener. It is a personal, sensuous delight that does not affect the freedom of others, nor sate the stomach.

To many people, music in one form or another has always been and remains an instinctual pleasure. And here, perhaps, lies the special value of Bach's sacred cantatas. Their fusion of text and music signals who we are: creatures whose brains are at home in a world of symbols but, despite all ambitions otherwise, are the sum-total of multiple physical processes. Melody, rhythm, harmony and architectural beauty are more convincing than the preacher. Or are they? The evidence must be left to the guide that follows.

Brief Glossary of Musical Terms

aria An extended lyrical setting of a text.

arioso A melodic passage of relatively short duration.

canon An exact, sequential imitation of one part by another.

cantus firmus The presentation of a chorale melody by one vocal part within a more complex texture.

chorale A traditional Lutheran hymn, familiar to the entire community.

chorale cantata A cantata whose text is based on the words of a chorale.

chromaticism Expressive deviations from the expected musical line, disrupting the sense of a secure key structure. It offers the contrast of tension and surprise, and in Bach's music is often a shorthand for thoughts of evil and death.

coloratura A rapid, virtuoso flow of notes on one syllable.

concerto A musical design in which one group of instruments – or a solo instrument – is contrasted with others.

continuo The bass line that provides the foundation of the harmony. It is almost always played by the organ, which adds improvised chords above, and is usually doubled by cello or perhaps double bass or bassoon.

counterpoint Combining rhythmically and melodically independent parts so that they converge harmonically while keeping their distinct identity.

da capo A widely used ABA formal design.

fugue A way of adding parts in imitative sequence at prescribed intervals, but with further free exploration of the melodic material.

homophony Combining a number of parts in block, i.e. rhythmically united, chords.

major and minor The two types of scale that are foundational to Bach's musical vocabulary. The lowering of the third and sixth degrees in the minor scale often brings a suggestion of melancholy.

melisma A decorative emphasis of one syllable, but less extended and brilliant than coloratura.

modulation A shift from one key centre to another. A move to the dominant key (the fifth note of the scale) creates a vibrant and positive effect, while a move to the subdominant key (the fourth note of the scale) sounds more subdued.

obbligato An essential instrumental solo part.

pizzicato The plucking, rather than the bowing, of a string instrument.

recitative A quasi-speech like way of singing a text without the regular patterning or lyrical appeal of melody.

ritornello A recurring musical passage that acts as a binding structural element

tonic key The scale that provide the aural anchorage of a movement, allowing for a sense of departure and then homecoming.

A Note on Performance

There are many recorded performances of Bach's sacred cantatas, each one reflecting the director's interpretation in terms of tempo, balance of instruments and voices, and tone colour. For at least half a century, there has been a shift in interest toward reviving the kinds of sounds that were current in Bach's time (though whether or not he would have preferred something richer and fuller we can never know).

Similarly, some favour a choir of male voices, as Bach had at his disposal, though female singers are now the norm, at least for the soprano line. There is also the question of the size of the chorus, about which it makes no sense to be dogmatic. Bach himself was nothing if not adaptable, cutting his musical coat according to his cloth, i.e. what performers were available to him. He was known to protest about the inadequate numbers in his choir. If some cantatas seem to work best with one to a part, others invite the drama of a fuller sound.

Each separate cantata account in this volume ends with a suggestion to the reader of a recording available at the end of 2024. This is not intended as prescriptive but rather as a starting point for exploration and comparison. In every case, the performance indicated has seemed faithful to the joint musical and conceptual intention of the work – but the same could be said of numerous others. There is limitless room for individual preference.

December: Prefatory Note

The start of the journey: cantatas for Advent and Christmas

December begins with the anticipation of the Nativity: the remembrance of the birth of Christ, supposedly the arrival of God on earth, on the 25th of the month. The date was first settled in the early fourth century AD, under the rule of the Roman emperor Constantine; current divergence in the date between Eastern and Western churches is the result of quirks of calendrical systems. It also coincides closely with the winter equinox, which across cultures has for millennia been associated with rituals that defy darkness and welcome the return of longer days. Nature-worshipping Mithraism, for instance, which attached great importance to midwinter, was an established presence in late imperial Rome. Whatever the mingled heritage, for the Christian, the arrival of Christ signals the coming of the redeemer of humankind: the bringer of light and life.

As with all great events, a large part of the excitement lies in the preparation. Bach's Church year therefore opened, not with Christmas day itself, but with the weeks beforehand: a period collectively known as Advent. It included potentially four Sundays – days on which believers were urged both to look forward and also to examine their own conscience. Their whole self, in thought and deed, must be purified in readiness for contact with God made flesh: the embodiment of the moral perfection to which all should aspire. There was abundant joy, but equally soul-searching penitence.

The following pages first give an account of the four existing Advent cantatas: BWV 61, BWV 62, BWV 63 and BWV 132. Bach had certainly composed others, though we can never know how much has been lost. Of these, three at least were expanded for future occasions. BWV 70a, for the second Sunday in Advent, was recast for the twenty-sixth Sunday after Trinity as BWV 70, Wachet! Betet! Betet! Wachet ("Watch! Pray! Pray! Watch!"). The early work BWV 186a for the third Sunday in Advent, Ärgre dich, o Seele nicht ("O soul, do not take offence"), was reassigned to the seventh Sunday after Trinity; while BWV 147a for the fourth Sunday in Advent, i.e. Herz und Mund und Tat und Leben ("Heart and mouth and deed and life"), was adapted later for a July festival: the Visitation of the Virgin Mary. All of these will be described in subsequent volumes.

Next come the cantatas for Christmas Day and the days immediately after: BWV 63, BWV 91, BWV 110, BWV 40, BWV 57, BWV 64, BWV 133, BWV 151. (The six cantatas that comprise the Christmas Oratorio are not included.) Finally, there is the Sunday after Christmas and a foretaste of the New Year: BWV 152, BWV 122 and BWV 28. In all, a total of sixteen cantatas for December are presented here, in a way that aims in each case to suggest the connection between the music and the conceptual foundation upon which the text is based.

1st Sunday in Advent

BWV 61: *Nun komm, der Heiden Heiland*

(Now come, Saviour of the Gentiles)

Librettist: Erdmann Neumeister

Date: 1714

And let us, ciphers to this great accompt
On your imaginary forces work.

William Shakespeare: *Henry V*

Though their backdrop was the interior of a church – usually ornately decorated to inspire awe and reverence – Bach's sacred cantatas were innately theatrical. They glamorised theology with music that, like pictures and statuary, helped to bridge the gap between the senses and the more abstract concepts of religious faith. They were part of a communal performance: the weekly church service designed to unite the private and the public self in an aspiration towards a shared life of the spirit. As the key to such a life was thought to lie in biblical texts, a central function of these services was to expound the meaning of scripture. Music also took its place alongside the sermonising and ritual, for Luther himself had endorsed it as an aid to directing the mind to God.

Bach began composing cantatas at least as early as 1707, using the format and styles then usual in a religious context. His dramatic options, however, were greatly expanded by a new approach to the writing of cantata libretti, pioneered by the Lutheran pastor Erdmann Neumeister (1671-1756). This enabled more variety, so that alongside traditional hymns and biblical references, there were verses that could be set as more overtly emotional, operatic-style arias. In musical terms, secular and sacred could collaborate in the impulse to worship, and the stylistically omnivorous Bach took every advantage of the potential for theatrical contrast. Creating cantata libretti became a literary industry of its own, and Bach used texts from multiple writers. Evidently he took a close interest in the words, sometimes altering them to suit his purpose.

BWV 61 was composed in 1714 when Bach was concertmaster (leader of the court orchestra) at the court of Weimar; the inclusion in his score of two viola parts rather than the later convention of one marks it as a relatively early work. The libretto is from a collection published by Neumeister in 1711 and it is designed for the first week in Advent: the start of the Church year in December, when the believer looks ahead to celebrating the Nativity. This marked the birth of Christ, when God and mortal were believed to have become one. It brings the message that, however humble the human condition, within it lies the possibility of the sacred.

No 1 Chorus

A chorale chorus such as this unites old and new. At its musical heart is Luther's hymn, *Nun Komm, der Heiden Heiland* ("Now come, Saviour of the gentiles") – but with its ancient plainsong contours newly clothed in magnificence. Bach integrates the simple melody into the studied, formal brilliance of a French overture, with its slow-fast-slow structure. Christ may have renounced earthly power, but his status in the eternal, invisible universe of the spirit speaks in the language of secular glory. Just as the French opera overture announced the entry of the most powerful monarch in Europe (Louis

XIV was yet to die in 1715) so Bach uses its style as a gesture to the heavenly king, his power and majesty compressed into the sprung energy of the upper string parts. Beneath them, cello, bassoon and organ continuo proclaim the iconic first phrase of the chorale tune.

It is the voices, however, who must make the meaning explicit: "Now come, Saviour of the gentiles, revealed as the virgin's child; all the world wonders at this, that God has ordained such a birth for him". The opening cry of "Now come, Saviour of the gentiles" passes successively to each vocal line, as if the spectators lining the royal route in turn acknowledge their king. Perhaps this also alludes to one of the day's prescribed gospel readings (Mt.21:1-9): a glimpse of Christ's last entry into Jerusalem, acclaimed by his followers yet refusing worldly privilege by choosing to ride on a donkey. The second line, "revealed as the virgin's child", changes to a solid four-part harmonisation to announce that the divine Redeemer of humankind was born like any other mortal.

The organisation of music and text ensures that the third line, "all the world wonders at this", coincides with the central portion of the overture structure. As the focus is now on the joy that Christ's birth brings, mood and tempo change into a high-spirited triple metre (Bach's instruction – *gai* – is appropriately French). A dance-like paraphrase of the chorale melody in the soprano line leads the rejoicing. All earlier stiffness has melted into lyrical ease as the parts flow in imitation, one after the other. The orchestral texture lightens, with the strings now doubling the voices; prolonged settings of "all" (*alle*) evoke the expanse of the world over which the Saviour is to rule. The final line, "God has ordained such a birth for him", completes the movement with a return to the manner of the opening; at the end, the unadorned vocal harmonies seem to absorb the miraculous into simple, unarguable reality: God became man, and that is that.

No 2 Tenor recit

Neumeister reflects on the Nativity in ten lines of rhyming verse. From these, Bach creates three distinct sections. The first four lines summarise the message that the chorale has already delivered: "The Saviour has come, has taken our poor flesh and blood upon himself and receives us as blood relations". A straightforward speech style in a major key underlines the would-be factual nature of the statement; only the dramatic leap at "as blood relations" (*zu Blutsverwandten*) betrays a sense of the extraordinary. A sudden rhetorical kick from both music and text then jolts the listener into an awareness of the deeper meaning, as the next four lines exclaim at God's sacrifice: "O most precious of all possessions, what have you not done for us? What do you daily not do for your own people?" The harmonies take an unsettled turn before a final *arioso* section full of melodic sweetness: "You come and let your light shine with its full blessing". The words refer to the second reading for the day (Rom.13:11-14), in which God is identified with light. Gently flowing descents for voice and continuo indicate the divine presence as it arrives to sanctify the human.

No 3 Tenor aria

With barely a pause, the continuo leads in a dance of happiness. Three is the significant number in this movement, possibly an allusion to the doctrine of the Trinity: God as Father, Son and Holy Spirit. Not only are there three beats in a bar, each of which is divided into three, but the texture of the whole is a trio, made up of continuo, unison violins and violas, and the voice. The structure, too, is in three parts – hardly unusual in itself, but particularly fitting here. The text beings with an open invitation: "Come, Jesus, come to your church and grant a blessed new year!". For this, the harmonies are predominantly in the major key. The next part is somewhat more troubled: "Promote the honour of your name, preserve sound teaching, and bless pulpit and altar". We hear the authentic voice of Neumeister, who had strong views on correct doctrine: he disliked, for instance, the intensely private orientation of the Lutheran movement known as Pietism. Bach's use of minor keys casts an appropriate shadow. The rhythmic animation, however, remains, and the aria ends with the delight of its beginning.

No 4 Bass recit

The words are a gift to the theatrically inclined composer. Neumeister has borrowed from the Book of Revelation (3:20): "See, I stand at the door and knock. If anyone hears my voice and opens the door, I will come into him and celebrate the evening meal with him, and he with me". The knocking persists throughout in the plucked (*pizzicato*) string chords; there can be no refusal. In case any listener has missed the point, "knock" (*klopfe*) is given three separate notes to indicate the threefold aspect of the deity. The abstract becomes physically real; the word is made flesh in music.

No 5 Soprano aria

Is this not a joyous exchange – the rich, noble, pious bridegroom Christ takes this poor, despised, wicked little whore in marriage, redeems her of all evil, and adorns her with all his goods?

Martin Luther: *The Freedom of a Christian*

From time to time, the intense religiosity of the cantatas, as here, expresses itself in sexual terms: "Open yourself to him, my whole heart, Jesus comes and draws inside me". The soul, represented by the soprano voice, responds with breathless excitement, depicted by Bach in terms of off-beat rhythms (the melodic phrases begin slightly askew). The aria is built as a da capo, and its slower (adagio) middle section becomes more overtly ecstatic: "Though I am only dust and earth, yet he will not spurn me and scorn to find his pleasure in me, so that I become his dwelling. Oh, how blessed I shall be!" The eroticism would not be out of place on the operatic stage.

No 6 Chorale

BWV 61 ends with the final lines of the hymn *Wie schön leuchtet der Morgenstern* ("How beautifully shines the morning star"): "Amen, amen: come, you beautiful crown of joy, do not delay long! I wait for you with longing!" Written by the Lutheran pastor Philipp Nicolai (1556-1608), it inspired a number of composers, and both words and music also provided the basis of Bach's chorale cantata, BWV 1. Beneath the simplicity of the soprano line, the lower parts spin out long phrases of yearning. A final touch of musical eloquence emphasizes the central theological point. A spectacular rising descant in the violins leads the imagination upward, to the transcendent realm opened by the miracle of the incarnation.

*

Suggested recording: Amsterdam Baroque Orchestra, dir. Ton Koopman

1st Sunday in Advent

BWV 62: *Nun komm, der Heiden Heiland*

(Now come, Saviour of the gentiles)

Librettist: Unknown

Date: 1724

BWV 62 was composed in Leipzig a decade after BWV 61, its predecessor for the same occasion. It owed its inspiration throughout to the same Advent hymn with which the earlier cantata began. This was Luther's *Nun komm, der Heiden Heiland* ("Now come, Saviour of the gentiles"). The heritage is ancient, dating back to the fourth century Roman bishop Ambrose. His *Veni, redemptor gentium* was translated into German by Luther and, set to an old plainchant melody, gained an enduring place in Lutheran worship. As these verses are the foundation of its entire text, BWV 62 accordingly belongs amongst Bach's chorale cantatas. The first and last movements use the beginning and end of the hymn verbatim, while for the inner movements an unknown librettist has paraphrased the remainder. The result, in words and music, is a series of tableaux that explore the meaning of the holy birth, seeing in the newborn infant the mighty champion of the human soul.

No 1 Chorus

Listening to Bach's music today, we marvel at the virtuosic range of technique that is the hallmark of his artistry. Yet the display of skill and the impression of beauty was for Bach integral to his purpose: to support a certain view of life's meaning. In the case of this chorus, charged as it is with unstoppable energy, the focal point is the nobility of the chorale that Bach weaves into his intricate texture. It brings with it the cry of welcome: "Now come, Saviour of the gentiles, revealed as the virgin's child; all the world wonders at this, that God has ordained such a birth for him".

In theatrical terms, the scene depicted is one of public excitement. The celebratory mood embraces not just the birth of Christ, but the subject of the day's biblical reading (Mt 21: 1-9). This described Christ's final entry into Jerusalem, surrounded by his followers. Triumphant but humble (as the story goes), he rode on an ass, conscious of his approaching death. The musical style is that of a brilliant, Italianate orchestral concerto. Groups of instruments – in this case a pair of oboes and the upper strings - separate out and recombine in a constant swirl of activity. The texture is always changing; the bustle is unending. The musical phrases begin off-beat, urging forward. Soon, though, the chorale melody announces its grandeur in the bass, moving at the unhurried pace of eternity.

In the organisation of this chorus, Bach displays his habitual mastery in weaving diverse elements into a coherent and yet varied whole. Without the voices the structure would be that of a self-sufficient instrumental piece, yet their words complete the sense of the music. One by one, the lines of the hymn emerge, alternating with the repeated material (the *ritornelli*) of the concerto. The soprano line, strengthened by the horn, slowly intones the melody, while the other voices complement its plainness with imitative part writing. Changes of rhythmic pace keep the chorale fresh throughout. On its first appearance, and when sung as the soprano *cantus firmus*, it proceeds at a stately two notes per bar. At other times – before all but one of the entries of the chorus - it is quoted at double speed (diminution). This is how it finally appears, as the chorus concludes with a repeat of the instrumental opening.

No 2 Tenor aria

The style of a courtly dance (the *passepied*) signposts the rank of the divine infant; its poised elegance distances Christ's origin from the pain and disorder of the mortal body. Lavish use of *staccato* (detached notes) brings a tiptoeing delicacy to the scene as the words point to the miracle of the birth: "Marvel, people, at this great mystery: the highest lord shows himself to the world." The timbres are bright, with two oboes doubling the first and second violins. Bach is also particular about dynamics, requiring a great deal of hush, as if not to wake the child. At the same time, the vocal line is exceptionally demanding, with great expanses of florid melody that flow upward to signpost the almost ungraspable elevation of the living God.

Yet as the middle section of this *da capo* aria reminds the believer, the apparently flesh and blood birth miraculously bypassed the sexual act: "Here the treasures of heaven are revealed, here heavenly food is set out for us; O wonder! Chastity is completely undefiled." Astonishment momentarily subdues the gaiety, and minor keys add a respectfully muted quality. For the final reference to Christ's nature, the texture reduces to voice and violin – the instrument that often features as a musical symbol of the Holy Spirit. A repeat of the first section of the aria restores the delight of the dance.

No 3 Bass recit

Moving ahead in time, the text turns to the full adult glory of the infant. Christ assumes the role of the warrior, destined to save the human race from its primeval opponent, death: "So from God's splendour and throne goes his only begotten Son. The champion of Judah breaks out, to run his course with joy and to redeem us fallen people". The vocal line strides, jumps and runs, evoking heroic physical presence. The last few bars are overcome with admiration and gratitude: "O bright radiance, O wonderful light of blessing!"

No 4 Bass aria

There is no distinction more serious than that of the warrior and the pacific inhabitant; no more is required to place man in the relation of master and slave.

Adam Ferguson: *An Essay on the History of Civil Society*

The music is a prolonged metaphor for power, with unison arpeggios and scale passages to demonstrate unwavering strength – much as in his operas Handel also presented masculine vigour, whether of the villainous or virtuous type. The continuo is doubled throughout at the octave by the upper strings; there is no softening or variety in tone colour: "Fight, conquer, strong champion! Show yourself to us mighty in the flesh!" Driving rhythms allow no rest to protagonist or listener; repeated sequences and straightforward harmonic progressions radiate confidence.

The central portion of the *da capo* design points to the contrasted helplessness of the human: "Be active to make our weakness strong!" Though the momentum continues, the key is now minor and the vocal line alternately cheers on its champion and wails and sighs over the vulnerable mortal. Believers must acknowledge their dependence on a superior being; humility is a precondition of heaven. A replay of the scene of battle completes the structure, yet the last phrase is a musical hint of the cost of victory. The tempo momentarily slows as the voice lingers in chromatic agony over *Fleische* ("flesh"). Christ too must eventually bow to the pain of subjugating the body to meet the demands of the soul.

No 5 Soprano/alto recit

After glimpsing the future, music and text return to their point of departure: the approaching birth of God incarnate: "We honour this glory and now draw near to your crib and praise with glad lips what you have prepared for us". Slowly moving string chords hover above, while the two voices spell out their awe and gratitude in a melodious duet. From this moment on, death need not be feared: "the darkness did not trouble us when we saw your everlasting light".

No 6 Chorale

Doubled by the instruments, a four-part setting of the final verse of Luther's hymn places Christ's birth in its theological context as a manifestation of God and his merciful plan for humankind: "Praise be to God the Father, praise be to God his only Son, praise be to God the Holy Spirit, forever and in eternity!"

*

Suggested recording: The Monteverdi Choir, dir. John Eliot Gardiner

1st Sunday in Advent

BWV 36: *Schwingt freudig euch empor*

(Soar joyfully on high)

Librettist: Uncertain, possibly Picander (Christian Friedrich Henrici)

Date: 1731

Although BWV 36 took final shape in 1731, much of its material (movements 1, 3, 5 and 7) comes from a secular cantata of 1726, written for the birthday of the princess of Anhalt-Cöthen. The original use, however, does not detract from the later religious intention, but rather shows the emotional fluidity of music. The point of departure in both versions of the cantata is celebration, and so the character of the music adapts itself easily to the joy surrounding the nativity. Christian Friedrich Henrici, who wrote under the pseudonym Picander, provided the words for the earlier cantata, and he may well have created the new text for BWV 36. Whoever the author was has inserted chorales instead of recitatives between the chorus and arias. The result is a substantial work, divided into two parts: one to be performed before and the other after the sermon.

No 1 Chorus

With the richness and variety of the concerto style, this movement is constructed as an alternation of instrumental episodes (*ritornelli*) with passages that include the voices. The first twelve bars – strings and continuo plus two oboes d'amore – set the scene. The first violin begins with a whirling triplet followed by an upward bounce. This becomes the motto for the whole movement: a musical transliteration of the impulse to fling the voice to heaven. The vocal lines rise in imitative sequence from bass to soprano, urging each other to musical worship: "Soar joyfully on high to the lofty stars, you tongues that now rejoice in Zion!" Accompanied by flourishes from the oboe, the interweaving of the voices continues until a moment of rhetorical contrast: "Yet stop! The sound need not carry far, for now he himself is drawing near to you, the Lord of Glory".

The choral texture solidifies as all four voices jointly emphasize the astonishing point: that God in human form is approaching his people. The overall structure of the movement is binary, as the two portions of text are then repeated in a similar way, along with intervening *ritornelli*. Similar, but not identical: for the surface of the music is constantly alive with changes of key. Within his tonal envelope of D major, Bach moves to the relative (B) minor halfway through the chorus, before journeying through a number of key shifts to arrive back to his starting point for the final proclamation of "he is drawing near to you, the Lord of Glory". The voices enter in sequence from highest to lowest, happily coinciding with the image of God's descent from heaven to earth.

No 2 Soprano/alto chorale

Any ambiguity about the sacred function of BWV 36 is instantly dispelled by Bach's reverent and creative treatment of Luther's Advent hymn: "Now come, Saviour of the gentiles, revealed as the virgin's child; the whole world wonders at this, that God has ordained such a birth for him". The full-bodied rejoicing of the chorus has contracted into the intimate format of a trio, and yet the musical riches are, if anything, greater. Two oboes softly double the solo voices, while the continuo below completes the ensemble. The singers linger over the text, line by line, in an imitative dialogue that extemporises upon the chorale melody. However, it is the third partner, the continuo, that adds the most elaborate improvisation, with each section introduced by the first four notes of the chorale. In this way, Bach ensures that the associated words of invitation to Christ ("Now come, Saviour of the gentiles") are kept constantly in mind, even as he embroiders the plainness of the old hymn. The ancient generates the eternally new.

No 3 Tenor aria

In this *da capo* aria, music and text represent the delight of faith as the mutual absorption of newly-weds: "Love draws its beloved gradually with soft footsteps. Just as a bride is enchanted when she looks at the bridegroom, so also a heart follows Jesus". The texture is refined, with the gentle, faintly melancholy flow (the key is minor) of a solo oboe accompanying the voice. A graceful and dance-like style implies a quasi-feminised depiction of the human soul as it yields to its Saviour.

No 4 Chorale

The first part of BWV 36 ends with the closing verse of a mystical hymn by the pastor Philipp Nicolai (1556-1608). He wrote both the words and music of *Wie schön leuchtet der Morgenstern* ("How beautifully shines the morning star") which became one of the iconic chorales of the Lutheran faith – and also inspired Bach's Annunciation cantata, BWV 1. In this powerful four-part harmonisation, each voice is reinforced by instruments.

The text brings together the themes of the cantata: the wish to worship God by making music, and the need to lose the self in the love of a deity who meets all needs – simultaneously an adorable infant, and the soul's spouse and protector. "Sound the strings in Cythera and let sweet music resound, that I may with my darling little Jesus, the wonderfully beautiful bridegroom of mine, move in constant love! Sing, jump, shout with joy, exult, thank the Lord! Great is the king of all honour!"

No 5 Bass aria

As with the other arias in BWV 36, new words have adapted the originally secular function of the music to a sacred purpose. The style is robust and energetic; the first violin part abounds in decorative brilliance, including a return to the bubbling triplets of the opening chorus, and in the same bright major key. Christ has entered the heart, and the believer greets the guest with delight: "Welcome, my dearest! Love and faith make room for you in my pure heart; come and dwell in me!"

No 6 Tenor chorale

There is, of course, work to be done. In Christian thinking, the reason for the divine incarnation was to provide a model of the power of spirit over flesh and thus to reveal the human capacity to transcend the limits of the body. The sixth verse of Luther's Advent hymn looks ahead to the Saviour's triumph over death: "You who are equal to the Father, lead on to victory in the flesh, so that your eternal divine power may be possessed by our sick human body." The melody is sung as a slow *cantus firmus* within the format of a trio sonata movement for two oboes and continuo. Moving at speed (*molto allegro*), the instruments urge on their champion; Bach makes merciless demands on the wind instruments, barely allowing them any breathing space – as if to say that all who embark on the Christian struggle will be stretched to the limit.

No 7 Soprano aria

Gently, BWV 36 approaches its goal. It is not so much the noise of outward show that brings closeness with the divine as the inner stirrings of faith: "Also with subdued, weak voices is God's majesty honoured". What seems weakness contains a strength that echoes through eternity, as the central portion of the aria makes clear: "When the spirit resounds like this, then, then it becomes a shout that he himself hears in heaven". The image comes to life through playful, bell-like imitation between voice and violin; the continuo joins in with its own staccato answering phrases. As ever, Bach draws on the sense perception of the material world to create a musical metaphor for a non-material reality.

No 8 Chorale

We can assume that the whole congregation took part in this sturdily harmonised setting of the doxology that ended Luther's hymn: "Praise to God the Father, praise to his only Son, praise to the Holy Spirit, for ever and ever in eternity". Music speaks to the individual, but also binds the group together. Did it – does it – make people better? That is another question.

*

Suggested recording: The Amsterdam Baroque Orchestra, dir. Ton Koopman

4th Sunday in Advent

BWV 132: *Bereitet die Wege, bereitet die Bahn!*

(Prepare the roads, prepare the path!)

Librettist: Salomon Franck

Date: 1715

The power of the compulsion to confess is almost always proportionate to the degree of anxiety with which individuals have initially felt impelled to conceal certain actions, impulses or desires.

Richard Webster: *Why Freud Was Wrong*

For the Christian, acknowledgement of sin is a precondition of the granting of eternal life in heaven; redemption is for those who know that they are undeserving. The stern libretto of BWV 132 is one of a collection of cantata texts published in 1715 by Salomon Franck, secretary to the council and court poet at Weimar. It is inspired by the day's prescribed Bible readings, which jointly suggest the tightrope of joy and penitence on which the self must maintain its precarious foothold. In the first of these (Phil. 4: 4-7), Paul exhorts Christians to rejoice and have no anxiety. The second (Jn. 1: 19-28) is taken from John's gospel and describes the interrogation of Christ's forerunner, John the Baptist, by the priestly establishment.

Franck transforms the incident into the self-examination that is required of every believer: the unflinching gaze into the conscience that will show how much the sinner has fallen short of the ideal. The rigorous text is animated by a musical language that signposts the psychological journey from summons to accusation, self-denunciation, confession and absolution. There are no choruses in this introspective work and the instrumental forces are modest: strings, organ, bassoon and (for the first movement only) an oboe.

No 1 Soprano aria

To understand the personal meaning of redemption requires constant and vigilant effort. The words of this *da capo* aria allude to verses from the Old Testament (Is. 40: 3-5) which were intended to console and inspire God's suffering people. A summons to attention – "Prepare the roads, prepare the path!" – occupies the entire first section. The oboe becomes the herald, beginning with a fanfare-like motto that anticipates the arrival of the voice. Bach makes enormous demands on the singer, whose winding heroism portrays the long road ahead. The texture alternates between solo and concerted instrumental sections; crisp reminders of the initial rhythm of the words punctuate the long vistas of the vocal writing.

The central section spells out the unremitting work for the conscience. All that deviates from the sacred ideal must be rectified: "Prepare the roads and make the footpaths in faith and in life completely smooth for the Most High, for the Messiah is coming". The opening three words are as before, but they are set differently, with jabbing repeated notes; an incessant rhythmic drive maintains the sense of urgency. For the climactic announcement – "the Messiah is coming" – Bach lets the instruments fall suddenly silent; the human voice alone proclaims the central tenet of faith. The reward and purpose of life is now in view, and with a return to the opening of the aria, humanity is once more focused on the need to ready itself for the event.

No 2 Tenor recit

Having pointed to the direction of travel, the librettist now spells out what the journey entails. Stylistically, Bach differentiates four portions of text, moving as needed from angularity to smoothness. The first requirement is that a true Christian must follow the example of Christ, whatever the personal cost: "If you would call yourself God's child and Christ's brother, then heart and mouth must freely confess the Saviour. Yes, O man, your entire life must give testimony of your faith! Even if Christ's word and teaching is sealed with your blood, devote yourself willingly to it!". For this, Bach uses the speech-like naturalism of recitative; discontinuities of rhythm and harmony imitate the dramatic pauses and changes of mood of the skilled public speaker.

Suffering, however, will bring its reward, promised in the lyrical sweetness of *arioso*: "For this is the Christian's crown and glory". Another transition returns to the uncompromising outlines of recitative for a reminder of the need for humility: "Meanwhile, my heart, prepare here and now the pathway of faith for the Lord, and clear away the hills and high places which stand opposed to him!" The final section compares the sin that separates humanity from God to the stone that blocked the entrance to Christ's tomb, and which could only be moved with the help of divine power: "Roll away the heavy stone of sin; accept your Saviour so that he might unite himself with you in faith!" An upward push starts off a rapid descent, and the continuo takes up the musical image. Then voice and instrument flow together as a token of the identity of the human with the divine.

No 3 Bass aria

The scene is a courtroom; prosecutor, judge and defendant fill the invisible space of the mind, now in imagination flooded with the glare of the accuser's lamp. One question haunts the listener: "Who are you?" Echoing the spoken phrase, Bach uses the musical motto of an octave leap to dominate the entire movement. The instrumentation is correspondingly rigorous: a solo cello allied with double bass (*violone*) and organ continuo. The tough arpeggiated figures for the cello act out the spiritual struggle.

First comes the challenge that looks ahead to the guilty verdict: "Who are you? Ask your conscience, then you are bound to hear the proper judgement on you, without any sham – whether you, O man, are false or true". The Old Testament provides evidence of original sin: "Who are you? Question the law, it will tell you who you are". Condemnation follows: "A child of anger in Satan's net, a false and hypocritical Christian". Serpentine chromaticism in both voice and continuo recalls the myth of the tempter in the Garden of Eden. At the end, syncopations in the vocal line represent the denial of truth and order, before the insistent opening motto brings the trial to its conclusion.

No 4 Alto recit

Sustained string chords place the listener in the self's inner sanctuary where full confession is made: "I freely admit to you, my God, that before now I have not truly committed myself to you. Although my mouth and lips call you Lord and Father, yet my heart has turned away. I have denied you with my life! How can you give a good testimony of me?" The instrumental pace is appropriately meditative, but there are sombre changes of harmony that reveal the agony of shame. Human shortcomings have severed the bond which baptism was intended to establish between sinner and God: "When, Jesus, your bath of spirit and water cleansed me of my misdeeds, I promised always to be faithful to you; but ah, alas...baptism's covenant is broken". The harmonic idiom remains dark as the soul, helpless and consciously unworthy, cries out for pity: "I repent my unfaithfulness! Ah God, have mercy, ah, help that I with unswerving loyalty may forever in faith renew the covenant of grace!" A final chord in the D major brings balm.

No 5 Alto aria

Baptism was from earliest times a reenactment of death and resurrection, made powerful and real by immersion, itself an active threat to life.

Richard Marius: *Martin Luther*

Reborn in penitence, the believer is now ready to receive Christ as the embodiment of God's reconciliation with the human. Both baptismal water and the stream of divine grace are symbolically united in the generous flow of a solo violin. While the librettist instructs the listener to be thankful – "Followers of Christ, ah, consider what the Saviour has given to you through baptism's cleansing bath" – Bach calls down blessing through music. The writing for the obbligato violin is idiomatic and graceful, its difficulties melting into melodious ease. The steady pace of the continuo provides a secure foundation for the ornamental style of both instrument and voice.

In Christian thought, the intimate connection of death and life is understood in terms of sin and redemption. The dross of earthly existence may be washed away by Christ's sacrificial blood and the pure water of baptism: "Through this fount of blood and water your clothes will become bright, though they were soiled with bad deeds" (note the chromatic disturbance of the vocal melody). The soul is to be made ready to welcome the newborn God with a rediscovered purity: "Christ gave you for new clothing crimson purple and white silk". While the structure of this aria is not a formal *da capo*, it is rounded off, as if in three parts, by a repeat of the opening violin solo that symbolises the descent of the divine spirit.

No 6 Chorale

Although Bach appears not to have attached a harmonisation, the libretto ends with the suggestion of a verse by the extraordinary Elizabeth Kreutziger. Born in 1500, she fled the convent to join Luther's circle in Wittenberg. Her hymn, "Lord Christ, God's only son", is also the foundation of BWV 96, composed for the 18th Sunday after Trinity, and its final stanza concludes BWV 123. It is a prayer for God's help in eliminating the sinful self: "Kill us through your goodness, awaken us through your grace; let the old mortal being sicken and die so that the new may live even here on this earth, and that our mind and all our desires and thoughts be directed to you". Could there be any merit in the idea of the human as endemically flawed? As long as the judge of virtue is not another citizen of this world.

*

Suggested recording: Netherlands Bach Collegium, dir. Pieter Jan Leusink

Christmas Day

BWV 63: *Christen, ätzet diesen Tag*

(Christians, engrave this day)

Librettist: Possibly Johann Michael Heinecke

Date: 25 December 1714

In July 1708, Bach was appointed Chamber Musician and Court Organist at Weimar. His abilities soon brought him an increase in salary and the esteem of the young Duke Johann Ernst. Conditions, however, were made difficult by the power struggles between Johann Ernst and his uncle and co-ruler, Wilhelm Ernst. The older man claimed supreme authority over the court servants, which included the musicians. Their working lives were hampered by a mass of conflicting regulations, prohibitions and commands.

By November 1713, Bach was looking elsewhere. He successfully auditioned for the post of organist at St. Mary's in Halle, but when he received his official letter of appointment in January 1714, he replied that he was unable to accept because he had not been formally released from service in Weimar. BWV 63 is likely to have been the piece with which he set out to impress his prospective new employers. From its style, the libretto is thought to be the work of Johann Michael Heinecke ("Heineccius"), the chief pastor at Halle, and Bach's bravura setting is a showcase for his own skills: his command of counterpoint, his dazzling play of texture, and his depth of emotional response.

What is notable about the text is how much it embraces the new approach to the sacred cantata that had been promoted by Erdmann Neumeister at the beginning of the century. In BWV 63, religious meditation is also a literary project. While steeped in theological assumptions about the meaning of Christmas, the libretto contains neither biblical quotations nor even a chorale. Instead, its seven movements are planned as a succession of recitatives that alternate with two arias in duet form, while the whole is bookended by sumptuous choruses. The writer takes the listener through a narrative that balances rejoicing with explanation. The central point is that the birth of Christ signifies God's gift of eternal life.

No 1 Chorus

The occasion is lavish – the arrival on earth of the divine prince – and clothed in appropriate musical splendour. Three distinct instrumental groups pay homage. Trumpets and drums, oboes and bassoon, and strings echo each other's C major fanfares, supported by the weight of the double bass (violone) and organ continuo. The enclosed space of the church building becomes a microcosm of a universe that reverberates with worship. Celestial pomp and power also imply control, coinciding neatly with the habitual symmetries of Bach's time. Not only is the overall design of the movement a three-part *da capo*, but its outer sections also divide into three. Passages of orchestral magnificence frame the verbal command: "Christians, engrave this day on metal and marble!". Trills ornament the vocal lines, dressed in their best for the great day.

The central section brings a change of text and atmosphere. The instruments fall temporarily silent, bringing intimacy to: "Come and hurry with me to the manger and show with joyful lips your thanks and duty".

As usual at this point in the *da capo* architecture, the key also changes – in this case to the relative minor, which suits the more introspective image of the birthplace. A short interlude, crowned with a prolonged trumpet trill, then ushers in the revelatory meaning of Christmas Day: "For the ray of light that streams in there will be a sign of grace to you". An imitative and gradually accumulating flow of voices and instruments suggests the radiance from above; a firm four-part vocal harmonisation completes the sentence before a return to the opening pageantry.

No 2 Alto recit

Although recitative generally implies the foregrounding of text with a minimum of melodic softening, in this case it glides constantly into the realm of the lyrical. The words grasp at the miraculous as Bach's setting (he instructs the accompanying string instruments to play quietly throughout) communicates deep wonder: "O blessed day! O amazing moment, when the salvation of the world – that sanctuary which God already in paradise promised to the human race – now comes in its perfection and seeks to deliver Israel from the captivity and slave chains of Satan". An imagined evil brings both a dragging tempo (*adagio*) and a writhing in the continuo and vocal line.

Now the listener must confront the unworthiness of the human in comparison with the divine. The change of direction begins with a poignant cry: "Dear God, what are we poor creatures?" To which the answer is: "We have fallen away and abandoned you, and still you do not hate us. For before we lie in ruin as we deserve" (the vocal line sinks) "the divine condescends to clothe itself in human form and on the earth" (another illustrative descent) "to become a child in the stable". The final bars turn to the melodic style of *arioso*, yet full of harmonic fluctuation to indicate the ungraspable nature of the miracle: "O incomprehensible yet blessed dispensation".

No 3 Soprano/bass aria

If BWV 63 has not quite reached its centre of symmetry – which arrives in the following recitative – there is a sense here of reaching the inner sanctum of the cantata. The reason is the quality of the music, whose bittersweet ambivalence is established by the timbre, both beautiful and melancholy, of a solo oboe; in a subsequent performance Bach gave the part to the organ – perhaps he could not resist playing it himself. The recurring musical motto, begun by the oboe and later imitated by the continuo, is a slow, gently ornamented descent: no doubt to indicate the blessing that floats down from on high. At the same time, the carefully phrased sighs seem to mingle penitence with longing: "God, you have ordained well what has now happened to us". With a relatively modest texture (two voices, oboe and continuo) this movement speaks of a withdrawal into private reverence away from the public celebration of the opening chorus.

The vocal parts – soprano and bass – are written in canon, i.e. they copy each other in sequence, leading alternately. The design is again a da capo, with a central episode that moves from the initial A minor to C major for the pledge of faith: "Therefore let us trust him constantly and build upon his grace, for he has bestowed upon us what will now delight us forever". This too is presented as a canon; the voices ascend in turn, united in reaching up to God.

No 4 Tenor recit

All is again positive: "Thus today the anxious sorrow that burdened Israel with fear is turned into pure salvation and grace." The librettist pivots toward the heroic, transforming the infant Saviour into the warlike defender of his people: "The lion of David's tribe has appeared; his bow is bent, his sword already sharpened to restore us to our former freedom." Bach mirrors the changing rhetoric with a shift to a confident C major, illustrating the arrow's flight with a dramatic surge of scales in the continuo. The voice rings out, and the key changes to the dominant (G) major, ready for the celebration.

No 5 Alto/tenor aria

Pourtant! dit-il, Dieux est bon; et l'univers qu'il a créé est bon. C'est l'attraction qui régit les mondes, et l'amour, et l'harmonie...Est-ce que les nuées d'orage qui voilent le soleil empêche que le soleil existe? Les nuées grossissent, la foudre tombe, et les hommes sont tremblants. Mais quelle lumière, après l'orage!

All the same, he said, God is good; and the universe he has created is good. Attraction rules the worlds, and love, and harmony...Do the storm clouds that cover the sun stop the sun existing? The clouds gather, the lightning falls, and men tremble. But after the storm, what light!

> Maurice Genevois: *Rémi des Rauches*

What can believers do but dance for joy? "Shout and call out to heaven, come, you Christians, come, join together in the dance. You should rejoice at what God has done today". The strings parts leap and bounce; the voices follow each other in energetic imitation; there is much musical twirling. Although not a formal *da capo*, the structure is the familiar ABA, which allows the central portion to present the rest of the text: "For his grace feeds us and covers us with so much well-being that one cannot thank him enough". With the repeat of the last phrase ("one cannot thank him enough"), Bach plunges into an exuberant inverted canon (the parts moving in opposite directions); a stream of notes on "thank" witnesses the overflowing gratitude of the human heart. With a slightly altered reprise of the opening, the aria ends with the high spirits of its beginning.

No 6 Bass recit

This dignified arioso-style recitative, accompanied by three oboes and strings, acts as a psychological bridge between the light-heartedness of the previous movement and the ceremonial grandeur with which BWV 63 ends. Punctuated by instrumental chords, it is a summons to renewed piety: "Let your hot flames of devotion redouble and strike against each other in humility and fervour." The vocal line rises as it exhorts the faithful to "Climb joyfully to heaven" and the movement ends with stately, reiterated calls to "thank God for what he has done!"

No 7 Chorus

Praise of God can be the only conclusion to this work for Christmas Day. The final chorus balances the opening of the cantata with, if anything, an even greater brilliance, both acoustically and technically. The full instrumental and vocal panoply returns for another large-scale *da capo* design that brings together triumph and humility. In the first section, a glittering preamble paves the way for the text: "Most High, look with favour upon these souls bowed in ardent love!" The words appear first in a solid chordal (homophonic) setting before being explored afresh in a double fugue. Bach has unpicked the sentence, giving a rising shape to "Most High, look with favour", as if to suggest the uplifted gaze to heaven, and a drooping quality to "these souls bowed in ardent love". These two musical phrases are interwoven in succession first by the voices and then with contributions from the instruments, to reach a climax that brings back the opening *ritornello*.

The B section of the movement brings a similar fusion of compositional bravura with expressive purpose. Its text divides into two parts. First alone, and then accompanied, the voices ask for divine approval: "Let the thanks that we bring make a pleasing sound to you and let us always walk in blessing". There is, however, a contrast of mood and tempo – now slowing to *adagio* – for a reminder of the mortal danger from which Christ promises to rescue humankind: "But let it never happen that Satan should torment us". One of the double fugues that follows is full of insistent repeated notes; the other is a sly, chromatic descent that emphasises the sinister nature of the enemy. Even as the voices make their last prayer for protection, reminders of the energy and optimism of the opening of the movement start to reappear, preparing the way musically for a return to the festive beginning. If music is a type of sacrificial offering, BWV 63 would surely be acceptable to the ear of any God.

*

Suggested recording: Münchener Bach-Chor,
dir. Karl Richter

Christmas Day

BWV 91: *Gelobet seist du, Jesu Christ*

(Praise be to you, Jesus Christ)

Librettist: Unknown

Date: 25 December 1724

BWV 91 is a little more introverted than BWV 63, which was written for Christmas ten years earlier in very different circumstances. At that time (1714), Bach was working at Weimar, uncertain of his future and eager to move on to a more congenial post. BWV 63 was a brilliant demonstration of his expertise, and its libretto differed from that of most later cantatas by not including a chorale. By December 1724, however, Bach was securely settled in Leipzig, where composing a weekly cantata was a regular duty. Their libretti were generally a mix of religious poetry with biblical quotations, with a place for at least one hymn – usually at the end. Sometimes, as here with BWV 91, the texts were based entirely on a chorale, either used verbatim or paraphrased. Here, the words are anchored to verses by Luther that had become a traditional feature of Christmas Day worship, for they summarise the meaning of the Nativity.

No 1 Chorus

The text – the first verse of the hymn – is exultant and thankful: "Praise be to you, Jesus Christ/that you were born as a man/of a virgin, that is true;/the host of angels rejoices over this/ Lord have mercy!" Each line appears separately, with the melody sung slowly as a soprano *cantus firmus*, while the lower voices repeat the words independently. All of this is enclosed within a musical context that conveys ceremonious joy. The imposing sound of two horns calls the world to attention, inspiring a rush of seven instrumental lines in turn: three oboes, upper strings and continuo. The volume gathers; drumbeats mark out the pace.

Bach makes use of three elements to maintain excitement: ascending scales, fanfare-like arpeggios, and a restless motto from the horns, as if turning on the spot. By weaving them together and passing them from one group to another, he generates a continuous flow of movement that colours our perception of the hymn. We understand from the outset that it will be full of urgent meaning. Unlike many of Bach's chorale choruses, in which the individual lines of a hymn are preceded by the interplay of other voices, here the steady soprano melody takes the lead almost every time. The lower voices then reinforce the message – most emphatically in the case of the third line, when they repeat "that is true"; the Christian must accept the miracle of the virgin birth. For the angelic rejoicing of the fourth line, Bach brings together his three main motivic building blocks: the scales, the spread chords and the twirling. The final *Kyrie eleis* ("Lord, have mercy") is a lingering cry to heaven.

No 2 Soprano recit

Part recitative, part hymn, this movement mingles Luther's second verse with theological commentary. It begins by identifying the Nativity as part of God's design: "The radiance of the highest glory, the image of God's essence, has at the appointed time chosen for himself a dwelling place". The first line of the hymn adds, as a gloss: "The eternal Father's only child". Here, as with each subsequent quotation from the chorale, the accompanying continuo part repeats the beginning of the hymn melody three times: Bach's reminder of the trinitarian nature of God.

The narrative continues with "The eternal light born of light" and completes the thought with a tenderly decorated version of the second line of the chorale: "is now found in the manger". A cry of astonishment – "O people, see what love's power here has done!" – takes us back to the hymn. "Our poor flesh and blood" (the librettist slips in: "and was this not cursed, condemned, lost?") "has become the clothing of the everlasting good". Bach responds to the librettist's interruption with a chromatic descent in the continuo and diminished harmonies, but with a last gesture to salvation ("so our nature has been picked out for blessing") the music ends with a firm cadence in preparation for the next movement.

No 3 Tenor aria

Three oboes in close harmony accompany the voice: "God, for whom the earth's circle is too small, whom neither world nor heaven can contain, chooses to be in the cramped manger". Bach's musical language implies compression. The metrical flow is bound by tightly controlled dotted rhythms; angular melody conveys a sense of discomfort, and both instrumental and vocal phrases are brought to an abrupt end by a leap of a minor seventh. In this deliberately awkward piece, the rhythmic straitjacket is barely loosened at the thought of the benefits brought by God's abasement: "if this eternal light appears to us, then henceforth God will not hate us, for we are now the children of this light". The voice is allowed to stay still for "eternal" (*ewge*), and there is quietness at the prospect of eternity, but the stiff outlines continue to remind mortals of the constraints to which God has subjected himself in accepting the limitations of the body.

No 4 Bass recit

The emphasis in this expressive accompanied recitative is on the nature of the gift that Christ's birth has brought (should humankind be disposed to receive it): "O Christendom! Prepare yourself to receive the Creator." Beginning with an octave leap to indicate the expanse of the Almighty, the message continues: "The great son of God has come down to you as a guest". Belief in the miraculous event will bring peace of mind, for the Saviour will lead the human soul to its heavenly destination: "Ah, let your heart be stirred by this; he comes to you to lead you before his throne out of this vale of tears". The tempo slows to *adagio* as the voice makes a laboured ascent to depict life's pilgrimage; the violins sigh in sympathy. After much harmonic wavering, the key makes its laborious way from A minor to C minor. The Christian path is one of struggle.

No 5 Soprano/alto aria

Music is able to bring together contrasting elements, not to dissolve their separate identity, but to reveal them as part of a united whole. Through its combination of melody, harmony and architecture – an expansive, orderly *da capo* – this aria reconciles the ambiguities of the Christian position: that though life necessitates sacrifice, a merciful transcendental power is on hand to crown it with joy. The paradigm is the figure of Christ himself: the immortal God who identified with humility and suffering and yet opened up the path to heaven.

This is the point made by the text, in which the message remains consistent throughout. The A section announces: "The poverty which God takes upon himself has brought us eternal salvation and the overflowing abundance of heaven's treasures", to which the B section responds: "His mortal nature makes you equal to the splendour of angels, and places you in their choir". Unison violins plus continuo determine the overall positive mood: the strings skip along, while the bass line maintains its steady progress. Against this backdrop, the vocal setting differentiates Christ's sacrifice from the redemption that it brings. *Die Armut* ("The poverty") brings lingering dissonance, while *ewig Heil* ("eternal salvation") is sweetly harmonious.

The B section continues to make the distinction between the living Christ's pain and the glorious future that awaits the faithful. At "his mortal nature", the vocal lines combine slowly ascending semitones (such chromaticism being a frequent musical shorthand for the influence of the devil) with stumbling syncopations. But at the vision of the angelic choir, the voices soften into a melodious flow. The intricate and finely blended part writing becomes an aural metaphor for a world in which the divine purpose includes both suffering and delight, and yet from which, in the end, a universal harmony will emerge.

No 6 Chorale

The full orchestra returns – horns, drums and oboes and strings – to add splendour to the triumphant last verse of Luther's hymn: "He has done all this to show his great love for us. Let all Christendom rejoice and thank him eternally. Kyrie eleis!"

*

Suggested recording: Collegium Vocale Gent, dir. Phillippe Herreweghe

Christmas Day

BWV 110: *Unser Mund sei voll Lachens*

(May our mouth be full of laughter)

Librettist: Georg Christian Lehms

Date: 25 December 1725

ridete, quicquid est domi cachinnorum
(let your house shake with all the laughter that is in it)

> Catullus

Christmas Day celebrates the fusion of the divine and the mortal, symbolised by the mystery of the incarnation: God made flesh in the newborn Christ. In this sumptuous cantata, music is, as ever in Bach, the conduit through which the imagination connects with its loftiest hopes. For the occasion of BWV 110, Bach drew on a libretto by the short-lived (1684-1717) Polish-born poet and novelist Georg Christian Lehms. It unfolds a panorama of God's eternal greatness and redemptive love for a consciously undeserving human race.

No 1 Chorus

O Freunde, nicht diese Töne! sondern laßt uns angenehmere anstimmen, und freudenvollere. Freude! Freude!

(O friends, not these sounds – let us instead strike up something more pleasurable and joyous. Joy! Joy!)

> Beethoven's call for the human voice to complete the message of his ninth symphony

In keeping with the idea of music as pleasing sacrifice, Bach begins BWV 110 with a personal offering. He places the magnificent opening of his fourth orchestral suite at the service of Lehms's text, so that what was originally purely instrumental fuses with the verbal; words and music form a continuum of meaning. The structural envelope is the French overture, in which the ceremonial grandeur of the beginning and end frame a central section of freewheeling energy. It is here that Bach adds the voices: "May our mouth be full of laughter and our tongues full of praise. For the Lord has done great things for us". The words are a quotation from Psalm 126, itself a song both of worship and of appeal for God's continuing help; the overall design of the movement, with the instrumental sections surrounding the vocal element, can perhaps be seen as a metaphor for the power of the divine to enclose and protect the human.

Large-scale orchestral forces dazzle the listener: strings, flutes (an addition to the original version), oboes, bassoon, trumpets and drums announce with processional formality the arrival of God on earth. As the cavalcade appears to halt, the voices arrive in turn, their high spirits integrated into the pre-existing patterns of the original instrumental piece. Bach's prolonged setting of *Lachens* brings us a whole world shaking with laughter. A change of texture and key then eases the full-voiced celebration into a more introspective mood. Three solo voices (soprano, alto, tenor), accompanied by woodwind alone, reflect on God's especial goodness: "For the Lord has done great things for us". The change of texture gives renewed impact to the return of the full chorus.

A solo bass voice at length emerges, gesturing to the favour granted from on high. The rising intervals of a fourth on *der Herr* ("the Lord") direct the inner gaze upward, while the sweeping octave descents on *Großes* ("great things") remind the listener that the celestial gift has been granted from above. A last outburst of praise draws in the whole ensemble of singers and instrumentalists, and leads to a climactic return of the original, stiffly choreographed ceremony. It is as if the closing instrumental section sweeps humankind in the train of the divine king.

No 2 Tenor aria

The glamour of public show gives way to private reflection, for which Bach provides a chamber-music context of two flutes and continuo. In this muted B minor aria, the flute parts wind softly around each other as the singer urges: "You thoughts and senses, soar aloft now from here, climb swiftly heavenward and consider what God has done!". The vocal line imitates the gently spiralling contours of the instruments; the rising of pitch acts out the mind's ascent to higher things. Each believer must meditate on the significance of the day: "He becomes human for this reason alone, that we should become children of heaven". At this point, the key moves to the subdominant (here E minor) – a tonal shift that brings a certain colouring of acquiescence and yielding. The offering that God requires is the submission to his purpose in redeeming humanity; the vocal phrases yearn upward, returning at last to the home key and followed by a repeat of the opening bars to round off the structure.

No 3 Bass recit

Another passage from the Old Testament (Jeremiah 10:6) brings a reminder of God's might: "There is none equal to you, Lord. You are great, and your name is great, and you prove this by your deeds". The string accompaniment adds its own imagery, as its climbing arpeggiated phrases accompany the strong leaps and runs of the voice.

No 4 Alto aria

The text sets out the paradox that underpins Christian belief. On the one hand: "Ah, Lord, what is mankind that you seek his salvation so painfully? A worm that you curse, when hell and Satan are about him." And on the other: "yet mankind is also your son, whom soul and spirit call to his inheritance through love". There is a seeming ambivalence in the human: morally flawed, and yet able to transcend its inherent unworthiness by leaning on an omnipotent yet self-sacrificing deity. Giving due weight to the theological complexity, Bach writes in a minor key and calls on the plaintive, dark timbre of a solo oboe d'amore, expressive of melancholy and seriousness. Christmas Day is a time of celebration, but also a reminder of the gulf between heaven and earth.

There is, too, an implicit tension in Bach's play of rhythm. He pits the angular vocal style, with which he characterises the corruption of human nature, against the more flowing quality of the oboe part – though this also conveys pathos in its chromatically coloured melodic contours. While, in Bach's day, what seemed on paper a clash of timing between beats divided into three (triplets) and those into four could be smoothed away in performance, there were occasions where rhythmic conflict was an intentional expressive device. Given Bach's keen response to text, this would make sense here, for it highlights the contrast between the dislocated human condition and the smooth course of the spirit. The second, more forgiving part of the text ("yet mankind is also your son etc."), is differentiated by a change of key and a softening of mood and style. The music lingers, with a certain poignancy, on the love (*Liebe*) that calls the human to the divine. Unfulfilled longing is never far from the religious belief of the cantatas.

No 5 Soprano/Tenor duet

Here, though, the vision is of a universe in which God and mortal are reconciled. The singers represent the angelic messengers who, in Luke's gospel (2:14), proclaimed the Nativity as the harbinger of a realm of peace: "Glory to God in the highest and peace on earth and good will to men!". As with the opening chorus, Bach calls on music that he had composed earlier: in this case, adapted from his 1723 setting of the Magnificat (BWV 243a). The close imitation and euphony of the vocal lines acts as a paradigm of the harmony to come when all align themselves with Christ; meanwhile, the continuo part gives buoyant support. The text appears in three sections, separated by short ritornelli. First, an extended, florid fanfare pays its homage ("Glory to God in the highest"). Gently cradling harmonies then bring the blessing of peace and, finally, universal goodwill flows vocally over the world, ending in a triumphant climax.

No 6 Bass aria

The connection between music and worship is made explicit in this summons to the communal project of gratitude: "Awake, sinews and limbs, and sing the joyful songs that are pleasing to our God". A solo trumpet leads the way, while three oboes strengthen the ensemble. The singer, too, enters with the musical athleticism of a second trumpet, taking on the role of the leader and preacher who rouses the world. A contrasting central section provides respite from the extrovert display, as text and music focus on the strings as symbols of the necessary inner devotion: "and you strings, full of quiet reverence, you shall prepare for him the kind of praise that makes heart and spirit rejoice". Yet here too there is nothing staid or solemn, as the violins busy themselves with their passagework. With a repeat of the opening material, the aria ends in heroic mode, as a celebration of the glorious future that the birth of Christ promises to all believers.

No 7 Chorale

Nothing remains but for the whole congregation to join together in thanks and praise. The words are the last verse of a Christmas hymn – "We Christian folk have now such joy" – by the sixteenth-century Saxon clergyman, Kaspar Füger (1521-c.1592). Bach enriches his setting by including all his instruments to reinforce the voices: "Alleluia! Praise be God! We all sing from the bottom of our hearts. For God has today brought us such joy that we shall never, ever forget". The sound of the packed church would have been, one imagines, reassuringly confident.

*

Suggested recording: J.S. Bach-Stiftung,
dir. Rudolf Lutz

Second Day of Christmas

BWV 40: *Dazu ist erschienen der Sohn Gottes*

(For this reason the Son of God has appeared)

Librettist: Unknown

Date: 26 December 1723

This day in the Church year, i.e. 26 December, both continues the celebration of Christ's birth and also commemorates the death of St. Stephen, the first Christian martyr. There are therefore two sets of associated readings from scripture. The first pair is specific to the Nativity: Luke's account of the shepherds' visit to the manger (Lk.2: 15-20), and an excerpt from Paul's letter to Titus (Tit.3: 4-7), emphasising God's redemptive mercy to unworthy humans. The second pair includes Christ's attack (Mt. 38: 34-39) on the Pharisaical rejection of God's true prophets and messengers, and an account of the death of Stephen in Acts 6 and 7. The librettist of BWV 40 has responded with a scenario which underscores the conflict between the forces of good and evil as they battle for the human soul. Bach's powerful setting is charged with psychological tension; the inclusion of three chorales – an unusually high number – looks to a tight-knit moral community.

Resplendent with drama, BWV 40 embodies a sermon on the meaning of the Nativity. For believers, God's arrival on earth in human form offers a release from mortal limits. It reveals that flesh and blood may be imbued with the divine and hence that the self might be perpetuated in eternity. The victory of life over death, however, can never be easily won, for in the theology of the cantatas struggle is endemic to the human condition. Yet while Christ's death on the cross is the ultimate paradigm of endurance, the text and music of BWV 40 leapfrog over suffering to focus the mind on the divine warrior's triumph over the forces of evil. To the believer, the Devil – the representative of death – is no mere cipher, but has real power to undermine faith, blocking access to eternal life and thus destroying both present and future happiness.

No 1 Chorus

The text is brief: "For this reason the Son of God has appeared: to destroy the Devil's work". Bach's musical exegesis unpacks and enlarges the verbal meaning in a virtuoso blend of the didactic and the rhetorically vivid. Each of the two main textural elements – the instrumental and the vocal – has its distinct task, while both are integrated into the overall fusion of mood, meaning and structure. A pair of horns, initiating a dialogue with strings and oboes, announces an atmosphere of the festive and the noble. The alternating phrases are simple enough, but the listener's attention is rewarded by variety both of phrase length and of instrumental groupings. A few bars later, the continuo part adds its own energy, with animated descending sequences below the slower-moving suspensions above.

A momentary silence from the instruments highlights the entry of the voices. Their opening rhythm follows the natural stress of the German words: *Dazu ist erschienen* (a rough English equivalent would be "that's why he's appeared now"). The horns respond immediately, and from now on Bach combines voices and instruments, letting the volume and intensity rise and fall as he plays with permutations of texture. In contrast to the rapid statement of the first three words (*Dazu ist erschienen*), the divine presence – *der Sohn Gottes* ("the son of God") – unfolds at a slower pace, with the emphasis on "God". Finally, the completion of the sentence arrives: *daß er die Werke des Teufels zerstöre* ("to destroy the Devil's work"). With this thought, the voices hammer out an insistent monotone, followed by furious activity in the bass: a portrait of the victor despatching the writhing enemy.

As ever, Bach must serve two masters: the dictates of artistic invention, and the need to expound the theological message. In a case like this, when a handful of words is full of compressed meaning, music must find a way to give the short text its due weight. For the central part of his design, Bach calls upon fugue as a device for repetition without monotony. In fact, he creates a double fugue: which is to say, he presents two themes for imitation. The first is associated with "For this reason the Son of God has appeared" and the second has a suitably serpentine character (present also in the continuo) for "to destroy the Devil's work". With Bach's mastery of counterpoint, both themes are developed simultaneously and draw on instrumental reinforcements to reach a climax. For the third and final section of the chorus (a division into three giving a familiar symmetry), Bach returns to the buoyancy of the opening: not as an identical repeat, as in the *da capo* format, but as a concluding assurance that the Devil's power is vanquished.

No 2 Tenor recit

The subject is the mystery of the incarnation: God's arrival in human form. "The Word becomes flesh and dwells in the world, the light of the world shines its beam over the circle of the earth". An upward flow of the vocal line on *bestrahlt* ("shines") gestures to the spread of divine light and is echoed by the continuo. The next portion of text pictures the Nativity: "The great Son of God leave his heavenly throne and it pleases his majesty to become a little human child". A descent of pitch indicates the divine humility. The rhetoric changes with a sudden leap of a minor sixth in the voice, accompanied by darker harmonies: "Consider this exchange, those who can. The king becomes a subject, the lord appears as a servant, and for the human race – O sweet word in everyone's ear" (emotion drives up the vocal pitch) – "is born to bring comfort and salvation".

No 3 Chorale

This is the third verse of a Christmas hymn by Caspar Füger (1521-1592). It is a reminder of the contrast between the unredeemed and the redeemed state of humanity. "Sin makes sorrow, Christ brings joy, because he has come to this world as comforter. God is now with us in our need: who can now condemn us as Christians?" Bach's bittersweet harmonies mark the contrast between the painful awareness of death, and joy at the thought of redemption.

No 4 Bass aria

Now that the rescuer has arrived, the monster – death and its associated terrors – can safely be taunted: "Hellish serpent, are you not afraid?". The first two words of the German text (*Höllische Schlange*, i.e. "hellish serpent") dictate the choppy rhythm and pitch contours of Bach's setting. The pace is fast and furious, with the strong outlines of the voice, oboes and lower strings surrounding the undulations of the first violin. Flashes of harmonic instability within an ultimately secure tonal context reflect the cut and thrust of battle. The outcome is never in doubt, as the text (with a change of key) adds: "The one who as victor crushes your head is now born". Nor does the energy slacken, as Satan's winding coils thrash around in the bass. There is, however, a moment of calm in the vocal line at the vision of a beatific eternity: "And the lost ones are now blessed with everlasting peace". A return to the headlong opening bars completes the structure.

No 5 Alto recit

As the divine purpose is to restore the original harmony between God and mortal, a vision of paradise regained follows the tumult: "The serpent that in paradise let the soul's poison fall upon all the children of Adam brings us no more danger. The woman's seed appears, the Saviour has come in the flesh and has taken away all its venom. Therefore take comfort, troubled sinner". The harmonic surface of this accompanied recitative moves imperceptibly, the vocal line gently sustained by the ripple of the upper strings, with minimal input from the continuo below. The final words of consolation – "Therefore take comfort, troubled sinner" – are, in musical terms, expressive of anguish rather than contentment. A rising minor sixth, followed by the fall of a diminished third, acknowledges the burden of sin that oppresses the human soul.

No 6 Chorale

Despite the good news, the Christian path demands a steadfast resistance to the power of evil. The undercurrents of disquiet are magnificently conveyed in Bach's setting of a verse by Paul Gerhardt (1607-1676). Having lived through much strife, encompassing both ecclesiastical infighting and the horrors of the Thirty Years' War, this Lutheran pastor had a keen sense of the harms of conflict, identified in the Christian consciousness as the influence of the Devil. His lines are full of resolute defiance and also hope: "Shake your head and say, 'Flee, you ancient serpent! Why do you try to renew your sting, and make me fearful and anxious? Now your head is snapped off and I, through the suffering of my Saviour, am snatched away from you and carried off into the hall of joy.'" The harmonisation is full of the kind of chromatic disruptions that are coded references to the influence of evil, with stealthy semitonal glides in the bass to indicate the presence of Satan. Words and music at last carry the believer safely to heaven and the D minor tonic.

No 7 Tenor aria

As part of Bach's musical homage to his first Christmas at Leipzig, nothing (one would think) could have dazzled more than this amalgam of the heroic with gratitude and relief. The vocal demands are almost superhuman, in the manner of an instrumental concerto. There are no string parts, but simply the penetrating sound of horns and oboes, which the athleticism of the voice must rival, and indeed dominate, for it crowns all with the summons: "Christian children, rejoice!". The intensity of emotion transmutes into prolonged coloratura on *freuet* ("rejoice"); music has its own vocabulary of feeling. As is usual, a second portion of text brings contrasting thoughts, partnered by changes in musical language. Danger can never be discounted: "Even though the kingdom of hell rages, and though Satan's fury terrorises you...". Disjointed gasps in the vocal line convey panic, as the continuo churns below, simulating the untiring energy of evil. But all is well: "Jesus, who can save, takes up his little chicks and covers them with his wings". The maternal imagery, taken from Matthew's gospel (Mt. 23:37) brings a quieter moment as the wind instruments fall silent and the voice soars in lyrical tenderness. Bach, however, does not linger, but returns his singer to the fanfare-like opening. A final display of vocal fireworks banishes – for the moment – all past fear.

No 8 Chorale

Having explained and inspired, BWV 40 ends with adoration of the deity who has the power to save his worshippers from death. The words are from a hymn by the Lutheran pastor Christian Keymann (1607-1662), and the melodic lines are reinforced by the instruments. The psychological comfort of faith is evident: "Jesus, receive your members henceforth in grace; grant all that one can ask to restore your brothers. Give the entire Christian flock peace and a blessed year. Joy, joy upon joy! Christ wards off all sorrows. Bliss, bliss upon bliss! He is the sun of grace." A last ascending sequence of fourths in the upper parts directs the believing mind upward to God.

*

Suggested recording:
Amsterdam Baroque Orchestra and Choir,
dir. Ton Koopman

Second Day of Christmas

BWV 121: *Christum wir sollen loben schon*

(We should praise Christ beautifully)

Librettist: Unknown

Date: 26 December 1724

The focus of this cantata differs from that of BWV 40, which was composed for the same point in the previous year. BWV 40 gave an account of the meaning of Christmas in terms of a battle between Christ as heroic redeemer and his arch-enemy, the devilish figure of death. BWV 121, on the other hand, looks to the intrinsic mystery of the incarnation and the need for the human mind to embrace the miraculous. It insists on the need for unreason, not (one would hope) as a universal principle of life, but in accepting the possibility of God in human form. Many of Bach's cantata texts wrestle with the negative implications of this idea, in terms of guilt that the embodied self falls short of its divine potential, but in BWV 121 the believer is, for the moment, directed to an open-ended faith that the two can become one.

No 1 Chorus

BWV 121 is a chorale cantata, i.e. based on a pre-existing hymn: *Christum wir sollen loben schon* ("We should praise Christ beautifully"). The outer movements use the first and last verses verbatim, and an unknown librettist has made a paraphrase of the rest. The ancient provenance of the chorale matters a great deal for the purpose of conveying a message that is untouched by time. First published in 1524, the hymn was Luther's translation of part of a Latin poem (*A solis ortus cardine*) on the life of Christ. This dates back to the fifth century CE, a thousand years before Luther's own day. The melody is of comparable antiquity, originating in plainsong, and hence is based on the modal scale system that was already archaic in Bach's time (see the introduction to this book).

In comparison with the major/minor tonal system, which remains the language of much of today's music, and in the development of which Bach played an important part, the return to a modal form of expression brings a sense of ambiguity. It hints at an eternal, ungraspable truth that transcends the divide between the material world and the intangible. In the case of this chorus, Bach also drew on the older style of the motet, with its clear-cut separation of the lines of text. For each one, the three lower voices begin in turn with the words and melody. At length, the soprano arrives, presenting the same material in longer (augmented) note values; here, the pace is slowed to half speed. The hymn calls for endless, far-flung celebration of Christ's coming: "We should praise Christ beautifully/The son of the pure maiden Mary/As far as the dear sun shines its light/Reaching to the ends of the world".

The part-writing combines movement with dignity. Each voice is doubled by instruments: strings, oboe, a trumpet for the soprano, and the solemn weight of trombones on the lower lines. An oscillating pattern of notes, first in the continuo, then passed to alto, tenor and bass, acts as a unifying feature. Its starting point is a reminder – an accelerated initial fragment – of the hymn tune, generating constant energy as a token of the life-giving influence that has arrived on earth. Bach prolongs it to emphasise certain words: *loben* ("praise"), *Magd* ("maiden"), *Sonne* ("sun"), *leucht'* ("light") etc. All the while, thanks to the modal character of the hymn, there is a sense of fluidity in which key boundaries are felt to shift and dissolve. We are not sure until the very end where the centre is to be found; even then, after a long-spun setting of *reicht* ("reaches"), the music comes to rest with the unanswered harmony of an imperfect cadence in B. God, the music implies, escapes definition.

No 2 Tenor aria

The Christian, we are told, should not puzzle too much over the incarnation, but simply believe: "O you creature exalted by God, do not try to understand, just marvel: God wishes through flesh to gain the salvation of the flesh". A charmingly syncopated, almost dance-like style and a light instrumental texture (solo oboe d'amore and continuo) help the believer escape the chore of rational thought. While there are no tonal uncertainties about this movement – the harmonies and *da capo* format are very much in Bach's contemporary idiom – rhythm and phrase structure are playfully varied as a token of the unexpected. For instance, the twelve-bar introduction is designed as two groups of three, followed by three groups of two. The text of the B section cautions the listener not to forget the proper order of things: "How great indeed is the creator of everything, and how despised and lowly you are – to think that you have been saved like this!". The drop in mortal self-esteem is signalled by an inversion of the musical idea that began the movement. As a result, the phrase drawing attention to the poor status of the human falls naturally (and suitably) lower than the phrase that celebrates God. A repeat of the gently buoyant A section, completing the *da capo* structure, leaves a final impression of lightness and hope.

No 3 Alto recit

There is an almost conversational intimacy to this simply accompanied recitative – except that, as ever with Bach, harmonic change drives the motor of the narrative. The text falls into three portions, each of them showing that God's nature lies beyond human logic and that heaven and earth are a continuum under his sway: "The unmeasurable essence of grace has not chosen heaven for his dwelling, because no boundary can enclose it". And then: "What wonder! All reason and intelligence are unable to fathom this mystery, when grace is poured into a chaste heart". In both cases, Bach's underlying trajectory is in the positive direction of the dominant key, though the bass line follows some unexpected paths. The miracle, though, is left to the end: "God chooses a pure body for the temple of his honour, so that he might, to mankind, turn in a wondrous manner". An extraordinary, completely unexpected chordal shift – a kind of harmonic jack-in-a-box – lands the living God on the solid ground of C major.

No 4 Bass aria

A simple, intuitive faith, bypassing rational niceties, must be the model for the believer. The text alludes to the biblical story in Luke's gospel (1:44), in which John the Baptist (forerunner of Christ) jumped for joy in the womb as he sensed the presence of the correspondingly unborn Saviour: "John's joyful leaping recognised you, my Jesus, already". Bach's rhetorical purpose is to arouse in the listener the same response of instinctive joy that is both the expression of faith and its reward. Hence the music is a display of guileless spontaneity, full of bouncing rhythms and undisturbed by complex harmonies. Leaping and twisting, punctuated with off-beat kicks, perhaps its style owed something to Bach's personal knowledge of the pregnancies of his two wives; he was the father of numerous children, though several died in infancy, as was so often the case in those times. The vocal part is as agile as the instruments, full of trills and long runs, as in the prolonging of *freudenvolles* ("joyful").

The structure is the familiar threefold *da capo*. Its central section moves to the relative (A) minor from C major as entertainment gives way to introspection: "Now just as a faithful arm holds you, so my heart wishes to leave the world and press on fervently towards your crib". Although a more lyrical style – a calmer rhythmic pace – and a sparer texture give a sense of quiet, the motivic material of the opening section is a constant reminder of the aria's intention to encourage a childlike trust; the syncopations become the kick of the mind rather than the body – the impatience of the soul to come close to God on earth. Adept as ever at making his craft conform to theological purpose, Bach ends his middle section with a shift to the key of the opening, and a repeat of the original boisterous delight.

No 5 Soprano recit

Bach follows the comparative earthiness of the aria with a contrasted, deeply spiritual moment. A leap of the imagination takes the believer to the scene at the crib. That the physical vulnerability of this child should clothe the unmeasurable divinity is a truth too deep for words: "Yet how should one look upon you in your crib? There is sighing in my heart" (the vocal line droops with a sympathetic semitone): "with trembling and barely open lips it brings its offering of thanks. God, who was so boundless, takes upon himself a servant's form and poverty" (pitch and status fall together). "And because he has done this for us, so with the angel choirs let a jubilant song of praise and thanks be heard". A ringing top B maps vocal effort onto the mind's aspiration towards a loftier model of the human.

No 6 Chorale

BWV 121 ends with Bach's setting of the last verse of the hymn on which the entire cantata is based: "Praise, honour and thanks be given to you, Christ, born of the pure maiden, with Father and the Holy Spirit, from now until eternity". The old modal character of the melody is subtly fused with the harmonic language of Bach's own time. Yet the cantata finishes, as it began, in mystery: a final lingering, unresolved chord points to an infinite expanse of time and space beyond human reach.

*

Suggested recording: J.S. Bach-Stiftung, dir. Rudolf Lutz

Second Day of Christmas

BWV 57: *Selig ist der Mann*

(Blessed is the man)

Librettist: Georg Christian Lehms

Date: 26 December 1725

[E]ver since the first struggle for survival during the persecutions of ancient Rome, going to one's death with fearless fortitude was the outward sign of a true child of God, of the confessors and martyrs

Heiko Obermann: *Luther*,
trans. Eileen Walliser-Schwarzbart

Martyrdom is a central element of Christian belief, which rests on the notion that God in human form sacrificed himself on the cross to save the human race from death. Not, however, from suffering, for it is essential for believers to validate their faith by following the example of their redeemer. But if accepting martyrdom – doubtless always more admired in others than practised by the self – is the high point of Christian ambition, it is nonetheless odd: it contradicts the instinct for survival which is the condition of all life (to which the Christian might add, "God-given").

There is, however, a sense in which all must face such a destiny, willingly or not. The universal drawback of life is that it must at some point end. How to accommodate oneself to this unwelcome fact is central to the texts of the cantatas. Their stance is not unique to Lutheranism, but representative of Christianity in general. It combines acceptance and denial, proposing that death is both physically real and yet not the annihilation that it seems, for it is the prelude to an eternally blissful, non-material existence. For this to be achieved depends on meeting one's last hour with confidence that, as Christ promised, it will bring release and reward.

The second day of Christmas – 26 December – commemorates St. Stephen, an early Christian stoned to death by opponents of his beliefs. His story, a familiar example of human intolerance (which all faith communities, sacred or secular, are inclined to inflict on others), appears in books six and seven of the Acts of the Apostles and is the inspiration for the text of BWV 57. The librettist, Georg Christian Lehms (1684-1717), refers only once to the particular case of Stephen, whose fate would most likely have been the subject of the day's sermon. Instead, the text recasts anxiety about death as a psychological drama: a dialogue between Christ and the soul. The distress concerns the mind rather than the body, and the self's resistance to the idea of its extinction is projected outward as persecution by others. Bach's music is in turn elegiac, intensely wretched, heroic and brittle with joy. There are, as usual, no pastel colours.

No 1 Bass aria

The singer represents the voice of Christ, using (anachronistically) words from the New Testament letter of James. This is considered to have been written around the turn of the first century and is in fact full of the sort of recommendations to do good works that Luther disapproved of as irrelevant to the question of faith. Lehms picked out an excerpt appropriate to the day: "Blessed is the man who endures trial, for after he has proved himself he will receive the crown of life". The music sets aside formal neatness in favour of an unbroken lyric flow, generated by the phrases in the introductory bars for instruments alone. Strings, continuo and three oboes (one of them the deeper-toned tenor version) combine suggestions of mourning and consolation. Beneath a poignant descending phrase, passed down the three string parts, the continuo remains steadfastly on the keynote – the movement is in G minor – before climbing to a cadence on the dominant in the fifth bar. The spontaneity of song rather than a mathematical tidiness of phrase length is the aim.

Violin and oboe then climb upward, suspended in yearning, before drooping in semitones to prepare for the entry of the voice. The divine reassurance ("Blessed is the man who endures trial") is melodically smooth, and yet it shares the subdued melancholy of the opening. There is a stoic calm in the predominantly stepwise contours and also in the frequent sustained notes: Bach lingers over such words as "blessed" (*selig*), "endures" (*erduldet*), "proved" (*bewähret*) and "crown" (*Krone*). There are to be no quick fixes for human suffering. Even so, hints of a brighter outcome filter through as the key bends a little to the relative major for the reiterated promise of eternity ("for after he has proved himself he will receive the crown of life"). In token of the permanence to come, the voice sustains the final "crown" over ten bars, ending conclusively on the key chord. A closing instrumental section echoes the earlier setting of "who endures trial" and prepares the listener for the agonised response of the human.

No 2 Soprano recit

The cornerstone of the therapeutic ethos is the belief that the defining feature of personhood is its vulnerability.

Frank Furedi: *Therapy Culture*

The soul wishes to be comforted by the word of scripture but finds itself still in torment: "Ah! this sweet consolation revives even my heart, which otherwise finds in grief and pain endless suffering and writhes like a worm in its own blood". A jagged vocal line and sinking harmonies partner the melodramatic language, full of self-pity and fear of persecution: "I have to live like a sheep amidst a thousand savage wolves" (note the shriek of terror on *tausend*, i.e. "thousand"); "I am a truly forsaken lamb and must surrender myself to their rage and ferocity" – this, though Lutheran Christian belief was obligatory in eighteenth-century Leipzig. Clearly the danger is from within the self rather than without. Worse is to come: an identification with the Old Testament figure of Abel, murdered by his brother Cain, suggests betrayal and abandonment even by those bound by the closest ties of affection and kinship - "What happened to Abel makes my tears flood out". Christ is the soul's only true friend: "Ah Jesus, if I knew no comfort from you here, then my courage and heart would break and, full of mourning, say ...". A descending diminished third distils the wretchedness of *voller Trauren* ("full of mourning") and points to the lament that follows.

No 3 Soprano aria

[S]uicide is the act of man and not of the animal; it is a meditated act, a non-instinctive, unnatural choice.

> Primo Levi: *The Drowned and the Saved*,
> trans. Raymond Rosenthal

The view familiar to the theology of the cantatas is that there are two versions of death: one is the ending of the physical self (which should be willingly renounced) and the other arises internally from an absence of faith, leading to deprivation of Christ's love and hence hope. The soul that feels itself distant from Jesus has lost all pleasure: "I would wish death for myself if you, my Jesus, did not love me". The theme of abandonment and loss is universal, and here, in musical terms, crosses the boundary between secular and sacred; the erotic is at home in both realms. The constant presence of the opening motivic material creates an aural cage from which there is no escape – but who would want to? There is a hypnotic beauty in the regular phrase lengths and the repeated patterns of lamentation.

The violin part sighs, swoops and sinks in grief, underpinned by the insistent mottoes of the bass line; the vocal line correspondingly mingles the lyric and the angular. There is an occasional glimpse of light in the gloom of minor keys: at the thought of Jesus, a momentary turn to the major warms the wretched soul with remembrance of the source of love and life. The second portion of text brings a change of key to the subdominant (F) minor and a brief melodious partnership in sixths between voice and violin: "Yes, if you would leave me grieving, then I would suffer more than from the pains of hell". The violin part soon resumes its sobbing phrases and an eight-bar interlude (again, emotion contained by pattern) returns to the original appeal to the absent lover.

No 4 Bass/soprano recit

It is a Lutheran axiom that to throw oneself on the mercy of God guarantees a gracious response. Christ turns to the supplicant: "I hold out my hand to you, and with it my heart also". The musical mood instantly transforms to the brightness of the major as the soul responds: "Ah! sweet pledge of love, you can overthrow my enemies and limit their fury".

No 5 Bass aria

This, then, is the war for the soul, and Christ appears in militant guise, inspiring defiance in his followers: "Yes, yes, I can strike your enemies who constantly accuse you because of me. Therefore compose yourself, oppressed spirit". Muscular and tonally straightforward, this *da capo* aria conquers depression and doubt with driving energy – in the major key, of course. Both voice and violin parts stand duty for brass fanfares: the call to arms against the primeval enemy who alienates the human from the divine. The clash of swords echoes in the choppiness of *schlagen* ("strike"). The central section of the aria is more sympathetic in mood and style, bending to the minor in its acknowledgement of the soul's suffering: "Do not weep, oppressed soul. The sun will still shine brightly, though it now shows only clouds of care". A repeat of the triumphant vision of the beginning completes the spiritual therapy.

No 6 Bass/soprano recit

Christ makes an offer that is hard to refuse: "In my lap is peace and life. One day I will give you this in eternity." The soul swoons in its longing for death: "Ah Jesus, if only I were already with you. Ah, if only the wind already grazed my tomb and grave, then I could withstand all trouble". Diminished harmonies on *Grab* ("grave") suggest the bleakness that must be confronted before the elevation to the life of the spirit. Even so: "Blessed are they who lie in the coffin and wait expectantly for the angelic summons! Ah, Jesus, open the heavens for me as you did for Stephen!" A positive and joyful wish for death pervades the soul; martyrdom is the soul's eager wish: "My heart is already prepared to ascend to you. Come,

come, delightful time! You may show me tomb, grave and my Jesus".

No 7 Soprano aria

The cantata has returned to its opening key of G minor, but the manner could not be more different. Fully convinced, the soul now appears to hop and skip, as in a lively *passepied*, to the accompaniment of death the fiddler: "I hurry to end my earthly life; I long" (the note extends over three bars) "this very moment to part with its joys". Rhythm and melody invite body and mind to enter into the spirit of the dance. The music brims with the energy of life, yet in the context – the urging forward of the moment of death – the gaiety seems febrile, almost macabre in its beauty. Although the violin stays continually busy, the vocal line lingers over its pledge to Christ in the next section of text: "My Saviour, I die with the greatest eagerness. Here is my soul - what will you give to me?". The aria ends with these words, and also with a questioning shift to the relative (Bb major). The goal must rest in the imagination.

No 8 Chorale

die Sehnsucht du, und was sie stillt
(you are both longing and the calming of it)

Friedrich Rückert: *Du bist die Ruh*

The believer can only, as ever, trust in the words of Christ, as imagined by the Saxon hymn writer Ahasuerus Fritsch (1629-1701). His dates tell us that he would in his early years have known of the horrors of the Thirty Years War, emblematic of the hell that humans can inflict on their own kind. Was it unreasonable to hope for a better world elsewhere? The communal voice, in four-part harmony, imagines the words of Christ: "Direct yourself, beloved, as it pleases me, and believe that I will remain your soul's friend always and forever. I delight in you and will take you into heaven from this tortured body". What more could be offered?

*

Suggested recording: Deutsche Bachsolisten, dir. Helmut Winschermann

Third Day of Christmas

BWV 64: *Sehet, welch eine Liebe*

(See, what love)

Librettist: Uncertain, possibly Johann Knauer, b.1690

Date: 27 December 1723

In the world of knowledge, the last thing to be perceived and only with great difficulty is the essential Form of Goodness. Once it is perceived, the conclusion must follow that, for all things, this is the cause of whatever is right and good; in the visible world it gives birth to light and to the lord of light, while it is itself sovereign in the intelligible world and the parent of intelligence and truth.

Plato: *Republic*, Book 7, trans. F.M. Cornford

Christ has only just arrived in the world and the Christian cannot wait to leave it. The overall inspiration for BWV 64 lies in the two scriptural readings for the day. Both of them (Heb.1: 1-14 and Jn.1: 1-14) proclaim the oneness of Christ with the supreme deity. In particular, the mystical beginning of John's gospel – a New Testament blend of Hellenistic with Jewish thought – identifies Jesus with the Greek logos: an embodiment of the divine essence and eternal source of light and life. The believer must accordingly turn from the values of temporal existence towards those of the spirit. Music and text in this cantata combine seriousness with radiant certainty. Rejecting what the world has to offer, the true Christian longs only to cast aside all that is impermanent and to become a citizen of an eternal, though intangible realm. Thanks to its inclusion of three chorales, BWV 64 also creates a sense of the communal weight underpinning individual belief, i.e. that life's meaning should be sought in a sphere other than material reality.

No 1 Chorus

The first letter of John (1 Jn:3:1) supplies the text: "See what love has the Father shown us, that we are called God's children". Combining thematic economy with a ceaseless flow of imitation, Bach's tightly constructed fugal setting offers a musical metaphor for a universe that is both controlled and yet life-giving. The fugal strategy brings several advantages: it enables the composer to give due weight to a short but important text by repeating it over time in various combinations and permutations; it allows different sections of the text to be presented simultaneously, as the musical fragments associated with individual units of meaning are designed to harmonise with each other; lastly, it brings intrinsic fascination through the inventive play of sound and thus (Bach's purpose) unites aesthetic pleasure with the religious impulse.

As the infant Christ is regarded as the centre of convergence between God and mortal, it is the commanding gesture *Sehet* ("See") towards this nodal point that generates and then constantly punctuates the stream of voices. Cutting through the continuous fabric of the fugue, it turns the mind's eye to the living Christ: to see is to know. In contrast to the brisk *Sehet*, the luxuriant play of sound on *erzeiget* ("has shown") suggests God's boundless love in reconciling himself with humanity. At the same time, texture and timbre indicate an austere strength: the four voices are reinforced by strings and brass and supported by organ continuo, either independent or otherwise doubling the vocal bass. Harmonically stable – no disturbing tonal adventures – this chorus builds to an intensely emotional conclusion. The continuo holds its breath with long pedal notes until it is swept into the marathon of the vocal bass on *erzeiget* ("shows"), punctuated with cries of *sehet* ("see"). An abrupt four-part chord suddenly stops the clamour, as the redemptive news is proclaimed for the last time: "we are called God's children".

No 2 Chorale

The seventh verse of Luther's hymn, "Praise be to you, Jesus Christ", reiterates the biblical message of the chorus and calls upon the world to give thanks to God: "He has done all that for us to show his great love; Let all Christendom rejoice over this and thank him through all eternity. Kyrie eleis!"

No 3 Alto recit

The incarnation – the appearance of God on earth – alters the entire mental landscape of the believer, who rejects the ephemeral world of the senses. A harsh rising interval of a seventh begins the catalogue of contempt: "Go, world! Just keep what is yours; I want nothing from you. Heaven is now mine and this will refresh my soul. Your gold is a transient possession, your wealth is borrowed. Whoever owns it is badly provided for". Rapid scales in the continuo sweep away the fake goods. The final sentence – "Therefore I can confidently say" – looks ahead to the next movement.

No 4 Chorale

In this second hymn, a verse by the German pastor Georg Michael Pfefferkorn (1645-1732), the tireless movement of the continuo suggests the resolve of the Christian throughout life, looking neither to right nor to left, the eye firmly fixed on heaven: "What do I care for the world and all its treasures, if I can only delight myself in you, my Jesus! All my pleasure is in you, and all my delight: what do I care for the world?"

No 5 Soprano aria

Can earthly and spiritual pleasures be distinguished? Arguably not in Bach's music. There is an infectious joy in this delicate gavotte, dedicated ostensibly to the self's withdrawal from the enjoyment of physical goods: "What the world contains must pass away like smoke, but what Jesus gives me, and my soul loves, is firmly fixed and stands for ever". A playful first violin part wreathes and spirals overhead, its descant doing double duty for the illusory nature of material things (flimsy scales vanish into the atmosphere) and the light heart of those who are immune to the world's allure. The B section of the *da capo* design begins with a change of texture, with the absence of the continuo releasing the soul's gaze to heaven. Protracted settings of *stehen* "stand" emphasize the enduring nature of divine gifts. A repeat of the A section once more lends musical sweetness to piety, as it steps out in its own delightful dance.

No 6 Bass recit

The vocal line strides confidently over the stave, assured of the place in heaven that Christ's birth promises to each believer: "Heaven remains certain for me, and I possess it already in faith. Death, the world and sin" (note the angular intervals of a diminished fifth and seventh) "yes, even the entire forces of hell, cannot now ever steal it from a child of God". The thought of heaven brings an impatient longing – the separation from the world cannot come soon enough: "Only this, only one thing still brings me sadness" (note the ever-expressive fall of a diminished fifth on *Kümmernis*) "that I must still linger in this world". Again, the essential meaning of Christ's birth – the elevated status of the human – is pointed out: "For Jesus intends to share heaven with me, and that is why he has chosen me; that is the reason that he was born as a person". With an emphatic trill on *Mensch* (Christ was indeed human) and an intake of breath before *geboren* ("born"), the composer adds his own gloss: this is the startling truth that should always galvanise faith.

No 7 Alto aria

The timbre of a solo oboe d'amore, both warm and melancholy, creates the emotional ambience for the soul's desire to repudiate life and reach for the promised, though as yet unattainable, bliss. Syncopated rhythms both of instrument and voice imply the dislocation of the mind from its current surroundings: "From the world I desire nothing, if only I inherit heaven". For the latter phrase, the music at length allows the imagination to soar to its celestial home in a more sustained and lyrical style. The B section of the aria similarly contrasts the disjointed present with the enduring life to come: "I surrender all else, for I am quite sure that I shall not eternally perish". Bach lays stress on the word *nicht* ("not"), which in the German text comes at the end of the phrase "I shall not eternally perish". It is the insistence on immortality that underpins the whole edifice of faith, enabling the believer to discount the present in the hope of a future transcendental ideal. Delayed gratification is a transferable skill, useful if not carried to excess.

No 8 Chorale

How weary, stale, flat and unprofitable
Seem to me all the uses of this world
William Shakespeare: *Hamlet*

Again, the voices are strengthened by brass and strings as the Christian community – the congregation – purges itself (in imagination, at least) of the trammels of existence. The farewell is taken from Johann Franck's *Jesu, meine Freude* ("Jesus, my joy"): "Goodnight, O life that the world has chosen; you do not please me. Goodnight sins; stay far behind and come no more to light! Good night, pride and pomp; to you, life of wickedness, let a final goodnight be said." Disillusionment is an all too familiar state of mind – Hamlet's lament speaks for many – though what it leads to varies with the individual. Bach's setting is full of heartfelt vigour, yet with a final chromatic twist. Parting is never simple.

*

Suggested recording: Bach Collegium Japan,
dir. Masaaki Suzuki

Third Day of Christmas

BWV 133: *Ich freue mich in dir*

(I rejoice in you)

Librettist: Unknown

Date: 27 December 1724

Quot homines, tot sententiae; suus cuique mos

There are as many opinions as people; everyone has their own way of thinking

Terence: *Phormio*

The interpretation of religious dogma reflects personal outlook. Although each Sunday in Bach's Lutheran church had designated biblical readings, there was much variety in the librettists' response to them. For instance, the writer of BWV 64, first performed a year before BWV 133, saw the incarnation (the assumed appearance of God as the infant Christ) as a reminder to shun the world of the flesh and to embrace the thought of death; yet BWV 133 thinks only of rejoicing at the arrival of the new-born brother of mankind.

It is a chorale cantata, with a text based on four verses by Caspar Ziegler (1629-1690): jurist, poet, and rector of Wittenberg university. The first and last verses are used verbatim; the others are recast to create the words for two pairings of aria and recitative. The focus throughout is on the adorable presence of the child and rapture at speaking his name. With only strings and a couple of oboes d'amore at his disposal (though an additional trumpet reinforces the hymn melody) Bach's canvas is relatively small – perhaps some of his musicians needed time off at Christmas. Yet with charm and brilliance he achieves his object: the portrayal of delight in the living God.

No 1 Chorus

Unlike many other chorale choruses in which the voices have their own complex part in the overall texture, here Bach makes relatively few demands of his singers; again, their numbers may have been depleted on this occasion. Their task is to deliver the separate lines of the hymn, dispersed throughout the movement, in four-part harmony: "I rejoice in you/And bid you welcome/My dearest little Jesus!/You have taken it upon you/To be my little brother./Ah, what a sweet sound!/How friendly he looks/The great son of God!". Sweetness of sound inspires the musical vision; the entire movement could stand alone as an instrumental concerto, with a leading role for the first violin. Dazzlingly energetic, the opening material radiates an excitement that is sustained throughout, reappearing between (*ritornelli*) and alongside the vocal sections.

The aural image is of bells: an initial threefold peal (an allusion to the doctrine of the Trinity?) leads to a protracted carillon, where the oboists are given the strenuous task of doubling the second violin and the viola. Although the music of this chorus is particularly highly patterned and full of repeated sequences, it avoids monotony. The violin part rises to the glittering heights of a top E, and the setting of the chorale becomes more elaborate. The soprano line, reinforced by trumpet and viola, clings to *Ton* ("sound"), while the other voices repeat the words below. The last line of the chorale, "The great son of God", is signposted with equal care. This time, the violin pitch falls (perhaps in imitation of God's descent to earth) before the voices continually marvel at the divine status of the child. A final *ritornello* ends with the flourish of a scale, underpinned by one last threefold chime in the bass.

No 2 Alto aria

Referring to the beginning of Ziegler's second verse, the text proclaims the transformative nature of the nativity: "Take comfort! A holy body holds the incomprehensible essence of the Most High. I have seen God – how blessed I am! – face to face". The instrumental context is a trio sonata for two oboes and continuo, which introduce the three main expressive features of the movement. A fanfare-like beginning, in which the natural stress of the German *Getrost!* ("Take comfort!") dictates the crispness of the rhythm, is followed by an exultant cascade in the oboes, and this in turn leads to a quiet, rocking sequence. Flowing vocal passages – as so often in Bach there is little difference between instrumental and vocal virtuosity – create the impression of boundlessness both of the promised comfort and of the ungraspable (*unbegreiflichs*) nature of God; the cradling harmonies attach themselves to "how blessed I am!" (*wie wohl ist mir geschehen!*). The last part of the text – "Ah! my soul must now become healed" – brings a sudden solemnity: the vocal line is punctuated with cries of relief at restored spiritual health. But Bach does not linger here, instead gliding effortlessly to a return of the summons to happiness.

No 3 Tenor recit

The librettist slips in a reminder of the sombre history behind Christ's coming. It was human sin that first alienated God from man: "Adam, full of terror, may hide before the face of God in paradise". The wonder, then, is that the Almighty has deigned to reappear: "The all-high

God" (the vocal line climbs with astonishment) "himself lodges with us". A slowing of tempo to *adagio* – here acting as the musical equivalent of quotation marks – signals that these words are derived from the hymn; Bach also uses a fragment of its melody. The pattern is repeated: first, a comment from the librettist ("And so my heart does not take fright; it knows his merciful cast of mind. From his immeasurable goodness"), and then lines from Ziegler add: "He becomes a little child and is called my dear Jesus". Another change to *adagio* acknowledges the excerpt from the chorale.

No 4 Soprano aria

A paraphrase of the next verse of the hymn forms the text: "How delightfully these words ring in my ear, that my Jesus is born". The tone colours (upper strings and soprano) are delicate and the parts are ornamented with trills; the continuo is similarly airy, lightened by rests and flourishes. This God is to be tender rather than coercive. The aural image of bells that featured in the opening chorus returns here in the first violins' rapid alternation of open and stopped notes (the "spattering" technique of *bariolage*). For the all-important message – "my Jesus is born" – Bach turns to an unadorned declamatory style, as if to make a distinction between the unvarnished truth (so to speak) and the emotional pleasure that it brings.

But no truth impresses without knowledge of its contrary. The central section of the *da capo* slows to a funereal *largo* to consider, more in sorrow than in anger, those who lack faith: "Whoever does not understand the name of Jesus, and whose heart is not moved by it, must be hard as a rock". As the continuo falls silent – non-belief, the musical language suggests, is without foundation – the texture dwindles to upper strings and high voice. As a token of the flint-hearted deniers, life and warmth ebb away in the chromatic descents for the second violin and viola. At the same time, diminished thirds cast their shadow over the vocal line. All this, however, disappears with a return to the transparent joy of the opening section.

No 5 Bass recit

Eternal life is the pay-off for faith: "Well then, death's fear and pain" (death – *Todes* – as usual signposted by diminished harmonies) "does not concern my comforted heart". The pitch drops with God's journey to earth, followed by an ascent for the soul's consequent resurrection: "If he brings himself from heaven to earth then he will also think of me in my tomb". The conclusion, in the more melodic style of *arioso*, points to the talismanic power of Christ. The words are Ziegler's: "Whoever truly knows Jesus does not die when he dies, as soon as he calls him by name".

No 6 Chorale

Faith sustains hope and helps to make sense of the believer's journey through life. "Well then, I will hold fast to you, Jesus, even if the world should break into a thousand pieces. Oh Jesus, in you only will I live; in you, only in you, my Jesus, will I fall asleep".

*

Suggested recording: Amsterdam Baroque, dir. Ton Koopman

Third Day of Christmas

BWV 151: *Süßer Trost, mein Jesus kömmt*

(Sweet comfort, my Jesus comes)

Librettist: Georg Christian Lehms

Date: 27 December 1725

The two earlier cantatas for this day – see BWV 64 and BWV 133 – had their own distinct response to the meaning of the incarnation. The first emphasised the need to distance oneself from the lure of the material world, and the second drew attention to the shared humanity of the infant God with the onlooker. The libretto of BWV 151, however, moves in another direction still. With paradise now open to the elect, the text views the hardships of life as training for heaven. By choosing to arrive as the lowest of the low, the reasoning goes, the heavenly prince has transformed self-abasement into a mark of divine status: to accept Christ-like poverty helps one's chances of resurrection after death. The living God offers himself as inspiration to all who endure weary servitude. There are no choruses in this introspective work, which calls upon four solo voices – who doubtless led the singing of the final chorale.

No 1 Soprano aria

While the format of BWV 151 does not offer the high drama of large forces or overt mental conflict, there is psychological theatre even in the intimate setting of this aria. Pondering the Nativity, the believing soul is infused with an ecstatic calm that prefigures the bliss of heaven: "Sweet comfort, my Jesus comes, Jesus is now born!" To depict a concentrated stillness in music is a challenge. Some variety is needed to maintain the listener's interest, but not so much as to dispel the overall aura of tranquility. Bach's solution is to convey a state of inner rapture through a combination of a very slow pulse (*molt'adagio*), gently rocking melody, and a leisurely - barely perceptible - pace of harmonic change. To this, he adds emotional intensity through the beauty of a virtuoso flute part. Ornamenting the outline of the vocal melody, the exceptionally elaborate writing for the solo instrument tells the listener that surface simplicity can contain great depth of feeling.

The design of the aria is a three-part *da capo* – a structure that Bach exploits to create maximum contrast. The central section brings a sudden arousal from the trance-like state of the beginning. It is as if the self, lost in contemplation of the nativity, becomes newly conscious; able to observe its own state and explain the reason for it: "Heart and soul rejoice, for my beloved God has now chosen me for heaven". The music is full of brisk, staccato energy, dancing its way through the outpouring of coloratura on *freuet* ("rejoices"). As is usual, the key has changed for the middle part of the aria: in this case to the relative (E) minor. There is always a serious undertone to the vision of heaven, for as yet it can only be the object of yearning. The vocal line accordingly leaps upward to its celestial goal (*zum Himmel* – "to heaven"). A repeat of the idyllic peace of the opening transports the listener back to the vision of paradise.

No 2 Bass recit

Luther emphasised that our redemption through Christ is entirely compatible with our lack of freedom on the earth.

Bernhard Lohse: *Luther*, trans. Robert C. Schultz

Religion has practical consequences. The promise of immortality is conditional in the first place on faith, but the narrative of the incarnation also implies a moral and social subtext: if Christ took his place on earth in the form of a low-born child, he showed that spiritual merit attaches to the humble, and that the experience of poverty and hardship is a bond between believer and God. The continuo remains steady as the voice explains the lesson: "Rejoice, my heart" (the surge of happiness becomes an ascending scale) "for now the pain eases which has oppressed you for so long" (the allusion is to the fear of death). "God has sent his dearest son, whom he holds in such high affection, into this world. He leaves the throne of heaven to deliver the entire world from its chains of slavery and servitude" (the unspoken tyrant is the devil who brought death into the world). For the last part of the recitative, an increased pace of harmonic change, with dramatic descents in the continuo, signals the extraordinary turn of events: "O wonderful deed! God becomes man, and on this earth chooses to become even lowlier and much poorer than we are". The implication is clear: we should be satisfied with what we have, however little.

No 3 Alto aria

The value of the redemption shared by those who believe in Christ has to be proved in their imitation of Christ. It is by following in the footsteps of their redeemer that they show whether or not they have inwardly overcome the world and have willingly taken up their cross. True human freedom is, in practice, to be found in man's ability to suffer humbly. How can the redeemed believer even want to live better than the Lord, who suffered and yet was innocent? We, on the other hand, are guilty and richly deserve all the suffering we meet in this world.

Joachim Kahl: *The Misery of Christianity*, trans. N.D. Smith

The believer may have to wait a while before attaining the Elysian bliss suggested by the opening aria, but at least the present becomes more endurable when one can attach meaning to it: "In Jesus's lowliness I can find comfort, and in his poverty, riches". Style and timbre are appropriately restrained, workaday rather than a delight to the ear. Violins, viola and oboe proceed in dogged unison - except that the strings reduce to a solo violin at each entry of the voice. The melodic line is dour, lacking variety in rhythm or phrasing, and its limited contours match the restrictions of human life; music subjugates itself in a sequence of descending phrases. Although not a formal *da capo*, there is a three-part structure, with a more hopeful central text, now in a major key: "For me, his poor status brings only well-being – yes, his wondrous hand will weave only wreaths of blessing for me". Even the weaving of blessings, however, takes a musically downward as much as an upward turn, and the Christian gaze is soon returned firmly to earth.

No 4 Tenor recit

Despite all, the overriding – and heartening – message is of human exceptionalism. Why else would God send his son on his mission of rescue: "You precious Son of God, now you have opened the doors of heaven for me, and through your lowliness brought the light of salvation!". The trill that draws attention to the first syllable of "God's son" (*Gottessohn*) links the cantata text to the day's Bible readings (Heb. 1:1-14, and Jn. 1:1-14), each of which proclaims the identity of Christ with the supreme deity. The conclusion is clear: "Because you now, quite alone, left the Father's city and throne out of love for us, for this we wish to hold you in our hearts".

No 5 Chorale

The words are by Nikolaus Herman (1500-1561), an early supporter of Luther and prolific writer of hymns. His verse celebrates the nativity as a sign of the reconciliation of the divine with the human: "Today he opens the door again to lovely paradise; the cherub" (i.e. the angel who stood at the gate to block the return to Eden of Adam and Eve) "no longer stands before it. Glory to God, honour and praise". Bach's uncomplicated four-part setting speaks only of the certainty of faith.

*

Suggested recording: J.S. Bach-Stiftung, dir. Rudolf Lutz

Sunday after Christmas

BWV 152: *Tritt auf die Glaubensbahn*

(Walk on the path of faith)

Librettist: Salomon Franck

Date: 30 December 1714

It is true, that a little philosophy inclineth man's mind to atheism; but depth in philosophy bringeth men's minds about to religion: for while the mind of man looketh upon second causes scattered, it may sometimes rest in them and go no further; but when it beholdeth the chain of them confederate and linked together, it must needs fly to Providence and Deity.

Francis Bacon: *Of Atheism*

Bach composed BWV 152 while he was employed as a musician by the Duke of Weimar. His libretto was one of a collection by Salomon Franck, a learned and devout official at the same court. The topic of the cantata relates to the biblical readings for the day, both of which point to faith as the supreme requirement for the Christian. The first example is in Luke's gospel (Lk.2: 33-40), which recounts how the elderly Simeon and the old widow Hanna instantly recognised the transcendent quality of the infant Christ when, shortly after his birth, he was brought to the temple. The other excerpt is from Paul's letter to the Galatians (Gal.4: 1-7), written in the early decades of Christianity, a time when its adherents had yet to agree upon the precise nature of their beliefs and practices.

The roots were Judaic, and the question to be decided was which of the old beliefs should be carried forward into the new. Jewish followers of Christ expected Gentile (i.e. non-Jewish) converts to accept the laws enshrined in books of the Old Testament. Paul thought otherwise, and his letter to the Galatians (now somewhere in modern Turkey) is a passionate plea for faith in Christ's divinity and resurrection to be the sole passport to the Christian community. His wish in principle to dispense with legalistic baggage influenced the entire course of Christianity, up to and including – notably – Luther. The distinction, however, between the organised and the undocumented inclination to God has historically counted for little when political uniformity is the goal. The power to, as Elizabeth I put it, "make windows into men's souls" has routinely been usurped by the less than divinely qualified.

The drama of Franck's text lies in an opposition between faith and what he sees as the spurious wisdom of reason. He presents reason as the easy option, while belief in God is the difficulty: identified as the mind's stumbling block (a figure of speech with antecedents in the Old Testament). The contribution of Bach's setting is that its sheer musical charm seems to smooth over all obstacles to faith. The text is addressed to the individual, not to the community; hence the intimate scoring – even if this (who knows?) happened to be a necessity for Bach at that moment – happens to fit perfectly with the personal tone of the message. The sound-world of BWV 152 combines the silvery with the warm in a quartet of recorder, oboe, viola d'amore (treble viol) and viola da gamba (bass viol) – the whole supported by the organ continuo. There are no chorales, nor choruses; a bass voice moves from a prophetic role to the voice of Christ, while the soprano acts as the mouthpiece of the soul.

As there was a discrepancy between the pitch of the organ at Weimar and that of wind instruments, the original score writes their parts in different keys; modern performers have to choose a compromise between the two – the needs of the singers perhaps being the most urgent.

No 1 Prelude

An openness to chance influences loosing thought from preconceptions is indispensable to creative thinking.

> A.C. Graham: *Disputers of the Tao*

In his earlier cantatas, Bach experimented with a greater variety of format than in his later practice at Leipzig. Open to all kinds of musical influences and styles, he chose the model of the Italianate *canzona* to begin BWV 152. This is typically a lively imitative piece, preceded by a slow introduction. Here, the first four bars speak of yearning. Harmonically speaking, they constitute a prolonged imperfect cadence, eloquent with anticipation. Above, a highly decorated, quasi-extempore, lyricism for the three upper instruments (recorder, oboe, viola d'amore), spins out its longing. The answer arrives in a light-footed fugue that suggests the abundant life enjoyed by the believer. Nothing discordant or heavy oppresses the mind; the technical ingenuity and playful syncopations aim to give pleasure. Different blends of colour and texture intrigue the ear as Bach intersperses fugal conversations with free-running episodes. Around the mid-point of the movement, the viola da gamba and organ fall silent as recorder and viola d'amore flit around the fugue subject in the oboe. After this cadenza-like moment, the bass instruments reappear so that the whole ensemble may join in an intricate coda. Overlapping entries (*stretto*) of recorder and oboe create the illusion of increasing pace as the fugue dances to its conclusion.

No 2 Bass aria

The text of this aria contains a triple message: "Walk on the path of faith!"; "God has laid the stone that holds and carries Zion"; "O man, do not stumble against it!'. Each of them is associated with a different musical idea, though it is the command to walk on the path of faith that recurs most often. It opens and closes the movement with its simple stepwise descent, followed by a melodic flourish to shows the path's triumphant endpoint; one might imagine the upward gestures of the preacher. Changes of phrase length mark out the various sections. For instance, the instrumental introduction (oboe and continuo) begins with multiples of two bars, while the stern "God has laid the stone that holds and carries Zion" appears first in two sets of three bars and later requires nine. In warning not to collide against the imperative of faith, the vocal line lurches against the underlying pulse. As the order of the German text is "stumble you must not!", Bach makes much of the final *nicht* with an ornamental trill. The movement ends with a repeat of its orderly beginning.

No 3 Bass recit

The beliefs we have received from our ancestors – beliefs as old as time – cannot be destroyed by any argument, nor by any ingenuity the mind can invent.

Euripides: *The Bacchae,* trans. Philip Vellacott

In turn threatening and hopeful, the rhetoric of the libretto is matched by Bach's emotional setting. The text begins with a scriptural quotation (Lk. 2:33-35): "The Saviour is set for the fall and rising of the people of Israel". At these words, the vocal line plummets by a tenth, only to ascend by the same dramatic interval. As usual, the blame rests with the human: "The noble stone" (i.e. Christ) "is without fault, even if the wicked world injures itself against it, yes, falls over it into hell" (the vocal line takes an ungainly tumble) "because it runs evilly against it and does not recognise God's favour and grace". The outlook for the believer, however, is sweet – conceptually and musically: "But blessed is an elect Christian, who bases his faith on this cornerstone, for through this he finds salvation and redemption". The voice part follows in the footsteps of the continuo; the faithful Christian may expect a serene and certain future.

No 4 Soprano aria

The shimmering tone-colours of recorder, viola d'amore and voice speak of celestial aspirations: "Stone, which surpasses all other treasures, help me, through faith, always to make you the foundation of my salvation, and not injure myself against you". High-pitched sustained notes in both recorder and voice parts indicate the enduring nature of divine truth, and also that the rock of belief (*Stein*) will elevate rather than crush the human spirit. Gentle harmonies of thirds and sixths between recorder and viola d'amore enhance the mood of beatific calm – a foretaste of paradise.

No 5 Bass recit

You can only form the minds of reasoning animals upon Facts: nothing else will ever be of any service to them.

Charles Dickens: *Hard Times*

Though you seem, by your glib tongue, to be intelligent, yet your words are foolish.

Euripides: *The Bacchae*

Implicit in BWV 152 is a debate on the rival claims of the rational and the irrational. For the librettist, the imperative of faith demands suspension of the rules of material evidence: "Let the clever world be annoyed that God's son leaves his high throne of honour to clothe himself in flesh and blood and to suffer as a human being. The greatest wisdom of this earth must, before the counsel of the Highest, become the greatest foolishness. What God has ordained, reason cannot fathom; the blind guide leads the spiritually blind". Bach's setting is correspondingly fierce. The voice plunges in with a leap of a diminished seventh and continues with strongly contoured declamation in minor keys; Christ's suffering (*leidet*) is prolonged musical agony. The blind leader (*die Leiterin*, i.e. reason) wanders along a disjointed harmonic path before a final chord prepares for the next movement.

No 6 Soprano/Bass duet

What, after all, is the cross of Jesus Christ? It is nothing but the sum total of a sado-masochistic glorification of pain.

> Joachim Kahl: *The Misery of Christianity*,
> trans. N.D. Smith

A love duet between the soul and Christ sets the seal on faith. The musical manner is dance like, but the divinity is exacting. As the soul asks: "How should I embrace you, beloved?", the response is: "You must renounce yourself and forsake all else". Similarly, to the question: "How should I recognise the eternal light?", Christ replies: "Acknowledge me in faith without resentment". The soul is eager: "Come! Teach me, Saviour, to scorn the earth! Ah, draw me beloved, that I may follow you", despite a somewhat uncompromising response: "Come, Soul! Through suffering attain joy. I shall grant you a crown after affliction and shame!" The solo instruments – all three, significantly, in unison – make their own contribution to the interwoven texture. The imitation, between the voice parts especially, is an obvious pointer to the closeness of the soul with its Saviour. With its infectious pulse, this movement returns BWV 152 to the high spirits of its prelude. The text speaks, the music convinces.

*

Suggested recording: Concentus Musicus Wien, dir. Nikolaus Harnoncourt

Sunday after Christmas

BWV 28: *Gottlob! nun geht das Jahr zu Ende*

(Praise God! Now the year comes to an end)

Librettist: Erdmann Neumeister

Date: 30 December 1725

The ending of the old cycle was understood to be a time of acute jeopardy, making a moment when the world could erupt into chaos if the precious balance of the great sustaining forces of this Fifth Sun should lurch out of control, and men, world, and gods vanish all together...While Mexican ritual can be usefully considered as a technique of propitiation or an attempted regularisation of "nature", the major thrust was not instrumental, but rather aesthetic, expressive, interrogative and creative.

Inga Glendinnen: *Aztecs*

Days, months and years calibrate the lifespan of the individual; these arbitrary markers remind us of the cycles of life, death and decay which govern our existence. Religious belief, however, proposes an all-powerful being that not only transcends boundaries of time and space but also takes particular care of the human species. In BWV 28, it is God as ruler and protector of his people who takes centre-stage; faith in his power and kindness cushions the self against the fears of mortality that slip through the chink between the old year and the new.

The text of BWV 28 is from a collection by Erdmann Neumeister (1671-1756), the Lutheran divine who in the early years of the eighteenth century did much to shape the cantata libretto as a literary genre. Although performed not long after Christmas, BWV 28 looks not so much to Christ as to the Old Testament Jehovah. It evokes a world in which authority is sanctified by tradition and – treated with respect – is sure to act for the common good. This cantata is both celebratory and placatory, acknowledging God's past gifts and looking forward to their continuation in the year to come. No darkness or depression clouds the mood, and the impulse to give praise and thanks inspires in Bach a rich variety of musical forms and styles.

No 1 Soprano aria

Gratitude is the theme: "Praise God! Now the year comes to an end. The new one is already close. Think of it, my soul: how much good your God's hands have done for you in the old year! Strike up a happy song of thanks to him. Then he will think of you further and give you more in the new year." Music colours the words with delight. A staccato bass bounds in to establish a dance-like pulse; above, two groups of players – three oboes, and strings – alternate and echo each other in the varied textures of an instrumental concerto. A twirling melodic fragment is the subject of their musical conversation; after a dozen introductory bars, this is taken up by the singer as the motto of praise (*Gottlob!*). The vocal part does double duty: it has a verbal message to deliver, but its role is also akin to a solo instrument within the context of the concerto.

For Bach, words and music converge in meaning, sometimes in subtle and sometimes in more obvious ways. For instance, at the first full vocal statement of "Praise God! Now the year comes to an end. The new one is already close", the glimpse of the future happens to coincide with a turn to the brightness of the relative major. At the instruction to reflect ("think of it") the melodic pace slows; there is a serious purpose to the rejoicing. And, as one would expect in music of this period, decorative runs illustrate the abundant happiness of the song (*frohes Danklied*). There is, however, a contractual subtext, for a benefactor who is thanked is more likely to repeat the favour. An extended setting of "he will think of you further" (*so wird er ferner dein gedenken*) looks to God's unwearying concern; although, to be sure the Almighty has understood the point, the instruments fall silent for a last repetition of "and give you more in the new year". A final *ritornello* – a repeat of the opening bars – completes this high-spirited movement.

No 2 Chorale

Mind and music now focus on the eternal God, whose presence is evoked in a traditional hymn. "Now praise the Lord, my soul" was written by the learned Johann Graumann (1487-1541), an early and distinguished Lutheran figure. His words rephrase the beginning of Psalm 103 so that, by Bach's time, the entire hymn was swathed in layers of antiquity. Accordingly, the musical treatment here makes a startling contrast with the more modern Italianate brilliance of the opening aria. In keeping with the chorale's heritage, Bach sets it in what to him was the consciously historic style of a motet. This gives each line of text its separate ceremonious dignity, with its melody anticipated in an imitative play of voices. In comparison with one of Bach's typical chorale choruses, the texture is relatively spare, as instruments are here brought in to double the singers rather than to provide thematically independent surroundings. Strings and four brass players – trumpet and three trombones – add their weight to the voices as the great conveyor belt of counterpoint rolls out an exploration of each short line, before its arrival as a slow-moving soprano *cantus firmus*.

The first two pairs of lines are set identically: "Now praise the Lord, O my soul,/whatever is in me, praise his name!", followed by: "He increases his benefits more and more/– do not forget this, my heart!". The next section of text moves from praise of God to his tender care: "He has forgiven your sin/and healed your great weakness,/saves your poor life,/and takes you into his bosom". In reference, perhaps, to the Christmas theme of reconciliation, there is a particularly lengthy treatment of "He has forgiven your sin"; all the while, an ascending chromatic figure insinuates its way into the texture as a reminder of the Devil's serpentine nature. Awkward diminished intervals gesture toward human fallibility (*Schwachheit*), to which the response is an insistent repetition of "saves your poor life" (*errett' dein armes Leben*). The last four lines offer a vision of human flourishing under divine rule: "he showers rich comfort upon you,/rejuvenates you like an eagle;/the King creates justice/and protects those who suffer in his kingdom". Suffering is painted with lingering descending phrase, stretched over a long series of suspensions, as it waits patiently for divine redress.

No 3 Bass recit and arioso

God's pledge in the Old Testament book of Jeremiah supplies the text of this movement: "Thus speaks the Lord: it shall be a pleasure to me to do good to them, and I will plant them in this land faithfully, with my whole heart and soul". A melodious style and regular patterns, including imitation between continuo and voice, give this movement the lyrical character of *arioso*, rather than the standard heightened speech of recitative. The predictability of repetition also points to a deity who is reliable, bringing a future without disruption. The great spread of *pflanzen* ("plant") becomes the musical symbol of the deep-rooted security that only God can provide. A concluding triple vow ("with my whole heart and soul") leaves the listener assured of God's commitment to his followers.

No 4 Tenor recit

Neumeister adds his preacherly gloss to the previous biblical quotation: "God is a fountain where pure goodness flows. God is a light where pure grace shines. God is a treasure that is called pure blessing. God is a Lord who intends what is true and heartfelt". Hushed string chords accompany the singer, telling of intense inner devotion. The second part of the text moves on to conclude: "Whoever loves him in faith, honours him in childlike love, listens to his word from the heart and turns from evil ways, God gives himself with every gift". Hence the clinching argument (QED) for faith: "Whoever has God must have everything". At this, the voice makes an exultant leap, for it is true that, given the premise of scriptural authority, faith's gift is a sense of completeness. To believe that one has access to the supreme good (i.e. the support of the cosmic benefactor) makes the possessions of this world seem of little value.

No 5 Alto/tenor duet

Worship appears to have achieved its object – the continuation of divine favour – but there is no harm in one last request; an exuberant dance (the style of a *gigue*) both celebrates the deity and gives him a final nudge. The continuo is an active member of the trio (the others being the two voices); it introduces the melody and then showers the ear with arpeggiated confetti to illustrate the blessings that rain down from on high. It also provides the *ritornelli* that separate the portions of text, which are set initially as a playful canon between the voices. The singers begin with an appreciation of recent kindness from on high: "God has blessed us in the current year, so that good actions and good health have come together". Bright major keys endorse the picture. The tenor then considers the view from the present: "We praise him from our hearts, and ask in addition that he would also grant us a fortunate new year". The confident energy remains, while a key shift here to the minor gives the overall design a three-part tonal structure (shaping the musical architecture is always second nature to Bach). Wheedling semitones begin the last part of the prayer: "We hope for this because of his persistent kindness, and we praise it in advance with thankful minds". As wishful thinking transmutes once more to certainty, the key returns to its original C major; the display of gratitude throughout BWV 28 has surely guaranteed goodwill from on high.

No 6 Chorale

The concluding hymn is the work of another early Lutheran theologian, the conciliatory Paul Eber (1511-1569). It is the last verse of his *Helft mir Gotts Güte preisen* ("Help me to praise God's goodness"), written for the New Year. It summarises the entire theme of BWV 28, and adds a reference to the divinity of Christ: "All such goodness of yours we praise,/Father on heaven's throne,/As you show us through Christ, your son,/And we pray you further:/Grant us a peaceful year,/Preserve us from all suffering,/And nourish us abundantly!". A full complement of brass, wind and strings supports the voices. Bach's God enjoyed the sound of music.

*

Suggested recording: Münchener Bach-Chor, dir. Karl Richter

Sunday after Christmas

BWV 122: *Das neugeborne Kindelein*

(The newborn little child)

Librettist: Unknown

Date: 31 December 1724

So that the great mass of men may never hit on the idea of taking their history into their own hands...the *Christological teaching* of the churches tells them explicitly that...The decisive problems of human existence (in a word, man's salvation) cannot be solved by men themselves, but only by the redeemer who God as sent to men as an act of pure grace.

Joachim Kahl: *The Misery of Christianity*, trans. N.D. Smith

As time leads us all from birth to death, the human clock is periodically reset to create the sense of a new beginning. The celebration of the birth of Christ falls between two such moments: the winter solstice, after which the days increase in length, and the calendrical turning point of the new year. For Christian believers, however, the Nativity marks another type of renewal: it is the occasion when the cosmic purpose is fulfilled, so that corrupted humankind can once again claim its long-lost kinship with the angels – those bodiless courtiers of the deity.

This is the subtext of the hymn upon which BWV 122 is based. Its four verses were written by Kyriakus Schneegaß (1546-1597). Born to a peasant family in Thuringia, he eventually studied at the university of Jena and became a Lutheran pastor. His prodigious output of hymns is a reminder of the important role these apparently modest products played in the collective

Lutheran consciousness. In them, the meaning of scripture could be summarised in a rhyming form that was as easy to memorise as the associated melodies were to sing. For those who had little time or theological expertise, the conceptual value of the hymns is obvious. More than that: singing helps to embed the words in the memory, while the sharing of music creates an emotional bond that unifies the community of believers.

Hence, as with chorale cantatas in general, BWV 122 rests on what would for its listeners have been a familiar foundation, verbally and musically. The challenge for the composer was then to preserve the traditional hymn while presenting it afresh in a wider context devised by his artistic imagination. The task of the librettist was similar, in that the brevity of the hymn verses had in places to be expanded and re-modelled to fit the demands of a large musical scheme. In creating a narrative that could be unfolded through a variety of choral and solo numbers, the librettist – here, as so often, the identity of the writer is unknown – added his own emphases. With BWV 122, the rejoicing of the hymn is spliced with reminders of human unworthiness; only the goodness of God is able to cure the human spirit of its alienation from heaven.

No 1 Chorus

Style and structure convey an artless joy, in keeping with the view of Christ as small child rather than endowed with his full majesty: "The newborn little child/The darling little Jesus/Brings once again a New Year/To the chosen Christian throng". As the hymn is in triple time, Bach adapts it to the rapid steps of a *passespied*: a lively dance of French provincial origin, fashionable at the court of Louis XIV. A catchy instrumental beginning – with violins and viola doubled by oboes and with echo effects to keep the audience on its toes – sets the lighthearted mood and subsequently alternates as a *ritornello* with each line of the hymn. While the soprano steadily sings the melody (the *cantus firmus*), the lower voices repeat the words in ever-changing imitative counterpoint. On each occasion, the gradual accumulation of parts adds weight to the words. In addition to the regular patterning of instrumental and vocal passages, there is a further shaping brought about by the underlying harmonic progressions. The third line leads naturally to the relative major (Bb) of the G minor key of the hymn, lending an extra brightness to "brings once again a New Year". An especially active bass line extends the setting of the final "to the chosen Christian throng", emphasising the redemption of the favoured few.

No 2 Bass aria

A secular society...misunderstands the nature of religion: to console, but, first of all, to challenge and confront

Christopher Lasch: *The Revolt of the Elites*

The second verse of the hymn looks toward heavenly rejoicing. Bach's librettist, however, insets a reminder (how could a true believer ever forget?) of human wickedness: "O people who daily sin, you shall be the angels' joy." It is the accusation rather than the pleasure that appears to inspire the setting. Voice and continuo enter into an angular partnership, relentless in its repetition. The angelic joy (*Freude*) is – conventionally enough – allowed to spread its wings over four bars of vocal coloratura, though the austere energy of the continuo never relaxes. The aria is designed as a *da capo*, bringing the usual change of text for the central section: "Their exultant cry that God is reconciled with you is a proclamation of comfort". Even so, and despite a key change to the relative major, the musical manner barely changes. Quite possibly Bach was mindful of the overall dramatic shape of the cantata, aware that its positive message needed the spice of contrast.

No 3 Soprano recit

Here at last is the celestial music, in the form of a recorder trio that hovers above the voice. The words again take the second hymn verse as their starting point, but with a long theological footnote from the librettist: "The angels, who before shrank away from you as the damned, now fill the air in their choir above as they rejoice in your salvation". The tone colours are as ethereal as the timbre of the previous aria was dark and earthbound, for, as the librettist explains, past failings can be set aside: "God, who drove you from paradise out of the company of the angels now lets you be perfectly blessed on earth again, through his presence". The vocal line is all sweetness as it urges the listener to express gratitude for the new dispensation: "Then be thankful now with full voice for the wished-for age of the New Covenant".

No 4 Soprano/alto/tenor aria

If music is to be the means by which mortals show their kinship with the spiritual beings above, Bach shows the way in an exquisitely crafted setting of the third verse of the chorale. There are three main constituents, in order of appearance. First, there is the rhythmic envelope, introduced by the skips of the continuo part. As with the opening chorus, Bach takes delight in the dance; this time, however, his reference is to the *Loure* – again, French in origin. The chorale, meanwhile, is given to the alto voice, strengthened by violins and viola in unison. At the same time, soprano and tenor surround the hymn with a duet that sets a separate text by the librettist. In other words, each of the four lines of the chorale is given its own simultaneous commentary.

The pairings are as follows: "If God is reconciled and our friend": "Oh, blessed are we who believe in him". Next, "What can the wicked foe do to us?": "His fury cannot rob us of our comfort". The third lines are: "Despite the Devil and hell's gates" (this, incidentally, is a softening of the original, which placed the Turks and the Pope next to hell): "Their raging will be useless". Finally: "Little Jesus is our refuge": "God is with us and will protect us". Bach uses the new portions of text to enlarge his musical scheme, extending the space between each line of the chorale verse. The remarkable feature of this movement is the coexistence of separation and integration. Each element of text (of whichever authorship) has its distinct presence, and yet flows seamlessly into the whole. That is one of the special gifts of music – at least, in the hands of a master.

No 5 Bass recit

Quiet string chords signal a mood of deep contemplation: "This is a day that the Lord himself has made when he brought his son into the world." Yet despite the evident rapture – "Oh blessed time that is now fulfilled" – the vocal line is full of the intervals that speak the musical language of yearning. "Oh faithful waiting, from now on assuaged! Oh faith, that sees its goal! Oh love, that God draws to himself! Oh joy that breaks through sorrow and brings God the offering of our lips".

No 6 Chorale

As music director, Bach would surely have led straight into the fourth and last verse of the hymn – *attacca subito*, as a later composer might have instructed. All the instruments – strings, oboes, continuo – join in the lilting melody as partners of the human voice: "This brings the true Jubilee year! Why then should we ever be sad? Jump up! It's time to sing; little Jesus turns all sorrow away." This is the unconditional fervour of Kyriakus Schneegaß, passing to future generations his certainty of divine love and redemption from death. Bach was surely of the same mind; we may not be, but can still feel kinship with his belief in music as a delight of the world as it is and possibly – who knows? – a token of a better world to come.

*

Suggested recording: J. S. Bach-Stiftung, dir. Rudolf Lutz

January: Prefatory Note

Embarking on the New Year

The following selection of twenty cantatas for January shows the believer moving from the festivities that celebrate the Redeemer's birth to a mounting sense of vulnerability. The New Year's Day cantatas (BWV 190, BWV 41, BWV 16, BWV 171) resonate with the imagined presence of Christ - especially as that same day coincided with the circumcision of the infant in accordance with Jewish ritual. Yet the Sunday after New Year brings the background hum of the Christian sense of beleaguerment in BWV 153 and BWV 58. Epiphany Sunday, however, which marks the arrival of visitors from the East to pay homage to the newborn God, invites the faithful to renew their own commitment in the resplendent mysticism of BWV 65 and BWV 123.

The remainder of the month contains cantatas for the first four Sundays after Epiphany. They begin with the insecurity and longing of BWV 154, BWV 124 and BWV 13. Themes of patience and mental hardship similarly dominate BWV 155, BWV 3 and BWV 13. The third Sunday after Epiphany advocates submissions to God's will (BWV 73, BWV 111 and BWV 72), while the final group (BWV 156, BWV 81 and BWV 14) is full of awareness of death and the need of the human psyche to lean on a transcendent power. In so doing, the mind fortifies itself against its own helplessness.

New Year's Day/Circumcision of Christ

BWV 190: *Singet dem Herrn ein neues Lied*

(Sing to the Lord a new song)

Date: 1 January 1724

Librettist: Unknown

The main purpose of the cantatas for New Year's Day is to proclaim in music a commitment to God and thus to obtain his protection for the year to come. BWV 190 was the first of such works that Bach composed in Leipzig. The surviving manuscript for its first two movements is incomplete, containing parts only for violins and voices. However, the scoring for the opening chorus may be inferred from the closing chorale. This includes three trumpets, three oboes and drums, and as it was quite usual for Bach to call on his full forces at the end of a cantata, one can assume that all these instruments took part at the beginning – especially as the words summon everyone to praise God with "drums, strings and pipes". Modern performances must rely on musically informed editing to fill in the gaps. An unknown librettist has compiled a substantial text that brings together excerpts from Old and New Testaments. The Psalms – themselves part of an ancient tradition of singing to God – are a notable resource throughout, but for the Christian the real cause for rejoicing is the arrival of Christ as the supreme token of God's love for humankind. One of the Bible readings for the day (Lk. 2: 21) tells of the naming of the infant Jesus. Uttering his name becomes for believers a conduit to the ear of God and all the benefits that he might bestow; it is the talisman of faith.

No 1 Chorus

In the religious ritual and the resultant worship of a god, the cohesiveness and continued existence of a group and its culture are best guaranteed through one supreme and permanent authority.

Walter Burkert: *Homo Necans*, trans. Peter Bing

The use of music and dance to ward off evil spirits has a long history, noise in general being considered a prophylactic, up to and including the present: for instance, in the folk customs of the Bulgarian Kikeri (not to mention the curious practice of pot-banging in the UK when a novel respiratory virus spread amongst the population). In this chorus, even without the full score, the artistic purpose is clear. The occasion and the text call for musical worship of the divine: "Sing the Lord a new song! Let the assembled saints praise him! Praise him with drums and dancing!" (the latter more of a group ceilidh than a tango); "praise him with strings and pipes! Lord God, we praise you! All that has breath, praise the Lord! Lord God, we thank you! Alleluia!".

Loud volume and a fast tempo are music's basic tools for creating excitement. Both of these are used here, assuming (as we might) that trumpets and drums added their power to the ensemble. At least there is no doubt about the scintillating energy of the violin parts, and the insistence of the voices as they call on the world to join in the singing and dancing. The object is to praise God: the setting of the word *loben* ("praise") is spun out with decoration as a sign that no time or trouble can be too much. The tonal palette is bright and clear, avoiding ambiguities of harmony and key. It is, however, through the shaping of his design that Bach gives the text its maximum impact. The meaning of the whole can be summarised in the two imperatives: to praise and to give thanks. The impulse is both immediate and age-old, because each present act of worship links believers to a shared heritage of belief that waves away the passage of time.

Hence the "new song" that arrives halfway through the chorus is a renewal of the old: a quotation from Luther's version of the Latin *Te Deum*: "Lord God, we praise you" (*Herr Gott, dich loben wir*). Moving at the slow pace of one syllable per bar, the simple plainsong melody claims attention in its busy and sumptuous musical context, giving fresh impact to the words. Bach then adds his own homage of two fugal settings of "All that has breath, praise the Lord!", climbing from bass to soprano entries, and then reversing the order. After a short gap, the next phrase of the *Te Deum* appears, delivered with the same solemnity as before: "Lord God, we thank you" (*Herr Gott, wir danken dir*). Finally, an elaborate "Alleluia" completes the structure; intention – the desire to worship – and action have met in music.

No 2 Chorale and recit (bass/tenor/alto

The same two lines of the *Te Deum*, set in four-part vocal harmony, alternate with sections of explanatory recitative. The bass voice begins with the reason for praise: "since you, with this new year, grant us new prosperity and blessing and still look on us with favour". A glance at Leipzig's fortunate history inspires the tenor with thanks, "since your kindness has in time past protected the entire land and our dear city from famine, pestilence and war". In the same vein, the alto continues: "for your fatherly faithfulness is still endless; it is renewed every morning. For this, then, merciful God, we fold our hands humbly and throughout our lives express our thanks and praise with mouth and heart".

No 3 Alto aria

From this point on, the manuscript is complete. Violins, viola and continuo cradle the singer in peace; "Praise your God, Zion, praise your God with joy. Rise up! Tell the glory of the one who in his sanctuary will from now on feed you as your shepherd in green pastures". No doubt the text suggested to Bach the quasi-rustic style of the rocking pedal in the continuo. The strings proceed in close harmony, in easy partnership with the voice. Similarly, the tonal surface barely stirs: although Bach moves to the relative (F sharp) minor in the central part of the aria, this seems more for the sake of aural variety than to create a change of mood, as would typically be the case in a *da capo* aria. Faith promises an undisturbed tranquillity of heart.

No 4 Bass recit

Yet if this is the ideal, the text here implies that it is not easily achieved. The librettist has combined elements of the Old and New Testaments; the spiritual longing of Psalm 27 v4 ("One thing only I ask") can now only be satisfied by identification with Christ. The prayer to distance the self from the attachments of the body brings the first hint in BWV 190 of inner struggle: "Let the world desire what pleases flesh and blood; only one thing, just one, I ask of the Lord". Praise and worship have a particular end in view: "This one thing I greatly wish, that Jesus, my joy, my true shepherd, my comfort and salvation and my soul's best part, would embrace me as a little sheep of his pasture, in this year too, and never more let me go from his arms".

The recitative style is conversational, as if the believer is thinking aloud. The listener overhears the revelation of need – the vulnerability that lies beneath the communal dazzle of sound. Fear of death is the subtext, for consistent faith is the condition of eternal life. The last few bars settle into a more melodic style and a steady rhythm as they underwrite the believer's hope for the future: "May his good spirit, which shows me the way to life, govern and lead me on a level path; thus I begin this year in Jesus's name".

No 5 Tenor/bass aria

Though the key returns to the D major of the opening chorus, the scene has shifted from the public to the private – from the outer to the inner self. Faith looks only to Jesus, whose name begins each of the six lines of verse: "Jesus shall be my all, Jesus shall be my starting point, Jesus is my light of joy, To Jesus I commit myself, Jesus helps me through his blood, Jesus makes my ending good". The style is intimate and tender as in a love duet – which in fact it is. One solo instrument (the range of the part suggests an oboe d'amore or possibly violin) accompanies the voices. Its lyrical, upward-winding phrases suggest the soul's yearning to be one with Christ. A gentle homecoming is the goal, and this is implied in the constant repetition of stepwise descents in both instrumental and vocal parts.

Although no longer swept along by an exultant crowd, the believer is never alone; the imitative and harmonious writing for the voices depict the soul endlessly shadowing, and shadowed by, its Saviour. As with the alto aria, the mood is consistent throughout, though Bach creates harmonic shaping. At "To Jesus I will commit myself" (*Jesu will ich mich verschreiben*), the arrival of the relative (B) minor seems to initiate a central section. A further move to its subdominant (E minor) hints at acquiescence in the death that awaits all, sooner or later. The Christian may remain composed and cheerful as Christ's sacrifice grants the possibility of eternal life. Repeated assertions of "Jesus makes my ending good" ("*Jesus macht mein Ende gut*") lead the music safely back to its home key.

No 6 Tenor recit

Oh! Thank you, God, for a lovely day.
And what was the other I had to say?
I said "Bless Daddy", so what can it be?
Oh! Now I remember. God bless Me.

A.A. Milne: *Vespers*

After the pledge of faith, the moment has come to ask for a reciprocal token of God's love. To a thoughtful background of string chords, an all-inclusive prayer points out all the local institutions and individuals deserving of divine protection: the believer and his family, church, school and teachers, council, law courts, every household – the list goes on. The message is clear: in a world subject to God, humankind may here and now enjoy a foretaste of heaven.

No 7 Chorale

The second verse of Johann Heermann's New Year hymn, *Jesus nun sei gepreiset* ("Let Jesus now be praised") provides a concluding (and conclusive) reminder of the link between obedient piety and social order. If God's word prevails, then peace and prosperity are sure to follow. One can only admire, and sympathise with, the positive spirit of Heermann (1585-1647), who endured a lifetime of ill health and tragedy, surviving the plague and the Thirty Years' War. One must hold on to something amidst pervasive violence and destruction. What that might be differs from one mind to another; therein lies the problem.

Let us complete this year
In praise of your name,
That we may sing of it
Within the Christian community.
Help us to survive life
Through your almighty hand,
Preserve your dear Christians
And our fatherland.
Turn your blessing toward us,
Grant peace in every part;
Grant us, untarnished in this land
The blessing of your word.
Bring hypocrites to ruin
Here and everywhere!

A ceremonial flourish of trumpets and drums punctuates each phrase; thus, the final vision of God is embellished with the aural regalia of power, inspiring the soul with courage to enter the year ahead.

*

Suggested recording: Monteverdi Choir and Orchestra, dir. John Eliot Gardiner

New Year/Circumcision of Christ

BWV 41: *Jesu, nun sei gepreiset*

(Jesus, now be praised)

Date: 1 January 1725

Librettist: Unknown

To have survived the crossing from the old year to the new inspires gratitude in the believer and thoughts of a future stretching into eternity. The previous New Year's cantata (BWV 190) took for its ending the middle verse of Johann Heermann's hymn, *Jesu, nun sei gepreiset* ("Jesus, now be praised"). For BWV 41, however, the entire hymn forms the basis of the libretto. Its verses are unusually long (fourteen lines); the first and third are used for the opening and closing choruses, while the words of the second provide the material, in altered form, for two pairs of aria and recitative. There is, therefore, much in common between BWV 41 and BWV 190, chief of which is the need to praise and thank God for his continuous protection. Yet there are some differences of emphasis. For instance, in BWV 190, a significant theme is the talismanic power of the name of Jesus – an allusion to one of the day's biblical readings (Lk. 2: 21). With BWV 41, on the other hand, the impression is of the fullness of life amidst time without end. The renewal of the calendar brings a reminder not only of the infinite grandeur of God, but also of the self's chance of eternity, as faith promises a share in the nature of the divine. If the New Year marks the discontinuities of bodily time, Christianity, with its promise of resurrection after death, proposes to abolish them.

No 1 Chorus

Bach's approach to his hymn text – with its melody unadventurous enough to be acceptable (one would imagine) to Calvin himself – is a model of how the artistic imagination can transmute words into musical gold. They begin with: "Jesus, now be praised/ at this New Year/ for your goodness, shown to us/ in all distress and danger,/ so that we have lived to see/ this new happy time/ which hovers about us, full of Grace/ and eternal blessedness". The cry to worship becomes a dazzling tribute to the divine, complete with his earthly retinue of three trumpets and drums, three oboes, strings and continuo.

From these massed forces, Bach constructs a great formal edifice, using his opening *ritornello* as its framework. He does not overdo the use of his aural shock troops (the trumpets) but, varying the texture, periodically puts strings and woodwind at the forefront. Rooted in the C major tonic key, brass fanfares suggest God's might, while octave-spanning descending scales in the continuo suggests his limitless being – the interval of an octave acting as a metaphor for the boundless. The chorale is sung as a soprano *cantus firmus* that holds fast above the activity of the lower voices.

So far, text and music have looked upward to celestial power, but the following two lines turn to the human context: "so in tranquil stillness we have completed the last year". The change of perspective brings a contrast in style that satisfies the aesthetic need for variety. Bach accompanies the new thought with a change of pulse: a slow-moving (*adagio*) triple rhythm. The vocal parts join in solid harmony – and note the prolonged setting of *Stille* ("stillness"). Meanwhile, the trumpets stay silent as oboes and strings follow their gentle path. The key has changed to the relative (A) minor, for what could be more poignant than the desire for continuing peace?

The setting of the remaining lines brings further change. Technique and expression merge in the fugal treatment of the words – "We want to give ourselves to you/ now and for evermore" – as the continuous succession of entries acts out in music the endless dedication of the Christian community. The lower voices now precede the appearance of the soprano hymn melody, in contrast to the earlier part of the chorus, when all the singers entered much at the same time. A similar imitative treatment leads in the final plea: "Protect body, soul and life/henceforth throughout the whole year!" (the year – *Jahr* – extends over five bars). To complete his design, Bach repeats these last two lines, all the while easing the key back to its original C major for so that the movement can end with its the triumphant opening *ritornello*.

No 2 Soprano aria

The faux-rustic style, with its almost folksy tune and a trio of instruments in close harmony, recalls the alto aria (No. 3) of BWV 190. Here, though, instead of violins and viola, the pastoral mood is more conventionally implied by the sound of oboes. In both cases, the aim is to give an impression of human sincerity and meekness. Yet despite its air of simplicity, this aria is structured as a lengthy *da capo*. Its outer sections are all smoothness, with almost no decoration of the parts – just the occasional trill – and a leisurely pace of harmonic change.

Calmness reigns, as the lack of musical turmoil mirrors the hope of an untroubled future: "Let us, Oh highest God" (a direct quotation from the second verse of the hymn) "so complete the year that it may end as it began". In his score, Bach reminds the instrumentalists to play more softly when the singer – it would have been a choirboy – enters. The B section looks to the fulfilment of the prayer: "May your hand be with us, so at the year's end we may, amidst the abundance of blessings, as now, sing an alleluia". The vocal line spills over with joy before returning to the demure delivery of the A section. The Almighty's favour must not be taken for granted.

No 3 Alto recit

Throughout BWV 41, the text treads carefully between respect and hope. This recitative begins with a bow: "Ah! Your hand, your blessing alone must be the Alpha and Omega," (note the C major octave interval) "the beginning and end". God is all-seeing and all-caring: "You carry our life in your hand, and our days are ordained by you; your eye looks over city and country; you count our good things and know our sorrows" (the harmonies darken). The human can only yield to a power beyond its comprehension: "Ah! distribute both however your wisdom wills it and wherever your mercy directs you".

No 4 Tenor aria

To illustrate the bounty that flows from heaven, Bach's chosen instrument here was a smaller version of the cello: the *violoncello piccolo* (which was most likely held across the chest rather than balanced on the floor). The part consists of a virtuoso succession of leaps and flowing, ornamented phrases, above the continuo's harmonic support. The vocal line is melodically uncomplicated, though often with a rising pitch to denote the direction of thought upward: "Just as you have granted a noble peace for our body and condition of life, so continue to give our soul the blessing of your word". As the central section of the *da capo* points out, faith is the precondition of a good life both now and in the hereafter: "If we have this means of salvation, then we are blessed here and your chosen ones there!". Is there an advance whiff of prosperity theology? Despite Luther's resistance to the idea, faith necessarily involves a transaction of sorts. The ultimate lure is the hope of immortality, but if it also brings an agreeable life in the present, so much the better.

No 5 Bass recit

However, with no visible means of support, belief is always vulnerable to attack. Every type of opposition is attributed to the plotting of the Devil – hence the final request to God for the strength to repress all wavering. The text of this recitative derives from the last two lines of Heermann's middle verse: "Yet since the enemy watches day and night to harm us and wants to destroy our peace, then please listen, Lord God, when we pray in the holy congregation, 'Let Satan be trodden underfoot'". The latter appeal is part of Luther's German Litany, performed here as a fast and furious interpolation from the massed choral voices, while the continuo heads for the depths below. One last pledge leads from subservience to God in suffering and death to the ultimate destination beyond: "Then we remain, to your renown, your chosen property, and can also, after cross and pain," (the crunch of chromatic harmonies) "depart from here to glory".

No 6 Chorale

Praise, gratitude, hope, dutiful humility, and an awareness of the spiritual context of mortal existence are woven together in the complex fabric of BWV 41. The last verse of Heerman's hymn unites all these elements; it is both a concluding prayer and, in Bach's setting, an imposing summary of what has gone before. Each of the first pairs of lines alternates with a reminder of the opening fanfare: "Yours alone is the honour/yours alone is the praise;/teach us patience in bearing the cross/rule all our doing/until we happily depart/into the eternal kingdom of heaven/to true peace and joy". The next two lines appear more simply, to match their humble intention: "Meanwhile, deal with us all/as it seems best to you". Such implicit trust in God is to be the means of happiness – as Bach shows in the rhythmic twirl that follows: "This is what we Christian believers sing, in all sincerity, wishing with mouth and heart a blessed New Year". After a last repeat of the expression of goodwill, the trumpets add their own splendid Amen.

*

Suggested recording: J.S. Bach-Stiftung, dir. Rudolf Lutz

New Year/Circumcision of Christ

BWV 16: *Herr Gott, dich loben wir*

(Lord God, we praise you)

1 January 1726

Librettist: Georg Christian Lehms

Whenever a new step is taken consciously and irrevocably, it is inevitably connected with sacrifice.

Walter Burkert: *Homo Necans*, trans. Peter Bing

In the Christian religion, worshipper and worshipped are bound together by reciprocal ties of sacrifice. As Christ shed his own blood to redeem a sinful race of mortals, they in turn are required to offer themselves to their divine king. New Year's Day is a reminder of this relationship. It coincides with the occasion of the infant Christ's circumcision: the ritual sacrifice of the flesh that dedicates the male child to God and, in this particular case, hints at the blood that will be spilt at the crucifixion. It is, therefore, the moment to submit once more to God as guarantor of life's continuation in this world and the next. In BWV 16, music and text combine in tribute; the words pay their respects, but music is the route to the self-forgetfulness that ritual demands.

No 1 Chorus

The *Te deum* – the ancient Latin hymn of homage to God – has featured in Christian worship for almost two millennia. Luther's own version, first published in 1529, achieved iconic status amongst his co-religionists: to allude to it was to tap into the roots of the entire belief system of Christianity in general and Lutheranism in particular. It becomes the "new song" (*neues Lied*) of the opening chorus of BWV 190 - a previous cantata for New Year's Day - and supplies the text of the first movement of BWV 16: "Lord God, we praise you,/Lord God we thank you:/You, God the Father in eternity,/the world honours far and wide". Though the custom was to sing these lines antiphonally, i.e. a single voice alternating with the group, Bach gives them here to the soprano line as a *cantus firmus*.

While the *Te deum* proceeds with unhurried dignity – the melody doubled by a hunting horn – its musical surroundings tell a different story, of underlying emotional excitement. The continuo gallops along in the long-short-short (dactylic) rhythm that propels the movement from beginning to end. With the arrival of the *Te deum*, the lower voices gather in rapid-fire imitation; the texture soon builds as the upper instruments (violins, oboes and viola) join in the apparently spontaneous music making - though (as with jazz) Bach's easy brilliance in the weaving of parts comes from long practice. All the while, he notes the musical implications of his text, as with the octave leaps in the setting of "God the Father in eternity" (*Gott Vater in Ewigkeit*) and the long vocal span to represent everlasting time. The ancient tonal idiom of the *Te deum* appears to oscillate between minor (A) and major (C); it is in this last key that the rejoicing comes to rest.

No 2 Bass recit

The Lord said to Moses, "Consecrate to me all the first-born".
Exodus 13:1

New Year's Day symbolises the rebirth of time, the beginning of a fresh episode of (as it seems to the believer) God-given life: "So we give voice at this happy time with burning devotion, and lay before you, O God, at this New Year, the first offering of our hearts". The Old Testament Jehovah may have required blood, but the Christian God contents himself with words of appreciation: "What have you not done already from eternity for our salvation, and how must our hearts feel even now your faithful love! Your Zion enjoys perfect peace, prosperity and blessing". Words make their greatest impact, however, when paired with music and thus lifted into the realm of the sacred: "The temple echoes with the sound of strings" (the German alludes to the biblical "psalteries and harps"), "and our souls well up when the heat of devotion warms our hearts and mouths. Oh! Should we not strike up a new song and with ardent love begin to sing?"

No 3 Aria for bass and chorus

On with the dance; let joy be unconfin'd

> Lord Byron: 'Childe Harold's Pilgrimage'

Ritual allows for self-abandonment within a secure structure. Both conditions are met in this piece of religious theatre, which seems to draw in the listener as both onlooker and – in spirit at least – as participant. The overall design is in three parts: choral at the beginning and end, and with a bass soloist (plus one communal interjection) in the centre. It begins with a summons from all the bass singers together: "Let us exult", repeated by a clamour of instruments – including a triumphant horn – and voices. The next phrase, "Let us rejoice", follows similarly. There is no essential difference between vocal and instrumental parts, for both of them arise from one of music's simplest elements: a fanfare built from the notes of a chord. The setting of the vowel sounds – the *au* of *jauchzen* ("exult") and the *eu* of *freuen* ("rejoice") – turns them into infectious peals of laughter, though tight rhythmic patterns hold the wildness in check.

Having established a context of almost manic joy, Bach moves at last to its cause: "God's goodness and faithfulness are renewed each morning". A short passage for the upper instruments creates a transition to the central solo with its sermon of hope: "Since his hand crowns and blesses, Ah, then, believe that our condition will be for ever and ever fortunate". The key moves to the relative minor and the accompanying texture is lighter, to give more prominence to the message. It contains, after all, the main point: that God will grant eternal bliss to his followers. The vocal line is both rhetorical and expressive, with decorative emphasis on "crowns" (*krönt*), an insistent urging of surrender to faith (*ach so glaubt*), and a long glimpse into eternity (*ewig*). Now, at the centre of symmetry of the movement, the massed voices interrupt with another call to rejoice; the horn trills its approval. The solo voice returns, ending with a grand, swooping cadence and followed by a return of the high-voltage style that began the movement.

No 4 Alto recit

In the Old Testament we find blessing as the source of all good things, and the withdrawal of blessing as the source of all dangers. The blessing of God makes the land possible for men to live in.

Mary Douglas: Purity and Danger

Humankind has fulfilled its obligation to God through the sacrifice of the spirit and can now expect something in return. The first item is the continuation of the structures of belief that integrate Church and society:

"Ah, faithful refuge, protect henceforth your precious word: protect Church and school, so that your kingdom is increased and Satan's cunning is foiled". The vocal contours rise over a diminished seventh to soften "our beloved calm", while gently descending intervals accompany the gift of "complete wellbeing". The ultimate source of blessing, however, comes from the self. Faith enables immortality; it brings the strength to endure life, with the inner gaze fixed on a transcendent good: "Blessed are we if we trust in you for ever and ever, my Jesus and my salvation".

No 5 Tenor aria

The tender style of this aria follows logically from the preceding recitative. As with so many of the cantatas, the trajectory of BWV 16 is from extrovert to introvert: from the loud communal voice to the intimate connection of the individual with God, which is often represented, as here, as a love song. A simple promise forms the A section's text: "Beloved Jesus, you alone shall be my soul's wealth". There are no abrupt transitions of melody, key or rhythm to disturb the soul's tranquillity. Above the regular pace of the continuo, one mellow-toned instrument – either the viola or the *oboe da caccia* (a proto-cor anglais) – partners the singer. The key is F major which (as the subdominant of the earlier C major) contains a hint of yielding.

The B section begins with a rising sequence of longing for the Saviour: "We would place you before other treasures in our faithful hearts". Conventionally enough, the key has changed to differentiate the central part of the musical structure, and Bach's choice of the relative (D) minor fits the implied poignancy of the text. Its real preoccupation is the moment of death, a subject that eventually emerges with: "Yes, yes, when life's cord breaks, our spirit, content with God, will speak the same yearning words as our lips…". Symbolising the continuity of mortality with immortality, the singer continues without a break to the "Beloved Jesus" of the A section. Thus the recurring cycle of time – the New Year – is bound to the deeper question of eternal life.

No 6 Chorale

The librettist, the short-lived Georg Christian Lehms (1684-1717), had not added a final chorale, and so Bach made his own choice: the last verse of a new year's hymn by the theologian Paul Eber (1511-1569). Its lines epitomise the message of the entire cantata: "All such goodness of yours we praise,/ Father on heaven's throne/ as you show us /through Christ your son,/and we pray you further/to grant us a peaceful year/preserve us from all suffering/and nourish us gently".

*

Suggested recording: Netherlands Bach Collegium, dir. Pieter van Leus

New Year's Day/Circumcision of Christ

BWV 171: *Gott, wie dein Name, so ist auch dein Ruhm*

(God, as your name is, so is your renown)

1 January, probably 1729

Librettist: Christian Friedrich Henrici (Picander)

Bach had composed several cantatas for New Year's Day before BWV 171. Three of them – BWV 190, BWV 41 and BWV 16 – have already been discussed in the pages of this book. They all focus on the need to praise and thank God so as to ensure his care in the year to come, and they all include references to a long heritage of sacred music – dazzlingly reworked, of course. The libretto of BWV 171 is conceptually taut and more closely connected than its predecessors to the day's two biblical readings. The first of these (Lk. 2:21) tells of the naming of the infant Jesus, which accompanied the ritual of circumcision. To name is to establish identity. Both the name and what it represents then merge in the imagination, so that to call upon one's God by name becomes a token of belief in his actual presence.

The companion passage of scripture is Paul's assurance (Gal. 3:23-29) that all who follow Christ may count themselves Abraham's heirs and God's chosen people. Christ and the Old Testament God are one and the same; to affirm the name of either is to ally oneself with the indissoluble deity and hence ensure his continuing oversight. The writings of the Old and New Testaments are thought to be a combined revelation of God's nature and power; from such a grand perspective, human demarcations of time are minuscule punctuation points, mere blips of mortality. They remind the physical being of its limits, impelling the believer to implore God for his protection now and in the future, when death threatens to undo the self.

No 1 Chorus

Picander – who wrote, amongst other things, the words of Bach's St. Matthew Passion – supplied a brief text for this opening chorus. It is a verse from Psalm 48: "God, as your name, so is your renown to the ends of the earth". As with the other New Year's Day cantatas, Bach has a large ensemble at his disposal, resplendent with brass (three trumpets), drums, and the penetrating sound of oboes. He uses them, however, with calculated restraint - mostly to double the voices; the Old Testament Jehovah is not one for flummery. More important, perhaps, is Bach's use of form. He turns the strict protocols of fugue into a display of energy and brilliance: a musical homage to the God of Ages. The continuous flow of parts becomes a metaphor both of God's infinite being and the endless human impulse to worship.

The fugue subject itself, with its reiterated keynote, is austere, even elemental (and in fact Bach included it in the Credo of his Mass in B Minor); its beginning and end encompass an octave, i.e. an interval that opens the possibility of endless renewal. The overall musical architecture comprises two separate fugal expositions with an intricately worked episode as a connecting arch. Here, at last, Bach brings in the trumpet – not merely to gild the sound, but also as an active participant in the fugue. All the while, the voices – the sopranos especially – spin out the setting of *Ende* ("ends") to depict God's boundless influence. With the second appearance of the fugue, its subject is slightly altered (for variety's sake?) so as to rise before its end, and the order of vocal entries is changed. Finally all three trumpets and drums join the singers in a great coda that powers its way to the security of the key chord.

No 2 Tenor aria

The urge to praise takes on a more personal aspect as chorus and orchestra give way to a solo voice and a pair of violins plus continuo. Again, Picander's text borrows from Old Testament psalms that praise the name of God: "Lord, as far as the clouds go, so goes your name's renown". The key is in the major; the style sparkles. As the mind's eye looks to the skies, so ascending figures and leaps characterise the violin parts, with far-reaching arpeggios that extend over the territory of the stave. The vocal line also reaches upward; as so often, Bach favours illustrating the words above the comfort of the singer, who must grapple with the lengthy setting of "goes" (*gehet*). The aria follows a three-part design, with the music of the central section turning to minor keys as the words point to the universal imperative to honour God: "All that moves its lips, all that draws breath, shall exalt you in your might". Strenuous rising patterns make increasing demands on the voice, especially at *erhöhen* ("exalt"); the continuo too has – temporarily – to make as much effort as the upper strings. But this is pre-eminently a day for rejoicing, and so the movement returns to the consistent brightness of its beginning.

No 3 Alto recit

While God the Father may overwhelm with his grandeur, in his human form he appears as comforter and intermediary between heaven and earth. The name of Christ brings calm and resilience: "You sweet name of Jesus, in you is my repose, you are my consolation on earth; how, then, can I be troubled when I have my own cross to bear?" A change of harmonies from minor to major mirrors the positive direction of the believer's thoughts. Life is portrayed as a battle to be fought: "You are my stronghold and my banner; I run to it" (note the scuttle of *da lauf ich hin*) "when I am hounded". The name, and what it signifies, means everything: "You are my light and my light, my honour and my confidence, my support in danger, and my gift for the New Year.

No 4 Soprano aria

The music is a borrowing from an earlier secular cantata, where it invoked the soft west wind. A gently rocking pulse underpins the soaring of a virtuoso violin, while the lilt of the vocal melody suits the contentment that the soul derives from thoughts of Christ: "Jesus shall be my first word in the New Year". The structure and tonality of this movement are correspondingly transparent: two D major outer sections offset a central portion which confronts the thought of death. The name of Jesus, however, brings the strength to face one's end: "Again and again, my mouth smiles at his name, and in my last hour Jesus shall also be my last word". The violin arpeggios continue throughout, wafting the divine spirit from on high.

No 5 Bass recit

God will favour and bless the community provided they keep His commandments and obey His law. This significantly qualifies the original absolute promise of blessing and possession. If they fail in their witness and adherence, they will be punished by God withdrawing His favour from the people.

Anthony D. Smith: *Chosen People*

Even so, the believer looks for final reassurance. In this colourful recitative, Bach differentiates four stages of a psychological process that alternates hope with fear. The text begins with a prompt from scripture (Jn.14: 13-14): "And since you, Lord, have said: Just ask in my name, and the reply will be always be 'Yes' and 'Amen'". A poised, melodic style sets apart the words of Christ – to which the response is a sudden disruption of mood. Accompanied by the lamentation of a pair of oboes and the wildness of diminished harmonies, the voice cries out: "Then we beseech you, Saviour of all the world, do not reject us; protect us this year from fire, plague and the danger of war!". The cure for all these horrors is, of course, to bring community and individual under God's guidance. Bach steadies the rhythm and smooths the harmonic language for a vision of social stability: "Let your Word, that bright light, burn pure and clear for us; let our government and the entire land acknowledge the blessing of your salvation. Grant at all times good fortune and welfare to every walk of life". A final, orderly *arioso* urges Christ to keep his promise: "We ask, Lord, in your name, to say 'Yes' to this, to say 'Amen'".

No 6 Chorale

Bach turned here to another self-borrowing: from his earlier New Year's cantata, BWV 41. This work was based on Johann Heermann's hymn: "Jesus, now be praised," and Heermann's last verse appears there at the end in full musical finery (brass, wind, trumpets etc.). The same splendid setting concludes BWV 171, though now the words are of the middle verse, which fits perfectly with what has gone before: "Let us bring the year to an end/with praise of your name/that we may sing of it/in the Christian congregation./If you wish us to make our way through life/under your almighty hand,/support your dear Christians/and our native land!/Send your blessings to us/grant peace everywhere,/keep pure in the land/your blessed word,/destroy the devils/here and in every place!". The sense of threat – the underlying insecurity – is palpable. Human life is inevitably uncertain; the religious belief of the cantatas can be understood as one example amongst many of the attempt to appease a power beyond comprehension.

*

Suggested recording: Concentus Musicus Wien, dir. Nikolaus Harnoncourt

Sunday after New Year

BWV 153: *Schau, lieber Gott, wie meine Feind*

(See, dear God, how my enemies)

Librettist: Unknown

2 January 1724

The previous day brought communal euphoria (see BWV 190, *Singet dem Herrn ein neues Lied*). Already, though, the calendar's illusion of a fresh start, and the picture of a society happily united in deference to God, has given way to the realisation that life goes on much as before. The usual demons must be fought; in fact, battle – of the inner rather than the outer variety – is essential for strengthening immunity against doubt. BWV 153 portrays a mind that feels itself under attack and, by a process of inner dialogue, finds a way to talk itself out of its waverings. The cantata is full of theatrical contrasts in its terrors, its sense of persecution, and the calm of faith restored.

For this psychodrama, Bach used only small forces, most likely because at that time of year there were so many demands on his choir and instrumentalists. As a result, there are no extended choruses in BWV 153, but rather a series of solo recitatives and arias, interspersed with three chorales in unadorned four-part settings. The libretto draws its life lessons from the day's gospel readings. Herod's persecution of the new-born Christ (Mt. 2: 13-23) becomes an allegory of the world's violence against the realm of the spirit, while the first letter of Peter (Pt. 4: 12-19) teaches that earthly agony is a sign of closeness to God. Difficulties are baked into the divine plan: if life is hard, that is how it should be, for the model is Christ's own suffering.

No 1 Chorale

This is the first stanza of a hymn by David Denicke (1603-1680), an esteemed academic, jurist and hymn writer, whose religious verses are still in use today: "See, dear God, how my enemies,/with whom I must endlessly wrestle,/are so cunning and powerful/that they can easily overcome me!/Lord, if your grace does not hold me safe,/then devil, flesh and the world/may easily cast me into misfortune". Bach and his congregation would have known (as few of us now would) the context of the entire hymn. It reads as a long polemic against the physical pleasures of life. The last line of the fifth verse conveys the general tone of Augustinian disgust: "My flesh incites me to sins" (*Mein Fleisch zur Sünde mich reizet*). In other words, the battle is between the material and the symbolic self, conducted with the usual passion of civil war. The chorale hovers at last on an imperfect cadence, waiting for the drama to unfold.

No 2 Alto recit

To the believer, God has objective reality. He is seen as the ally without whom it is impossible to suppress the inclinations of the body: "My beloved God, ah, pity me, ah, help my poor self! I live here amongst only lions and dragons, and these want, with their rage and ferocity, to finish me off completely". Both the language and the highly-coloured harmonisations – the so-called "satanic" diminished intervals – convey the violence of the struggle.

No 3 Bass arioso

The librettist looked for reassurance in the Old Testament book of Isaiah (Is. 41:10), with its message of God to his people: "Don't be afraid, I am with you. Do not give in, I am your God. I will strengthen you and help you with the right hand of my righteousness". The music inhabits the words with smooth and tight-knit authority. Its tonal structure aligns with the three statements of the text, bringing neat transitions from the tonic key (E minor) to the dominant (B minor) and back again to the tonic. The first four words of the German (*Fürchte dich nicht, ich* – "Don't be afraid, I") give Bach his initial rhythm and pitch contours. This two-bar phrase then becomes a recurring musical motto that binds the whole piece together both musically and also psychologically, as a constant reminder of God's protective presence. For the second part of the message ("Do not give in, I am your God"), Bach lets the vocal line soar, while in the final section God's right hand - symbol of his eternal power – spans an octave.

No 4 Tenor recit

The response from the believer is a classic "Yes, but ...": wishing to be convinced, yet not quite succeeding. The setting begins calmly enough with: "Truly, your words, dear God, bring peace to my soul and comfort in my sufferings". Soon, though, a high-pitched cry launches a catalogue of persecution: "Ah, but my troubles grow from day to day, for my enemies are so many; they are aiming at my life, bending their bow to unleash their arrows and destroy me". The vocal line rises and falls in panic, and the musical extension of *Bogen* shows the bow at full stretch. Despair comes from fear of an unredeemed death: "I will surely die at their hands". A slow, chromatic unravelling of *sterben* ("die") maps tonal breakdown on to the dissolution of the self. Words and setting then combine in a final outburst of helplessness: "God! My distress is known to you, the whole world becomes a den of torture for me; help, Helper, help! Rescue my soul!".

No 5 Chorale

If you lack faith, then clutch the last anchor. Have yourself carried to church like a child and then speak without fear to Christ the Lord: "I am undeserving, but I rely on the faith of the Church – or of another believer".

> Martin Luther, Maundy Thursday 1518, quoted by Heiko Obermann: *Luther*, trans. Eileen Walliser-Schwarzbart

In response, the communal voice offers the fifth verse of Paul Gerhardt's *Befiehl du deine Wege* ("Entrust your way"). It is set to the melody (*Herzlich tut mich verlangen*) that appears in Bach's St. Matthew Passion as *O Haupt voll Blut und Wunden* ("O sacred head sore wounded"). A Lutheran theologian, Gerhardt (1607-1676) was a prolific writer of hymns, aware of their contribution to the teaching of the Church. As with the opening chorale above, the entirety of *Befiehl du deine Wege* would have been familiar to Bach's world. Its twelve verses preach complete surrender to the idea that one's life is being ordered for the best by an invisible higher power.

   The therapeutic value of this is evident; it finds a place in many belief systems and is enough to account for the widespread human inclination toward religion. In addition, based on the premise that the deity plans nothing but good, it is natural to suppose that disturbances to one's happiness are caused by forces of evil. Personified as the devil and his agents, they are a fixture of the Christian belief of the cantatas, as in Gerhardt's verse here: "And though all the devils/would stand in your way/yet there is no doubt/that God will not retreat;/whatever he has decided/and whatever he wishes to have/must happen in the end/to fit his purpose and goal".

No 6 Tenor aria

While the emotional temperature is as high as ever, its fuel becomes defiance rather than fear: "Storm, then, storm, you tempests of tribulation! Pour your torrents over me!" Bach's setting unites the visual and the psychological. Dotted rhythms tell of the newly stiffened spine while the other parts (strings, and at times the continuo) swirl above and below in an evocation of chaos. The voice plunges into the maelstrom, swept along in a great rush of coloratura, yet keeping its head above water with its declaration of fortitude. Despite the appearance of wildness, Bach (like God, perhaps) has a controlling plan. Though the style – the integration of the spiky with the fluid – stays the same throughout, there is always an underlying tonal scheme. An initial section in A minor changes to the subdominant (D minor) for the next part of the text: "Strike, flames of misfortune, upon me! Disturb my rest" (note the lingering on *Ruh*) "you enemies!". But as the word of God comes to mind, the music returns to the home key: "For God says to me comfortingly: I am your refuge and your deliverer".

No 7 Bass recit

The main thing would naturally be the moral education of the little fishes. They would be taught that it would be the greatest and most beautiful thing if a little fish joyfully sacrificed itself, and that they must believe everything that the sharks said, especially when they told them that they would take care to provide a wonderful future for them.

Bertolt Brecht: *If Sharks were People*

Suffering, so goes this exercise in self-counselling, should not be regarded as the enemy; it is, on the contrary, a boon because it unites the soul with God. Those who wish to share an eternal existence with Christ must be prepared to accept their burden of sorrow: "Have trust! My heart, endure your pain and do not let your cross crush you! God will restore you at the proper time". A cadence in the major reflects the turn to optimism. In any case – continues the thought – how much worse it was for Christ himself, forced to flee into Egypt shortly after his birth. The harmonies cloud over (a sprinkling of chords of the seventh) to accompany the reference to the day's biblical story: "Indeed, his beloved son, your Jesus, when still a tender child, encountered much greater hardship, when the raging Herod threatened with murderous fist the ultimate danger of death! He had hardly arrived on earth when he had to become a fugitive" – note the brief fluster of the vocal line. A calm and elegantly decorated section of melody leads the listener to the right conclusion and the major key: "Come then, comfort yourself with Jesus and believe steadfastly: to those who suffer here with Christ he will grant the kingdom of heaven".

No 8 Alto aria

I'm wearying to escape into that glorious world, and to be always there; not seeing it dimly through tears and yearning for it through the walls of an aching heart; but really with it and in it.

> Emily Bronte: *Wuthering Heights*

With faith restored, the mind is back in balance; yet the believer cannot help some restlessness, when what is dreamt of is yet to come. The tempo quickens at the thought of that perfect realm beyond the present: "In that place is pure jubilation, where Jesus exchanges suffering for blessed gladness and everlasting joys". These (*Freuden*) extend over twelve bars as a token of eternity.

No 9 Chorale

BWV 153 finishes with the last three verses (16-18) of *Ach Gott, wie manches Herzeleid* ("Ah God, how much heartache"), written by the theologian Martin Moller (1547-1606). His hymn is full of mystic devotion to the figure of Christ; faith, with its promise of immortality, shapes the entire programme of existence:

Therefore I wish, while I live,
Joyfully to follow you, carrying my cross;
My God, make me prepared for that,
It serves for the best at all times!

Help me to deal rightly with my affairs
So that I can complete my course;
Help me also to master flesh and blood,
Protect me from sin and shame!

Keep my heart pure in faith,
So that I live and die for you alone;
Jesus, my comfort, hear my yearning,
O my Saviour, if I could only be with you!

A brisk tempo in performance gives a lilting quality, which fits the contented conclusion – though in BWV 58 the same melody is presented with the weight of sorrow.

*

Suggested recording: Netherlands Bach Collegium, dir. Pieter Jan Leusink

Sunday after New Year

BWV 58: *Ach Gott, wie manches Herzeleid*

(Ah God, how much heartbreak)

Librettist: Unknown

5 January 1727 (with later revisions)

Preposterous as it may seem in these pragmatic days, they clung to the quaintly outmoded view that there was too much cruelty and aggression in the world for it to be merely accidental, or solvable by piecemeal reform...For them, the flaw of the world ran so deep that it cried out for some thoroughgoing transformation, known in their jargon as redemption.

Terry Eagleton: *The Gatekeeper*

After the celebration of Christmas and the New Year, believers are obliged once more to confront the world as it is. The dismal experience of life in the present and the hope of better things to come coexist in a state of tension that in BWV 58 is presented as a dialogue between the troubled self and its own inner counsellor, represented by soprano and bass respectively. Theology and therapy work in partnership. As Bach generally uses a bass singer for the role of Christ, the voice here may be regarded as the internalised presence of the divine. The scoring of BWV 58 is comparatively light, probably because of the continuous demands of the New Year period. Apart from the two soloists, Bach calls only for strings and continuo, though for later performances he added three oboes as reinforcement.

No 1 Soprano chorale/bass response

Both verbally and musically, BWC 58 begins with two contrasting yet complementary impulses: the urge to despair and the need to resist it. The librettist took the first verse of Martin Moller's hymn *Ach Gott wie manches Herzeleid* ("Ah God, how much heartbreak"), and interspersed its lines with an encouraging commentary. This hymn appears in other cantatas - see BWV 3, for instance, and BWV 153 – bringing a message of enduring faith amidst present trials. Pastor and poet, Martin Moller (1547-1606) was noted for his intense personal devotion to Christ: the focus of hope throughout a life beset, amongst other things, by theological disputes – the occupational hazard of the intensely religious.

The sixteen-bar introduction creates the framework of the movement, both structurally and psychologically, preparing the listener for the text. The tempo is slow (*adagio*) and the musical context full of ambiguity in its fluctuations between (C) major and (A) minor. At this pace, the dotted rhythms convey heaviness, while drooping semitones in the melodic line portray the sagging spirit. Each line of the hymn, sung by the soprano, generates a response from the bass in a continuous musical conversation "Ah God, how much sorrow/I encounter at this time", answered by: "Only be patient, my heart,/it is an evil time". Evil (*böse*), as ever, casts its cloud with diminished harmonies.

At the mid-point of the hymn verse, Bach inserts the material of the opening bars, though this time with a change of key (G minor); it gives the structure its central arch. The remainder of the text follows: "The narrow way is full of tribulation/ by which I must make my way to heaven". Now the bass leads the mind to its imagined destiny above, as the vocal line climbs for "But the path to blessedness" and pours out its happiness for "leads to joy". The usual caveat remains, for this will only come "after sorrow", painted musically with a lingering chromatic descent. The final words are call for stoic resignation: "Only be patient, my heart, it is an evil time". Another repeat of the opening, this time in the original key, creates an overall symmetry; musical form stands firm against spiritual chaos.

No 2 Bass recit

A self-generated sermon appeals for renewed faith: "Even if the world persecutes you, you still have God as your friend, always at your back against your enemies". Where better to look for proof than in the word of scripture? The libretto finds evidence in the day's Bible reading (Mt. 2: 13-23), in which Christ's earthly father was prompted to escape King Herod's threat of murder: "Although the raging Herod passes a sentence of humiliating death upon our Saviour, an angel comes in the night" (note the swoop of the vocal line) "to bring Joseph a dream that he should flee the murderer and go to Egypt". The last section of the recitative opens with a rallying cry of a D major arpeggio, as it alludes to biblical promises from the Old and New Testaments: "God has a word that makes you trust him. He says: though mountain and hill collapse, though the flood waters are about to drown you, yet I will not" (a sudden jump of a minor ninth for emphasis) "leave you nor forsake you".

No 3 Soprano aria

BWV 58 is one of many examples in the cantatas of the process of auto-suggestion, with music acting out the transition from helplessness to empowerment. The words accept the individual's destiny – "I am content in my suffering, for God is my security" – but it is the character of the setting that transforms resignation into determination. A catchy two-bar theme, anchored in repeated notes, suggests positive rather than passive strength. The solo violin part is full of tumbling energy, though in a minor key and without the brilliance of its upper register. It depicts not so much the light-heartedness of liberation as a renewal of life's purpose. Bach creates a three-part design, placing at its centre the image of faith as the door that withstands the assaults of death: "I have a sure charter and seal, and this is the solid bolt which even hell cannot break". The rhythm of the vocal line judders a little but – in imitation of the Christian soul – stands firm. A repeat of the opening, modified so as to end in the home key of D minor, maintains the dogged optimism until the end.

No 4 Soprano recit

The myth of expulsion from Eden has had many interpretations; I prefer the symbolism of Everyman and Everywoman leaving the timeless garden of childhood for the realities of a finite and time-bound adulthood.

> Jonathan Kingdon: *Self-Made Man*

Faith teaches that the sufferings of a flawed and chaotic world are merely the preliminary to an afterlife of sublime perfection. But the comparison of present and future brings a tragic discontent: "Though the world cannot stop persecuting and hating me, God's hand shows me a different land". The vision of what is to be spills over into pure emotion as the vocal part flows from recitative into song (*arioso*). In other words, the free rhythms of speech settle into regular patterns, both in the continuo part and in the soul's repeated, minor-key yearning: "Ah, if only it could happen today, that I might see my Eden!".

No 5 Soprano chorale/bass aria

Again, a soprano chorale is paired with an independent response from the bass. Another Lutheran pastor, Martin Behm (1557-1662) wrote the words of the hymn: "I have a hard journey before me/to you in heavenly paradise;/ there is my true fatherland,/ for which you have spent your blood". Though Bach chose the same melody as in the opening movement, he entirely altered its character by changing its rhythmic shape. Not only that: he integrated it into the dashing style of an instrumental concerto, whose fanfare-like beginning is imitated by the call of the voice: "Just be comforted, you hearts;/ here is anguish" (a momentary musical shadow) "there is glory" (the vocal line spreads its wings). The remainder of the text for the bass contains a similar contrast: "And the joy of that time/outweighs all sorrow". Though Bach gives twice as many bars to happiness (*Freude*) as to present misery (*Schmerzen*), the shadows linger until the concluding: "here is anguish, there is glory". The contrast between what is and what will – or at least, might – be is the driving force for faith.

*

Suggested recording: Bach Collegium Japan, dir. Masaaki Suzuki

Epiphany Sunday

BWV 65: *Sie werden aus Saba alle kommen*

(All those from Sheba shall come)

6 January 1724

Librettist: Unknown

Epiphany Sunday celebrates the occasion when "wise men from the East" – as the story goes in St. Matthew's gospel (Mt. 2: 1-12) – came in search of the infant Christ. They believed that his birth as King of the Jews had been foretold in the stars and they had brought him gifts of gold, incense and myrrh. The event is seen by believers as the fulfilment of prophetic visions from the Old Testament, as for instance in the other scriptural reading for the day, from the Book of Isaiah (Is. 6: 1-6). This tells of the glory that God has in store for his people and, in an apparently prescient link with the gospel narrative, speaks of the tribute of gold and incense that other nations will bring to them.

Lutheranism places a particular emphasis on Christianity as a religion of the spirit: the conforming of the inner self to God's will takes precedence over all other virtues. Hence while the offering of material goods is a visible sign of worship, the gift of greatest value is the unseen dedication of the heart and mind. The subject of BWV 65 is therefore the definition of true riches, contrasting outer sumptuousness with the inner simplicity of spirit that is held to constitute the believer's real wealth - for it contains the promise of eternal life. At the same time, the opening scene of processional grandeur inspires glorious music from Bach, allowing the listener (however inwardly modest) to feel a participant in the great occasion.

No 1 Chorus

Luke told a tale of angels and shepherds, bringing some of the humblest people in society to Bethehem with news of Jesus's future…Instead of shepherds, Matthew brought Wise Men, following a Star in the East, and bringing gifts of gold, frankincense and myrrh…By c.200 Christian authors had already begun to upgrade the Wise Men from academics into kings or courtiers; early Christian mosaics and wall paintings show their adoration of Jesus on the model of barbarian envoys who offer golden crowns to a Roman emperor.

Robin Lane Fox: *The Unauthorised Version*

The importance of Epiphany in Bach's world shows in the rich and ample scoring of BWV 65. A full complement of musicians takes part, with pairs of horns, recorders and tenor oboes (known as the oboe *da caccia*) in addition to the strings and a four-part chorus. This sumptuous range of timbres becomes a surrogate for the visual magnificence implicit in the text: "All those from Sheba shall come. They will bring gold and incense". Constantly varied groupings of instruments entertain the ear with changes of texture, while the regular tread of the continuo underpins the stately sway of the rhythm.

The additional value to Bach of his large forces is that it enables him to layer their entries in such a way as to suggest an endless procession; as so often, his technique serves a theatrical purpose. The movement begins with the horns in the vanguard, bringing after them a combined following of strings and wind. The voices then arrive in turn, at first echoing each other, then continuing in an interwoven play of counterpoint. With such a short text, its impact is particularly dependent on the quality of the musical design. In this case, after the monumental display of chorus and orchestra, the instruments fall suddenly silent to highlight an elaborate vocal fugue – Bach's own artistic homage.

It begins with the voices in imitative sequence, from lowest to highest, in a spaciously decorated word setting. When each vocal line has taken its turn, the fugue continues to develop, combining and recombining its themes in different permutations, but becoming gradually weightier as the instruments return. At first doubling the vocal parts, they eventually have their own independent lines that enrich the whole tapestry. In this way, Bach builds the chorus to a climax, leaving the re-entry of the horns until the last. But it is not simply the horns that he has held back, for he has also kept in reserve the completion of the text, perhaps its most theologically significant part: "and proclaiming God's praise". In other words, the need to praise God is made to coincide with the height of the music's emotional rhetoric. Having made his point, Bach flows deftly back to a restatement of his opening bars; a last great unison for all the performers ends the movement with a communal emphasis on praising the Almighty.

No 2 Chorale

A simple Christmas hymn follows the pomp of the Magi. Its roots are ancient. It is the third verse of *Ein Kind geborn zu Bethlehem* ("A child was born in Bethlehem") – itself a translation of the medieval Latin hymn *Puer Natus in Bethlehem*. The writer was Cyriacus Spangenberg (1528-1604), an early follower of Luther and a noted theologian. Recasting religious texts – whether in Hebrew, Greek or Latin – into the vernacular was an essential element of the Lutheran project to bring the individual closer to the word of God. The old-fashioned repetitions and the modally inflected melody, with its oscillation between C major and A minor, evoke a state of unspoilt wonder: "The kings came there from

Sheba, came there; gold incense and myrrh was what they brought; alleluia, alleluia".

No 3 Bass recit

What can I give Him, poor as I am?
If I were a shepherd, I would bring a lamb;
If I were a Wise Man, I would do my part;
Yet what I can I give Him: give my heart.

Christina Rossetti

The role of teaching and preaching in Bach's sacred cantatas is most overt in the recitatives, in which the musical content, though moulded with care and conscious rhetoric, is clearly subordinate to the words. This recitative is full of theological content. It unfolds the sequence of thought that links the prophet Isaiah with the birth and death of the Saviour and the spiritual obligation of the contemporary believer. Old and New Testaments are called upon to validate each other: "What Isaiah foresaw has now happened in Bethlehem. The Wise Men present themselves at Jesus's manger, wishing to praise him as their king. Gold, incense and myrrh" (note the fall of the vocal line and the diminished harmonies that signify the use of myrrh for embalming Christ's body) "are the precious gifts with which they honour the child Jesus at Bethlehem in the stable". At this point, a further harmonic darkening looks ahead to the sacrificial destiny of the infant.

From here, the thought moves inwards to the obligation of the self: "My Jesus, if I now think of my duty, then I must also turn to your crib and likewise be thankful. For this day is for me a day of gladness, when you, oh prince of life" (a soaring vocal flourish) "become the light of the gentiles and their redeemer". The recompense can only be the dedication of the entire self to God: "But what might I bring to you, King of Heaven? If my heart is not too small a gift, then accept it graciously, for I can bring nothing nobler". A more expressive line, in both voice and continuo, colours the intention with warmth and fervour.

No 4 Bass aria

Though the style – now positively jaunty – differs from the preceding recitative, the direct influence of the words on the setting is just as clear. The binding motto of the music echoes the spoken contours of the opening words: *Gold aus Ophir* ("Gold from Ophir": a city famed in the Old Testament for its wealth). From this initial idea, Bach launches into what is essentially a written-out improvisation. It begins with a play on the musical material from two oboes da caccia and continuo, before the voice arrives to proclaim: "Gold from Ophir is too poor – away with those empty gifts that you mine from the earth". A great whirl of vocal coloratura tosses away the useless baubles. Within the short span of the aria, Bach changes key (to the subdominant – A minor – of the initial E minor) to mark the second half of the text: "Jesus wishes to have your heart. Give this, O Christian flock, to Jesus for the New Year!" All the while, the same motivic fragment constantly recurs as a unifying element, and the final bars recapitulate the opening.

No 5 Tenor recit

Some contractual details remain. First, the believer explains the nature and value of his gift, offered with the requisite humility: "Do not disdain, Light of my soul, the heart that I humbly bring you" (note the bowing of the vocal line on *Demut*). "It includes things that are the fruit of your spirit: the gold of faith, the incense of prayer, the myrrh of endurance" (a hint of torment in the continuo reminds the listener that suffering is part of the Christian lot) "are my gifts that you shall possess forever". There is, however, to be a reciprocal exchange: "But give yourself also to me and make me the richest person on earth; for if I have you then the greatest abundance of wealth must become mine one day in heaven".

No 6 Tenor aria

The full panoply of orchestral sound returns to celebrate the commitment of the soul to Christ "Take me as your own, take my heart as a gift. All, all that I am, whatever I say or do and think, shall, my Saviour, be dedicated to your service alone". Yet as the mood is now personal rather than grand, the horns take second place to the skips and sparkles of the recorders. The style is dancelike, brimming with discreet rather than triumphal joy – except that eventually there is no containing the delight. The vocal line overflows with its own riches in the shape of an embroidered setting of *alles* ("all"). Its rapid note values take their cue from the skittering phrases of the instruments – notably the recorders, but also the strings and sometimes even the horns – and then outrun them. Music imagines faith as irrepressible happiness.

No 7 Chorale

Bach provided a four-part setting of the melody of the hymn *Was mein Gott will, das g'scheh allzeit* ("What my God wishes, may that always be so"). He did not, however, add any words. Modern performances usually follow the suggestion of the musician (and key figure in the nineteenth-century Bach revival) Carl Friedrich Zelter (1758-1832). He chose the tenth verse of Paul

Gerhardt's *Ich hab in Gottes Herz und Sinn* ("I have given myself to God's heart and mind"). It confirms the self's dedication to a spiritual ideal: "Ah now, my God, I fall with confidence into your hands. Take me and accomplish your will with me until my final end, as you well know how; so that my spirit may benefit and your honour may be exalted in me more and more". Gerhardt's life (1607-1676) saw much hardship, both through the experience of the Thirty Years War and subsequent Protestant infighting; if he (and others like him) placed his hopes on a better world to come, one can only sympathise.

*

Suggested recording: J.S. Bach-Stiftung,
dir Rudolf Lutz

Epiphany Sunday

BWV 123: *Liebster Immanuel, Herzog der Frommen*

(Beloved Emmanuel, prince of the righteous)

6 January 1725

Librettist: Unknown

In the New Testament reading for the day, St. Matthew's gospel (Mt. 2:1-12) recounts the arrival of the Wise Men in Bethlehem, bringing rich gifts for the infant king whose birth had been predicted by a star. The previous cantata for the same occasion in the church year, i.e. BWV 65, impressed the listener with the theatrical splendour of the tribute bearers, and then expounded the distinction between mere worldly goods and the enduring wealth of the spirit. BWV 123 seems to take over where the earlier cantata left off. Without referring directly to the day's readings, it assumes an understanding of the central vision of Christianity and leads directly to the significance of Epiphany as a time to offer the soul entirely to God. The text of the cantata is based on a hymn by Ahasuerus Fritsch (1629-1701): legal scholar, public official and writer of religious tracts. Verses 1 and 6 enclose a series of recitatives and arias which paraphrase the sense of the rest, expressing, with almost mystic intensity, the believer's personal bond with Christ.

No 1 Chorus

Part earworm, part mantra, the opening two bars of the chorale and hence their associated words – *Liebster Immanuel* ("Beloved Emmanuel") – haunt the entire movement. The most striking feature of this chorus is not overt musical elaboration but the constant presence of this gently falling phrase, which appears close on fifty times as it passes from one group of instruments to another. In this way, the hymn is placed at the forefront of the listener's consciousness, concentrating the mind on the idea of Christ. The language is full of mystical-erotic longing for the Saviour: "Beloved Emmanuel, Prince of the righteous/you, my soul's salvation, come, come soon!/You, most precious treasure, have captured my heart/which burns and surges with love for you./Nothing on earth/can become dearer to me/than keeping my Jesus always with me."

As the entire piece is anchored to one fragment of melody, how does Bach make the repetition inspirational rather than tedious? The first means is through variety of texture. There are five groups of performers: flutes, oboes (specifically, the softer-toned oboe d'amore), upper strings, continuo and singers. The interplay of these elements produces shifting patterns of light and shade: sometimes by using the whole ensemble; or perhaps flutes and oboes answering each other; or again, the continuo may be silent as the other instruments continue above. The voices arrive, line by line, as an additional colour woven into the orchestral fabric; the difference is that they carry the verbal meaning, making explicit the associations already understood by Bach's listeners from familiarity with the hymn.

Another factor is the constant rhythmic energy. While the chorale itself is presented quite plainly, Bach adds impetus to it with an accompanying flow of triplets. There is never a moment without this onward propulsion to suggest the warmth and urgency of the call to Christ – whether in the groundswell of the continuo, the onward surge of the strings, or the descant of the flutes and oboes. Finally, there is a larger architecture that takes shape around the chorale. The long instrumental introduction, with its blend of melodic fragment and forward movement, contains the building blocks of the *ritornelli* that are interspersed with the voices and from which a unified structure is created. A final, repeated, profession of faith ("nothing can be dearer to me than keeping my Jesus always with me") leads elegantly into a return of the opening bars. The longed-for "Beloved Emmanuel" is also a symbol of a well-ordered universe.

No 2 Alto recit

And when the dew had gone up, there was on the face of the wilderness a fine, flake-like thing, fine as hoarfrost on the ground. When the people of Israel saw it, they said to one another, "What is it?" For they did not know what it was. And Moses said to them, "It is the bread which the Lord has given you to eat".

Exodus 16: 14-15

The presence of Christ on earth maps on to the gift of manna from heaven that sustained the starving Israelites during their flight from Egypt to the Promised Land: "He who is heaven's sweetness, the delight of the chosen one, already on earth fills my heart and breast, if I speak the name of Jesus and know his hidden manna". Faith transforms the inner self: "Just as the dew brings life to a parched land" (note the unexpected climb of a whole tone in the continuo), "so is my heart, even in peril and pain" (an awkward shift in the vocal line) "through the power of Jesus led to joy". At this, minor keys suddenly blossom into a cadence in A major.

No 3 Tenor aria

Yet suffering there must be. When stoically borne, it is a badge of authenticity for the Christian who wishes to follow the example of Christ. This *da capo* (i.e. three-section) aria is one of the many cases in Bach – and in music generally – where the expression of deep sorrow becomes a form of consolation; the shaping of tonality and form offers a safety net for the wildness of emotion. Before the voice enters, the first four bars alone speak of wretchedness. Two solo oboes d'amore, with their timbre of muted melancholy, follow a twisted path, full of awkward intervals, with much use of the augmented fourth and chromatic deviations. The continuo line below, though not as convoluted, shares the same tonal restlessness. It is not just that the key is in the minor (F sharp), but that it gives the impression of not being able to settle anywhere - which is precisely the point. At the same time, the music throughout is heavily patterned, both in terms of the imitation between the two oboes, and the repeated octave leaps in the bass.

The voice adds its lament – "Even the hard journey of the cross and the bitter food of tears" – only to conclude with the resolve of "do not make me afraid". At this point, Bach gives the vocal line a sudden rush of energy and a turn to the relative (A) major, underlining the message that there is a way for the believer to overcome the constraints of existence. Further contrast arrives in the central part of the aria. The pace quickens (*un poco allegro*), the key is resolutely major, and the torrents of the vocal line illustrate threatening storms: "If tempests rage". But as a different image follows – "Jesus sends me from above salvation and light" – Bach echoes the thought with a moment of lyrical calm for oboes and voice; undercurrents of distress linger in the continuo. What counts, though, is the vision of peace and healing that fortifies the listener psychologically for the return to the A section. Music makes space for both present anguish and hope of joy to come.

No 4 Bass recit

Belief in eternal life is a central tenet of the cantata texts. The arrival of Christ on earth signifies the abolition of death, understood as a divine punishment for human sinfulness. If believers pin their faith on Christ's redemptive power, they can discount the present in anticipation of infinite blessing in a timeless realm: "No hellish enemy can swallow me; the screams of my conscience are silent. How can the enemy's forces surround me? Death itself has no power, but victory is already planned, because my helper, Jesus, shows himself to me". With this, the key turns to D major: the bright sibling (in terms of key) of the B minor of the opening chorus.

No 5 Bass aria

A certain ambivalence, however, remains. On the one hand, the soft tone of a solo flute and the regular bounce of the continuo seem to depict a far securer mental world than that of the previous tenor aria. On the other, the price of inner contentment is a degree of alienation: "Leave me, O world, to your disdain" (note the flattening of the scale's leading note on *Verachtung*) "and to sorrowful loneliness". Against the busy foil of the flute part (a possible hint of the seductive charm of the world?), Bach turns Christian isolation (*Einsamkeit*) into long, held notes, and its accompanying sorrow gives a downward turn to the melody; in the outer sections of this *da capo* aria, the voice ends with a slow twist of regret. The inner portion – the B section – makes a clear reference to Epiphany: "Jesus, who has come in the flesh and accepted my offering, stays with me for all time". A prolonged setting of *bleibet* ("remains") signposts the enduring presence of Christ; and might the ornamented *alle* ("all") bring a hint of "alleluia"?

No 6 Chorale

The newborn Saviour signifies eternal values that transcend the temporary concerns of the body. Meditating on the infant, the believer looks toward the moment of death, when the physical being at last dissolves into the incorruptible purity of the divine. The final two lines are softly repeated as, in imagined private communion with God, Christians dedicate themselves to the life of the spirit: "Depart for ever, foolish concerns, for you, Jesus, are mine, and I am yours. I will prepare to depart from the world to you; you shall be in my heart and mouth. Let my entire life be surrendered to you, until some day I am laid in the grave".

*

Suggested recording: Bach Collegium Japan,
dir. Masaaki Suzuki

First Sunday after Epiphany

BWV 154: *Mein liebster Jesus ist verloren*

(My beloved Jesus is lost)

9 January 1724 (possibly earlier origin)

Librettist: Unknown

The gospel story has the power of all good stories to draw us into itself and to make us live it as we hear it...[it] is never a story told once and for all; it is always a story *being told*, always a story *in progress*. It is told powerfully in the sacraments – especially in the Eucharist.

> Richard Marius: *Martin Luther*

The two scriptural readings for this day comprise an episode from Luke's gospel (Lk. 2:41-52), and a passage from Paul's letter to the Romans (Rom. 12:1-6), which urges each individual to dedicate their particular gifts to the service of God. In Luke's narrative, Jesus is described as showing the sign of his calling at the age of twelve when his parents had brought him to Jerusalem for the Passover. As they were returning home, they realised that the boy was not with them and went back to look for him. They found him in the temple, where he had been showing a precocious understanding of religious matters. His response to his parents' anxiety was a calm: "Why were you searching for me? Did you not know that I must be in my father's house?".

Whoever devised the libretto for BWV 154 interpreted the lost-and-found story as an allegory of the continual need to connect the believer with the figure of Christ, both inwardly and also outwardly through the communal sacrament of the Eucharist. Consecrated bread and wine are for the Christian the tokens of the body and blood of the Saviour; if they are consumed in a state of sincere faith, then God's promise of the forgiveness of sin and of eternal life is, in the believer's mind, reaffirmed. The effectiveness of BWV 154 lies in its uniting of various perspectives: the listener takes part in the tale of loss both as a spectator and, thanks to the emotional prompting of its music, as an imaginary participant. This cantata is also – as so often – a demonstration of the plasticity of its Christian religious framework. While satisfying the personal hunger for moral meaning, independent of the world around, it insists upon a public commitment to those very inner values. If BWV 154 may be regarded as an advertisement for churchgoing (which, amongst other things, it is), it is also part of the perennial quest to reconcile the needs of the individual conscience with the imperative of social cohesion.

No 1 Tenor aria

Anxiety, terror, mourning: the musical message could not be clearer, with its tense, abrupt rhythms, its angular melodic lines and studied harmonic confusion. The continuo line, awkwardly chromatic, is full of the repeated patterns that suggest the funereal style of a ground bass; mortality, indeed, is the great fear of those separated from their faith. The mood recalls the tenor aria (No. 19) from the St. John Passion, which follows Peter's public rejection of Christ. Falls of a diminished fifth (the so-called "devil's interval") crowd the parts for instruments and voice: "My dearest Jesus is lost: O word that brings me despair". The vocal line is all discomfort, with its jagged contours and high leaps, to which the violin adds a commentary of sobs and sighs.

As the text moves on – "O sword that pierces my soul, O word of thunder in my ear" – further harmonic instability adds to the sense of doom. The words at this point are a quotation from Johann Rist's hymn "O eternity, word of thunder" – used also in BWV 20 and BWV 60. The juddering of strings and continuo act out the pounding of the the blood in the ears. Meanwhile, the continuo creeps up by semitones, arriving at last at the B minor tonic key. This enables a transition back the opening bars, so that anxiety lingers from beginning to end.

No 2 Tenor recit

"Where can I find Jesus? Who will show me the way?" The voice searches high and low, extending over a compass of almost two octaves. "Where has my soul's burning desire" – a leap of a minor ninth gapes with yearning (*brünstiges Verlangen*) – "where has my Saviour gone?". Without the solidity of faith, understood as the presence of Christ, there can be no mental peace: "No misfortune could trouble me so deeply as the loss of Jesus". At this admission, the key moves to A major: the brighter tonal sibling of the F sharp minor with which the recitative began.

No 3 Chorale

The response to the mental turmoil is a verse from a hymn. Set in four-part harmony and remaining serenely in A major, it is taken from *Jeus, meine Seele Wonne* ("Jesus, my soul's delight"). It was written in 1661 by the church musician Martin Jahn (1620-1682). He was one of the many millions personally affected by the Thirty Years' War, an event whose worst features - it ended only in 1648 - rank amongst the most horrific displays of human cruelty. Against the context of these events, it is not to be wondered at that faith in an ultimately benevolent divine power should have been an especial source of comfort. Jahn looks to Christ in his dual capacity as Saviour and vulnerable child, suggesting a bond of tender and mutually protective love: "Jesus, my refuge and deliverer, Jesus, my confidence, Jesus, strong serpent-crusher, Jesus, my life's light! How grievously my heart aches, little Jesus, for you! Come, ah come, I wait for you, come, oh dearest little Jesus".

No 4 Alto aria

Merging gospel story with theological metaphor, the libretto identifies Christ's disappearance with consciousness of sin: "Jesus, let yourself be found. Do not let my sins be a thick cloud where you, to my terror, would hide from me; appear again soon". If the text is still not entirely free of anxiety, the music takes a positive direction. Again in A major, its style is as smooth and sweet as the opening tenor aria was jagged and harsh. The quasi-pastoral sound of the two oboes d'amore and the conscious rusticity of pedal effects (i.e. one bass harmony per bar) look to Christ as the shepherd of his flock; the gentle flow of the melody suggests the trust that is the prerequisite of closeness to God. For extra softness, a harpsichord replaces the organ continuo, and its treble and bass lines in unison are doubled by the upper strings, giving an uncomplicated texture throughout. Touches of deliberate dissonance cast a brief shadow over *wo du dich zum Schrecken willst für mich verstecken* ("where you, to my terror, would hide from me") but barely disturb the calm surface of the music. Towards the end, the cries of *bald, bald* ("soon, soon") reveal the soul's urgent need, though a soothing repeat of the opening bars indicates that all will be well.

No 5 Bass arioso

To call out to Christ, acknowledging one's sins, is itself an act of faith, instantly confirmed by the recall of the divine voice from the day's scriptural reading (Lk. 2:49): "Did you not know that I must be in my Father's house?". The mental world of the believer is put to rights: order succeeds disorder, expressed musically in tight canonic imitation between the singer – as usual, the bass takes on the role of Christ – and the continuo. The effect is of controlled authority, with the constant ornamentation of *Vaters* ("Father's") emphasising the lineage of God in human form. The rhythms, as one might expect, are steady, and Bach's choice of the minor key (F sharp) adds appropriate seriousness.

No 6 Tenor recit

Wild joy and a sense of release combine with awareness of the lessons to be drawn from the drama of loss and reconciliation: it is through the biblical word and the sacrament of the Eucharist that God can be rediscovered. The vocal line bounds in with the new-found brightness of D major: "This is the voice of my friend! Praise and thanks to God! My Jesus, my faithful refuge, lets himself be heard again comfortingly through his word". A shift to the minor accompanies the glance back to the previous state of distress, in which mind and body suffered alike: "I was sick with sorrow, misery almost consumed the marrow of my bones". A return to D major brings spiritual recovery: "But now my faith becomes strong again, now I am supremely happy".

The contrasts between then and now continue, both musically and verbally: "for I see my soul's delight, my Saviour, my sun, who after my night of sadness" (a lean to B minor) "through his radiance makes my heart glad". There is work to be done, and a new strength: "Rise, soul, make yourself ready! You must go to him in his Father's house, in the temple". The continuo climbs with the growing excitement: "There he reveals himself through his Word; there he will refresh you in the sacrament". Yet while faith – any faith, in fact - brings its own reward of a secure mental framework, a distinguishing feature of the Christian belief of the cantatas is its insistence on self-awareness: in particular, a consciousness of personal imperfection. Moral modesty is required: "Yet to be worthy of eating his flesh and blood, you must also kiss Jesus in repentance and faith".

Alto/tenor duet

The time for self-torment is over. Bach again turns in a rustic direction, this time to signal the unaffected delight of those who have found Christ. Vigorous fiddle playing decorates the simple harmonic foundation of the continuo below, with its off-beat rhythmic impulse. Body and mind that were sick with fear now bound with energy. Bach divides the six lines of text into three groups of two, differentiated by key and (ultimately) tempo. First is the pure celebration for strings and voices in concert: "All is well, Jesus is found; I am no longer unhappy". The singers combine in melodious thirds and sixths, with their joy overflowing into decorative trills. A second pair of lines brings a key change to the relative minor, while the strings bustle a little less frequently: "He whom my soul loves appears to me at this glad time". For the last two lines, the strings fall silent as the voices gather pace for their final declaration: "I will now never more leave you, my Jesus. I will continually embrace you in faith". Prolonged settings cling to *umfassen* ("embrace"); finally, the strings join in again to round off the movement.

No 8 Chorale

A verse of a hymn by the Lutheran teacher and author Christian Keymann (1607-1662), underlines the commitment: "I will not let Jesus go from me,/I will go eternally at his side;/Christ leads me for ever and ever/to the stream of life./Blessed is the one who says with me/I will not let go of my Jesus". Faith brings both immediate and future blessing.

*

Suggested recording: Concentus Musicus Wien, dir. Nikolaus Harnoncourt

1st Sunday after Epiphany

BWV 124: *Meinen Jesum laß ich nicht*

(I will not let my Jesus go)

7 January 1725

Librettist: Unknown

In general, does not the class of things to do with the care of the body have less truth and reality than the things concerned with the care of the soul?

> Plato: *Republic*, Book 9 585D

"Do not be conformed to this world", urges St. Paul in one of the two New Testament readings for the day (Rom.12: 1-6), and it is the familiar Christian/Platonic binary of spirit and flesh that is the underlying theme of BWV 124. The other reading for the day (Lk.2: 41-52) makes a similar point, though with more human immediacy. It tells of Jesus as a twelve-year old, staying behind in the temple while his parents travelled home. By this action, he demonstrated the primacy of his bond with God over his earthly attachments. The parental search for the child became in Bach's earlier cantata for the same Sunday (BWV 154) the paradigm of every believer's longing for Christ as spiritual ideal. BWV 124, however, sidesteps the drama of fear, loss and reunion to proclaim from the outset a secure attachment to Christ – despite the knowledge that this will be tested to the full at the moment of death.

Though the psychological emphasis of the two cantatas is therefore somewhat different, an obvious link between them is the use of Christian Keymann's hymn *Meinen Jesum laß ich nicht* ("I will not let my Jesus go"). While BWV 154 ended with its last verse, for BWV 124 an unknown librettist has taken the whole of it as the inspiration for his text, making the work one of Bach's chorale cantatas. It follows the usual practice of quoting the opening and closing verses verbatim, while the inner four are paraphrased in a succession of recitatives and arias. Keymann's hymn is a fervent - and deeply moving – protestation of faith, for which Bach's musical setting creates an enlarged emotional hinterland: of cheerfulness and determination, despite the instinctive terror of the bodily self at the thought of its last moments.

No 1 Chorus

Long before the arrival of the text, the music is buoyant, stepping out in the dance-like style of a minuet, jaunty with trills and dotted rhythms; variations in phrase length (differing groups of two and three bars) add an element of surprise and freshness. The strings and continuo are instructed to play *staccato*, and from their energetic beginning a solo oboe d'amore emerges with concerto-like brilliance. Its coiling part, delightful in itself, is also an aural illustration of binding the self to Christ. Bach gives the hymn a triple pulse so that it can slip, line by line, into the instrumental envelope: "I will not let my Jesus go/since he gave himself for me;/thus my duty demands/ that I stick to him like a burr./He is the light of my life;/I will not let my Jesus go". A horn reinforces the soprano melody, and the four-part harmonisation is relatively simple. The voices, however, prolong each line at its end, as a token of the believer's intention not to let go. Meanwhile, the oboe barely pauses for breath throughout, either copying the bounce of the strings or spinning its own tireless thread, twisting and curling around the spot. The musical rhetoric is positive, persuading the listener that to renounce the world is gain, not loss.

No 2 Tenor recit

As each verse of the hymn is a variant of the same message, the text here expands upon the sense of previous movement: "So long as a drop of blood stirs in my heart and veins, Jesus alone shall be my life and my all. My Jesus who does such great things for me: I can indeed present him with nothing less than my body and life." The imagination is moving forward to the testing scenario of death; at the thought of giving up body and life (*Leib und Leben*), the voice strains upward – as if to heaven, but also perhaps with some of the high pitch of fear.

No 3 Tenor aria

The unease becomes explicit in an aria whose melodic and harmonic dislocation looks to the final wrenching of soul from body: "And when the cruel stroke of death weakens my senses and affects my limbs, when that day, hated by the flesh, brings with it only fear and terror ...". As with the tenor aria that opened BWV 154, the repeated patterns of the continuo line, with their descents of a diminished fifth, look to the musical language of mourning. The solo oboe above pours out its lament, punctuated by the hammering of the strings: a combination of death's peremptory knock, and the heart-stopping terror that it inspires. Restless and disjointed, the oboe part shares the torments of the vocal line. Such deliberate tonal disruption sets in greater relief a sudden lyricism at "yet this certainty comforts me: I will not let my Jesus go"; voice and oboe combine sweetly as the key changes to the major. The scheme of alternating terror and reassurance continues throughout the aria, and though the singer ends with the consoling prospect of faith, the final instrumental bars are unremitting in their anguish.

No 4 Bass recit

The immediate problem for the believer is that, while Christ is possessed by the mind as the object of faith, life in the physical world hinders complete union with the spiritual ideal: "Yet I still sigh! What severe hardships must my soul still suffer here? Surely my desperately afflicted heart can only be a wilderness and den of torment at the most grievous loss of Jesus?" Again, mental tension inhabits the music, with its jagged leaps for the voice and troubled harmonic progressions. The only remedy for life's inherent tragedy is a willed disposition toward the transcendent: "But yet my spirit looks up in trust to the place where faith and hope shine out and where I, after completing my course, shall eternally embrace you, Jesus". As the key settles at last in A major, an ascending run on *lauf* ("course", or "lap") gestures to an awaiting heaven.

No 5 Soprano/alto duet

Released from its connection with the body, the soul will be free of sorrow and hence Bach now sets to one side the melancholy associations of the oboe. This lighthearted duet even dispenses with the strings, using only the unison continuo instruments as a strong, swift accompaniment. The voices fly off together in a quick, dance-like tempo and imitative style: "Pull away quickly from the world, my heart; you will find your true happiness in heaven". The structure is the three-section *da capo*, with a change of text for its middle part: "When in the future your eyes see the Saviour, only then will your longing heart be restored to life – then it will be contented in Jesus". At this point, the key moves to the relative minor (F sharp); the shift to the minor, while not in itself unusual, adds a more sombre tint to the soul's yearning for a future good. Yet nothing slows the rhythmic pace, and the completion of the movement speeds the listener's imagination along the path from this world to the next.

No 6 Chorale

The last verse of the hymn, set by Bach with inventive vigour, summarises the whole lesson of the cantata. Steadfast faith, ideally alongside a community of the like-minded, will lead for certain to the transcendent goal: "I will not let Jesus leave me, I will be forever by his side; through Christ I am forever guided to the fount of life. Blessed is he who says with me: I will not let my Jesus go'". For the believer, as ever, the best is yet to come – though music brings a taste of it in the here and now.

*

Suggested recording: Bach Collegium Japan, dir. Masaaki Suzuki

First Sunday after Epiphany

BWV 32: *Liebster Jesu, mein Verlangen*

(Dearest Jesus, my desire)

Librettist: Georg Christian Lehms

13 January 1726

Then does not he, and every other who desires, long for what is not in his possession and not there; and what he has not, and what he is not himself, and what he lacks – these are the sorts of things that are the objects of desire and love?
Plato: *Symposium* 200e

Possibly Sigmund Freud's gaze was too narrow when he saw sublimated sex as the key to most human drives. Rather, it may be that the erotic is a subset of a deeper inclination: the urge to reach toward the hidden, to discover, to invent and create that is characteristic of the human animal. In this respect, religious yearning finds its own place – and has in fact often done so – in the taxonomy of desire. BWV 32 is a case in point. The third of Bach's cantatas for the first Sunday after Epiphany, it differs from its predecessors (BWV 154 and BWV 124) by its even greater personal intensity. The words are by the accomplished writer Georg Christian Lehms (1684-1717), employed for his literary gifts at the court of Darmstadt. He shaped his text as a dialogue in which the soul seeks union with Christ as the human face of the eternal and unchanging God. The soprano and bass voice take on the respective roles of seeker and sought. There are no choruses, though the final chorale is in four parts.

 The two scriptural readings for the day were the account in Luke's gospel (Lk.2: 41-52) of the time when Christ's parents searched for the boy only to find him in the temple, and Paul's instruction to believers (Rom.12:

1-6) to turn from the world to God. In his richly theological libretto, Lehms merged allusions to these excerpts with some of the fundamental preoccupations of Christianity: the opposition between the values of this world and the divine; the word of God as revealed in Old and New Testaments; and the reciprocal ties that bind believer, Church and Christ. The appeal of BWV 32 transcends its immediate religious context. It lies in its response to a widely shared yearning for the consolation of permanence in a world whose endless shape-shifting seems to deny the human psyche a settled home. It is Bach's gift in leading the listener from longing to reassurance and ultimately to liberated delight that gives BWV 32 its timeless emotional power.

No 1 Soprano aria

A tenet of Christian belief is that God will reveal himself at the moment when the mind feels itself succumbing to despair, defined as a felt separation from Christ: "Dearest Jesus, my desire, tell me, where shall I find you? Shall I lose you so soon and no longer feel you with me? Ah! my refuge, gladden me, allow yourself the delight of my embrace". The tempo is a slow *adagio*, and softly detached bow strokes in the strings (*piano e spiccato*) support the wordless song of a solo oboe. Its emotional power matches – possibly even transcends – the expressive effect of the voice which joins it in lamentation. Their shared melody exposes the anguish that invades the self, yet there are forward impulses in the music that counterbalance the static nature of grief. While the repeated patterns of the continuo hint at mourning, their underlying rhythm pushes on continuously in a slow, steady march of harmonic progressions, free of disturbing key shifts.

In addition, the sobs and sighs of the melodic lines for both voice and instrument are constantly inclining upward in small chromatic steps, as if actively imploring the return of what is known to exist but is temporarily absent. Prayer presupposes at least the possibility of an answer; this is not the death wish of an abandoned Ariadne. A gleam of the positive arrives, in fact, as the soul anticipates the joy of reunion and Bach moves to the major from the prevailing minor. Florid vocal decoration energises *erfreue mich* ("gladden me"), before the last appeal to the Saviour to let his presence be rediscovered. The compelling quality of this aria owes much to its finely balanced tension – typical of Bach – between the apparently free emotionalism of the soprano and oboe lines, and the quietly guiding hand of structure.

No 2 Bass recit

Christ's answer – a quotation from the day's reading from Luke's gospel - is swift and slightly impatient: "Why is it, why is it, that you have been looking for me? Do you not know that I have to be in that house, that house that belongs to my Father?"

No 3 Bass aria

praesentes namque ante domos invisere castas
heroum et sese mortale ostendere coetu
caelicolae nondum spreta pietate solebant

(for the gods used to come in bodily form to visit the pious homes of heroes and show themselves in mortal company – that was before religion was despised)

                Catullus: *The Marriage of Peleus and Thetis*

Taking his cue from the gospel story, the librettist shows how Christ's response to his parents applies to everyone who seeks him: "Here in my father's abode, a distressed spirit can find me". "Here" speaks directly to the congregation: the consecrated space of the church is where the believer can both unite with Christ and join in the fellowship of those who share the same faith. The vocal line is smooth and rhythmically straightforward, as befits divine assurance. Around and above, however, is the dance of a solo violin, whose cascades (note the abundant trills) suggest the outpouring of God's spirit. The texture is light, with a simple organ accompaniment; occasional chromatic shadows for *betrübter* ("distressed") darken the overall brightness of G major. The aria unfolds as an expansive *da capo*, with its central portion reinforcing the message: "There you will surely find me and unite your heart with me, for this is my dwelling". A smooth succession of key changes brings tonal variety, but the positive musical character is unchanged.

No 4 Soprano/bass recit

This is the climactic point of the cantata: the mutual pledge of devotion between the human spirit and its God. Hushed strings suggest the intimacy of the sacred, while the voices take their turn to create a symmetrical structure. The soul has heard and understood: "Ah, holy and great God, I will here in your presence continually seek comfort and help." To which the voice of Christ responds that there can be no compromise between material and spiritual values: "If you will curse earth's dross and only enter this dwelling, then you will pass the test in this world and the next". This brings before the soul a vision of heaven, for which Bach changes his style from speech-like recitative to a rapturous *arioso*. The words refer to Psalm 84 and unite the dreams of Old and New Testaments: "How lovely is your dwelling, mighty Lord of Hosts; my spirit longs for what shines only in your court. My body and soul rejoice in the living God:

Ah, Jesus, my heart loves you in eternity". The final exchange returns to recitative. Christ restates his promise: "Then you can be happy when your heart and spirit are on fire with love of me", and the soul now feels itself correctly aligned: "Ah! this word now tears my heart from Babel's land" (i.e. a place of confused understanding) "and I will place it devoutly in my soul".

No 5 Soprano/bass duet

For I intend to get to God
For 'tis to God I speed so fast,
For in God's breast, my own abode,
Those shoals of dazzling glory passed
I lay my spirit down at last

> Robert Browning: 'Johannes Agricola in Meditation'

The two lovers – the human and the heavenly – celebrate their restored closeness with a dance-like aria in the form of a duet. The formerly grieving oboe takes on a new musical guise, transformed by festive trills. It doubles the violin when it can, but that instrument tends to fly off with an excess of energy. The other parts, strings and continuo, bounce along in support. Imitative writing for the voices demonstrates their unity of feeling: "Now all torments vanish, and all grief and sorrow disappears". Again, the structure is a *da capo*. Its central section reiterates the pledge between believer and God. "Now I will not depart from you", inspires the response, "And I will constantly embrace you too". Contentment and joy lead neatly back to the initial section.

No 6 Chorale

As the communal expression of faith, the singing of this chorale completes the triangle of believer, God and society. It is the twelfth verse of Paul Gerhardt's *Weg, mein Herz, mit den Gedanken* ("Rid yourself, my heart, of the thought that you have been cast away"). Gerhardt (1607-1676) was not only a noted hymn writer – still highly regarded today – but his biography is full of personal and professional tragedy, encompassing plague, the period of the Thirty Years War, the deaths of his children, and theological infighting. The sentiments of the hymn as a whole are deeply moving, expressive of faith in an infinitely loving power that will, despite all trials, ultimately protect the suffering human. Such a belief, which underpins all of Bach's sacred cantatas, clearly brings comfort, particularly in the absence of other remedies. Gerhardt's prayer summarises the content of BWV 32:

My God, open to me the gates
Of such grace and goodness,
Let me always and everywhere
Taste your sweetness!
Love me and drive me onward
So that, as best I can,
I might embrace you and love you in return
And now no more grieve you.

*

Suggested recording: J.S. Bach-Stiftung,
dir. Rudolf Lutz

Second Sunday after Epiphany

BWV 155: *Mein Gott, wie lang' ach lange?*

(My God, how long, ah, how long?)

Librettist: Salomon Franck

19 January 1716

To receive trouble is to receive good fortune

> From the Zenrin Kushū, quoted by Alan Watts in
> *The Way of Zen*

The ethos of Bach's sacred cantatas is out of step with a world that aims to satisfy all wishes in the shortest possible time. BWV 155 is typical in its promotion of patience and of discounting the frustrations of the present in the hope of better things to come: in particular, the prospect of a transcendent existence free of the limitations of materiality and time. The text of BWV 155 is from a collection by Salomon Franck. He was an official at the court of Weimar where Bach was employed as a musician, and a writer of vividly sermonising poetry. Hence this is a comparatively early cantata, emotionally direct and less complex in overall shape than was usual in Bach's later output. The forces are small: soprano and bass soloists, two violins and viola, continuo, and an especially accomplished bassoonist.

Franck took his inspiration from one of the day's gospel readings (Jn. 2:1-11). It tells of Christ's first miracle, when he was a guest at a wedding and his mother had informed him that the wine had run out. After an enigmatic reply ("My time has not yet come"), he used his divine power to change six jars of water into wine of such quality that the bridegroom was complimented on keeping the best until the last. The lesson for the believer is clear: one must have faith that Christ will in his own time transform the wretchedness of mortal life into heavenly bliss. Until that moment, the human, unable to see the whole picture, must cope with whatever presents itself. Though framed in Christian terms, BWV 155 offers a model of self-counselling – an idealised version of how to transform a state of distress into a positive acceptance of life as it is.

No 1 Soprano recit

Although it is cast as recitative, i.e. obeying the contours of speech rather than melody, there is a distinctly lyrical quality to this emotional outburst. Lamentation and despair are the business of the text: "My God, how long, ah, how long? My misery is too great! I see absolutely no end to my suffering and sorrow". The continuo drags its feet in a prolonged tonic pedal, suggesting a spirit-deadening treadmill, while the vocal line above is full of poignant intervals as it continues its tale of misery: "Your sweet and gracious glance has hidden itself beneath night and clouds" (illustrated by a sinking of pitch), "your loving hand has, alas, been completely withdrawn, and I long anxiously for comfort". Musical weeping and wailing intensifies at "My poor self sickens each day as my cup of tears" (a tightening of the chromatic screw) "fills to the brim". Two contrasting musical images occupy the final bars. The first is an effervescent setting of "the wine of joy is exhausted", followed by the limping sighs of "my confidence has almost entirely sunk away". Yet the movement ends, as if enquiringly, on a major chord.

No 2 Alto/tenor duet

The soul has poured out its troubles, but now must find its own remedy. An encouraging message arrives (from without or within?): "You must believe, you must hope, you must calmly trust in God". All is harmony between the voices, and a solo bassoon bounds over the stave with warm authority. Bach has made it bubble over with virtuoso leaps and runs, reminding the listener of the heavenly refreshment that awaits in the fullness of time. The key may be minor (A) but the mood is all optimism. This brightens further in the central part of the *da capo* design, turning to major keys for: "Jesus knows the right moment to delight you with his help. When the sad times are over, his whole heart will be open to you". At *offen* ("open"), the vocal lines launch into a cadenza-like passage, partnered by elaborate roulades for the bassoon – a token of the overflowing joy to come. The A section then returns the listener to the original mix of encouragement and admonishment.

No 3 Bass recit

The librettist cum preacher argues for a more positive interpretation. He begins by asserting that what seems like abandonment by Christ is not really so: "Then be content, O soul! If it looks to you as if your dearest friend has left you completely" (Bach allows for a rhetorical pause), "O heart! keep your faith firm – it will only be a short while before he will, instead of bitter tears, grant you the wine of consolation and joy, and flowing honey instead of wormwood" (note the liquid surge in the continuo). What follows is conceptually rather less digestible: that pain is divinely inflicted as a necessary test of faith. "Do not think that he takes pleasure in causing you grief. He merely tests your love through suffering; he makes your heart weep in troubled times so that his light of grace may appear all the lovelier to you". The text ends with a glance toward the gift of the afterlife, for which endurance now is a small price to pay: "He has kept in reserve for the end the thing that comforts and delights you; then let him govern in all things, O heart!" The continuo winds its way smoothly down to a cadence in F which, as the relative major of the opening D minor recitative, signals a transformation of mood.

No 4 Soprano aria

The soul now skips away its doubts, as do the accompanying string parts: "Throw yourself, my heart, into the loving arms of the Highest, so that he may have mercy on you". The high spirits of the music melt into triplet rhythms in the remainder of the text: "Lay your yoke of cares and whatever has weighed you down till now, upon the shoulders of his grace." Salomon Franck was fluent in biblical turns of phrase.

No 5 Chorale

This is the last verse of an iconic Lutheran hymn, written by Paul Speratus (1484-1551). Ordained (as was Luther himself) as a Catholic priest, Speratus aligned himself with Luther's early attempts to reform the Catholic church from within. Dismayed at the practice of financing the Church through the sale of indulgences (i.e. buying oneself into God's favour), both men emphasised the purely spiritual content of the relationship between God and human. Speratus was sentenced to be burned at the stake as a heretic when he wrote his *Es ist das Heil uns kommen her* ("Our salvation has come to us here"); fortunately he was rescued from that terrible fate. The entire hymn sets out the doctrine of salvation by faith; its last verse appears here in a four-part harmonisation: "Though he appears unwilling, do not let it frighten you, for where he is most with you he would not disclose. Let yourself be more certain of his word, and though your heart says plainly 'No', do not let yourself be terrified".

*

Suggested recording: Bach Collegium Japan,
dir. Masaaki Suzuki

Second Sunday after Epiphany

BWV 3: *Ach Gott, wie manches Herzeleid*

(Ah God, how much heartache)

Librettist: Unknown

14 January 1725

...mystics may emphatically deny that the senses play any part in the very highest type of knowledge which their transports yield.

William James: *The Varieties of Religious Experience*

The basis of the text of BWV 3 – it is a chorale cantata – is a hymn by the mystically-inclined theologian Martin Moller (1547-1606). His eighteen verses, written in 1587, turn consistently in the direction of the divine, with a correspondingly weary aversion to the bodily life that must still be endured. The unknown librettist of the cantata clearly saw a connection between Moller's chorale and one of the gospel readings for the day: the account (Jn. 2:1-11) of Christ's transformation of water into wine, which symbolises his power to replace the poor stuff of mortality with eternal joy in the beyond. BWV 3, however, sets aside myth and metaphor to focus on the sense of discomfort for those pained by the gap between present reality and the heavenly ideal. While the vision of the latter inspires and consoles, it leaves a residue of distress, for the self must live out its time subject to the distractions of the body. Bach's music is correspondingly full of unease until the final depiction of a renewed and steadfast faith. BWV 3 ends, not with a dance, but a resolve to endure what, for the moment, must be.

No 1 Chorus

The text – Martin Moller's first verse – is brief and bleak: "Ah God, how much heartache/comes upon me at this time!/It is a narrow and sorrowful path/that I must travel along to heaven." Bach's setting looks beneath the surface of the words, exposing their emotional hinterland of suffering and resignation. He places the hymn within a musical context of deep melancholy that is thematically independent of it, though convergent in mood. His instrumental beginning (two oboes d'amore, strings and continuo) is troubled. The tempo is weary (*adagio*), the continuo is fixed for three bars on a solitary pedal note, and the twisting lines of the oboes are full of tonal contradictions, as if unsure of their home in A major. From here, the string parts ascend to a regular pattern of sighs, while the continuo begins to move steadily forward, and the key settles for a while in the brighter dominant (E major).

All these elements become the permanent background of the movement, and the continuous thread between the lines of the chorale. When this arrives, Bach gives it maximum impact through a type of aural layering. On each occasion, he begins with an imitative interweaving of the three upper voices, following the same winding style as the oboes. The bass, however, is held in reserve for the actual hymn melody. Its solemn weight – the vocal line in unison with continuo and trombone – cuts through the busy texture above. Moller's hymn would have been familiar to Bach's congregation, some of whom would doubtless have been intrigued by the long-awaited insertion of it into the intricate design. There are further, typically Bachian, instances of responsiveness to the text. For the third line of the chorale, the successive climb of tenor, alto and finally soprano depicts the journey along the narrow path, with creeping semitones indicating the pain and difficulty of the ascent. Yet the last line leads the imagination to heaven and the music to its keynote, as the soprano line ends on a high A. Music becomes the metaphor of faith: after much confusion and insecurity, earthly existence will surely lead to paradise.

No 2 Chorale/SATB recit

Moller's second verse, in a simple four-part vocal setting, alternates with passages of recitative that reflect on each line, while a recurring motto in the continuo, derived from the opening of the chorale melody, brings musical unity. The whole is an object lesson on the use of a hymn as an adjunct to scriptural understanding. Its opening words – "How hard it is for flesh and blood" – lead to a tenor aside: "which only seeks what is earthly and frivolous, and respects neither God nor heaven", before continuing chorally with: "to turn towards the eternal good". The alto voice sighs its regret: "Since you, O Jesus, are now my all, and yet my flesh is so opposed", to which the third line of the hymn responds with a rhetorical question: "Where, then, shall I turn?" This leads, in the soprano line, to the crucial admission of human need: "The flesh is weak, yet the spirit is willing; so help me, you who know my heart". The hymn ends with a declaration of faith – "On you, Jesus, my mind is fixed". Much the longest passage of recitative is then given to the bass voice, which concludes the movement with the promise of redemption, understood as release from death: "Whoever trusts your advice and help has surely never built on false ground, for you came to bring comfort to the whole world and have taken our flesh upon yourself, so that your death delivers us from final destruction. A believing spirit truly tastes the Saviour's friendship and goodness". In a word, faith becomes its own reward.

No 3 Bass aria

The symbolic water/wine opposition is embedded in the tonal design of this piece, in which alternations of major and minor contrast earthly suffering with the joys to come. The overall structure of the aria is the ABA *da capo*. It opens with a jagged continuo part, a rhythmic echo of the first three German words (*Empfind ich Höllenangst*) and full of spiky chromaticism that pushes at the boundaries of the F sharp minor key. The vocal line is similarly angular, with descending, doom-laden patterns and lingering cries of misery: "Even though I suffer hell's anguish and pain". A complete transformation, however, arrives with the completion of the sentence: "yet there must be constantly in my heart the true joys of heaven". The key changes to the relative (A) major – all chromaticism smoothed out – and the vocal phrases climb upward as they look to the promised bliss.

The B section of the aria continues the blend, verbal and musical, of the sorrows of bodily life with the miraculous transformational power of Christ: "I need only call on the name of Jesus, who can cast away even immeasurable griefs like a light mist". Although the underlying key leans to the major, there is a constant switching between the rootless chromaticism associated with *Schmerzen* ("griefs") and the easeful thought of the divine name (*Jesu Namen*); the mists *(Nebel)* float lyrically into the distance. Muscular rather than sensuous, this aria is a musical paradigm of a religious orientation that integrates suffering and intense happiness – at least the prospect of it, which is almost the same thing – into an all-encompassing narrative of life and death.

No 4 Tenor recit

True faith defies all fleshly weakness, as evidenced in this model declaration: "My body and spirit may fail, but if you, Jesus, are mine and I am yours, I will pay no attention to this". The words of this movement again recapitulate the foundational elements of faith, and Bach's setting of them is exceptionally expressive within the recitative, i.e. not primarily melodic, format. The vocal line and its underlying harmonies reflect a succession of emotions, from the sweetness of divine love to the joy that it inspires, and from the fearfulness of death to the confidence in transcending it: "Your faithful mouth and your unending love, which never changes, still keep for me your first covenant" (a reference to the immemorial promise of God's protection of his own) "which fill my heart with joy and also calms the fear of death, the terror of the grave. If need and want come upon me from all sides, my Jesus will be my treasure and wealth".

No 5 Soprano/alto duet

A serene unity of purpose now shines through the clear textures, steady rhythms and untroubled harmonic language. The instrumental envelope consists of two lines only: oboes and violin in unison above, and the continuo below. They encase the imitative and closely blended vocal duet: "When cares press upon me, I will joyfully sing to my Jesus". The text speaks of singing and Bach shows the way, for the Lutheranism of his time encouraged music as a way of transporting the soul to God. The key is E major: which is to say, the dominant – a gesture to the brighter side – of the A major of the opening chorus. The occasional turns to the minor – for where else would trouble and care (*Sorgen*) be found in music? – are not allowed to disrupt the positive spirit.

The shape of the duet is a lengthy *da capo*. Its central section brings a further thought: "Jesus helps to carry my cross, therefore I, believing, will say it serves for the best at all times" – i.e. present distress is part of a well-intentioned divine purpose. Recollection of the cross, with its double reference to Christ's self-sacrifice and the equivalent that is required of the believer, coincides with another shift to the minor (this time the relative – C sharp – of the duet's original E major). At the end of this B section, the insistence in the alto part of *Es dient zum besten* ("It serves for the best") emphasis the need to accept the inevitable. From present constraints, good things will follow.

No 6 Chorale

All that remains is the final verse of Martin Moller's lengthy hymn, expressive of the tragic human condition: "Keep my heart pure in faith, thus will I live and die for you alone. Jesus, my comfort, hear my longing; O my saviour, if only I were with you". The prospect of the perfect allows the believer to endure the imperfect.

*

Suggested recording: J.S. Bach-Stiftung,
dir. Rudolf Lutz

Second Sunday after Epiphany

BWV 13: *Meine Seufzer, meine Tränen*

(My sighs, my tears)

Librettist: Georg Christian Lehms

20 January 1726

As so often in Bach's sacred cantatas, there is an element of psychotherapy in BWV 13 – in the sense that a full acknowledgement of fear and sorrow precedes the coming to terms with life's limits. Anguish is translated into the language of music, on which the burden of feeling now rests; the composer may then direct and shape it in a way that combines artistic expertise with his own response to the solutions proposed by faith. BWV 13 takes its cue from the day's biblical reading: Christ's miraculous transformation of water into wine (Jn. 2: 1-11), which the librettist generalises into the theme of needing to wait for better things to come. Viewed through the religious lens, this means holding fast to belief in a divine plan that must, eventually, lead to a reward. In other words, faith can be seen as no more and no less than the universal tendency to optimism: psychologically, the defining condition of existence. Without it, the chances of survival are – literally – hopeless.

The libretto was devised by Georg Christian Lehms (1684-1717). Despite his relatively early death from tuberculosis, his literary output included poems and prose works (including the championing of female writers) as well as opera and cantata libretti. In the case of BWV 13, he created a succession of monologues of deep misery and self-rehabilitation that speak directly to the listener. While its narrative path is continuous, the cantata as a whole is shaped as two sets of three movements, with each pairing of aria and recitative punctuated by a chorale.

The first of these is by Johann Heermann (1585-1647). Ill health and catastrophe were his constant companions. They included the death of his first wife, plague, and the loss of all his possession in the Thirty Years War. The second hymn, ending the cantata, is by Paul Fleming (1609-1640): a notable, though again short-lived, German physician and poet. He was much travelled, disappointed in love and, like countless others, lived through a type of political turbulence that human societies have seemingly never learned to avoid. If BWV 13 is stoic, it cannot be accused of nihilism, for at least it looks at the last to a better-ordered world. On the other hand, if this must depend on divine power, what hope is there for the unaided human? The Lutheran message of the cantatas is: none whatsoever.

No 1 Tenor aria

The great achievement of this extensive *da capo* aria is to convey misery without monotony: in fact to transmute that very misery into the consolation of artistic beauty. The soul is in despair: "My sighs, my tears, cannot be counted". Tone colour makes an immediate and obvious contribution to the mood of melancholy; two recorders wail softly and repetitively above the long, winding lament of a tenor oboe, whose initial long-held note announces the theme of weary waiting. With its rocking rhythms, the style, metre and profound grief of this movement anticipate the opening chorus of Bach's St. Matthew Passion, which was composed in the following year. In both cases, the choice of performing tempo makes a difference to the listener's response: a well-intentioned dragging can lead to compassion fatigue, though the sense of spiritual exhaustion calls for appropriately slow footsteps.

While a barely changing D minor tonality adds to the impression of unending sorrow, Bach provides sources of musical pleasure through his constant variety of line and texture. Even so, the melodies display the authentic marks of anguish and despair; the vocal line begins with the same mournful sway as the recorders, and its sighs and tears (*meine Seufzer, meine Tränen*) are wrung out in the intervallic torment of the diminished third. The B section of the aria intensifies the gloom: "When each day is filled with woe, and misery does not go, ah then, this torment must already point the path the death". Changes of key and a more agitated vocal rhetoric indicate the danger to the soul; a descending sequence for the voice, trapped in minor intervals, reveals the sinking of the heart as it loses confidence in its final redemption. Bach's vocabulary of frustrated hope also includes long drawn-out endings of the harmonic sentences (i.e. cadences) as, for instance, in the last few bars of the B section. Though this is a familiar element in musical architecture, it works well here as a coded reference to the main point of the text: that much time must elapse before human wishes are fulfilled.

No 2 Alto recit

The deity appears unresponsive – though, in acknowledging his existence, the believer is actually at the first stage of regaining trust: "My dearest God so far has let me call to him in vain and, while I sob, no comfort appears. The hour seems a long way off, only I still in vain must implore him". The cry to God (*flehen*) twists in chromatic torment before extricating itself from minor to major.

No 3 Alto chorale

The words of Johann Hermann's hymn remind the believer of the supposed pledge of the divine to the human: "God, who has promised me his help at all times, is letting me look for him in vain in my present sadness. Ah! Will he then forever and ever be cruelly angry with me? Can and will he not take pity on the poor, now as before?" Bach's setting embodies a positive response. The simple chorale, with the voice part reinforced by the wind instruments (recorders and oboe), sits inside a musical framework of brightness and energy, from the violins in particular, and carried forward by the impetus of the continuo below.

No 4 Soprano recit

Two contrasted emotional states are depicted, with clear allusions to the water/wine dichotomy that underlies the religious meditation of the day. First, the continuo turns its back on the previous F major positivity by immediately flattening the seventh note of its scale. Existing troubles are again recounted: "My sorrow increases and robs me of all rest. My cup of grief overflows with tears. The need I feel has no consolation, leaving me dead to feeling. The grievous night of cares weights down my oppressed heart, and so I have only songs of woe." All of this is accompanied by the musical language of inner darkness: the harmonies are laden with diminished sevenths, and the last cry of *Jammerlieder* ("songs of woe") lands upon a cadence in Bb minor.

Yet in an abrupt demonstration of the act of will – the psychological turning point – that can lift the downcast heart, music and text change direction. The mind rallies itself: "Yet, soul, no, be comforted in your pain" (note the arpeggio fanfare), "God can transform the bitter wormwood" (the sudden sourness of the diminished seventh chord) "quite easily into the wine of joy and so give you many thousand pleasures". The final cadence is now Bb major.

No 5 Bass aria

The rhetorical oppositions of the text epitomise the conflicts of the entire cantata: on the one hand, life's lamentation; on the other, an inspiring vision of heaven. There is to be no easy mental victory, but merely a never-ending struggle to redirect the mind from present to future: "Groaning and pitiable weeping are not the least help for the sickness of sorrow". Bach points out the contrasts between what is and what – with the right effort – might be, underlining them with the alternation of two related keys: G minor and Bb major. Recorders and solo violin in unison begin with a sighing, chromatically inflected melodic line for the portrayal of misery. But soon enough a transformation arrives: the rhythmic pace seems to gather speed with rapid scale passages, and the key turns to the major. These alternations of light and shade set the pattern for the entire aria.

While not a formal *da capo*, there is three-part structure, enclosing a message of hope: "But whoever looks toward heaven, and strives for comfort there, a light of joy can easily appear in his grieving heart". The instruments add their ornate and animated commentary, and there is an overspill of musical delight on *Freudenlicht* ("light of joy"). With his return to the opening, Bach ends the aria exactly as he started. Until the final moment, the mood is poised between tragedy and hope, for faith demands endless mental toil.

No 6 Chorale

BWV 13 ends with a four-part setting of a verse from Paul Fleming's *In allen meinen Taten* ("In all my actions"). The entire hymn, written in 1642, expresses unswerving commitment to the dictates of God's will, as evidenced in the unfolding of life. The excerpt here advises: "Then, soul, be true to yourself/and trust him alone/who has created you./Let things go as they will,/your Father on high/knows the right counsel for everything". Passive, perhaps – or an active way to defend the self against despair?

*

Suggested recording: J.S. Bach-Stiftung, dir. Rudolf Lutz

Third Sunday after Epiphany

BWV 73: *Herr, wie du willst, so schick's mit mir*

(Lord, as you will, order things for me)

23 January 1724

Librettist: Unknown

The hunger for faith in God that pervades the texts of Bach's sacred cantatas is an expression of the search for life's meaning. It includes, naturally enough, the quest to make sense of death, which Christianity interprets as the approach to a new and infinitely better existence – provided that one trusts in God's power to grant it. Accordingly, the intended lesson of BWV 73 is the need to work constantly at keeping the mind in alignment with the divine will, both as a present comfort and as the basis of hope for the future.

The libretto is inspired by the day's gospel reading (Mt. 8: 1-13), which tells of miraculous bodily cures made possible by faith in Christ's ability to work wonders. These become the metaphor for the healing of souls, i.e. the inner rather than the outer self. Bach's setting is its own musical miracle of tautness and variety. Two chorales by different writers frame the cantata, while the overall key structure implies the path of submission: the movements descend from the G minor of the opening chorus, through the Eb major of the tenor aria, to the C minor of the last three numbers. Everything points to the need to bow to God's will as the goal and guiding principle of life.

No 1 Chorale/STB recits

Conceptually and musically, this movement rests on the first verse of a hymn by the learned Lutheran theologian Caspar Bienemann (1540-1591). Its opening words ("Lord, as you will") are a direct allusion to the day's scriptural story, in which a man afflicted by leprosy called out: "Lord, if you will, you can make me clean". Bienemann recast the cry as: "Lord, as you will, order things for me both in life and in death", for the two represent a unity. The melody of the first four words – *Herr, wie du willt* – becomes a recurring motto and a binding element of the musical architecture. Crisp and powerful in the horn, these four notes are a perpetual reminder to align the self with God. They punctuate the flowing style of two oboe, while the strings bound with rhythmic energy. The play of instruments throughout gives the texture the colour and contrast of an instrumental concerto.

The lines of the chorale, in a plain, four-part setting, alternate with commentaries from the librettist. Bach presents these in the declamatory style of recitative, though within a musically regular context. The response to the hymn begins with a lament: "Ah, but I still sigh at how much your will lets me suffer. My life is the target of bad luck, since misery and vexation keep tormenting me while I live, and my suffering will hardly leave me in death". At this, the chorale resumes with a plea: "You alone are what I long for - Lord, do not let me perish!". An appeal to God's goodness follows: "You are my helper, consolation and refuge, who counts the tears of the distressed and does not break the fragile reed of their confidence; and because you have chosen me, speak a word of comfort, a word of joy". All the while, the horn adds its prompt of "Lord, as you will".

The last two lines of the chorale are purely compliant: "As long as you keep me in your favour, do as you will; give me patience, for your will is best". A final soprano recitative adds a little sermon: "Your will is indeed a sealed book of which human wisdom understands nothing; blessing seems to us often a curse, and correction seems like angry punishment" (much use of diminished harmonies to signal pain). "That rest which you have appointed for us one day in the sleep of death seems an entrance into hell". Dread distorts the (C minor) key with an unexpected flattening (Db), while the oboes mimic the collapse of confidence. Faith, however, rallies: "Yet your spirit sets us free from this error and shows that your will can heal us". The movement ends with a modified repeat of its beginning, as the voices three times insist: "*Herr, wie du willt*".

No 2 Tenor aria

Text and music turn to the benefits of faith as a source of healing and delight. A solo oboe part overflows with runs, leaps and staccato lightness, imitated and paired by the voice: "Ah, pour the spirit of joy, I beg, into my heart". The design is a modestly-scaled *da capo*, with a brief central section that acknowledges episodes of soul-sickness: "I am a spiritual invalid; joy and hope often falter in me and I become timid". Music and verbal sense unite in the chromatic stutters of *Zaghaft* ("timid") and the prolonged vocal waverings on *wanken* ("falter"). A return to the A section waves aside all reservations.

No 3 Bass recit

Those who submit to God may also enjoy a sense of superiority toward those who do not consider their soul's welfare. A diminished seventh chord – the harmonic token of everything out of joint – introduces the admonishing rhetoric: "Ah, our will remains perverse, now defiant, now despondent" (note the downward creep of the continuo and its expressive clash with the vocal line); "it never wants to think about death! Only a Christian, schooled in God's spirit, learns to submerge himself in God's will, and say...". And so to the next movement.

No 4 Bass aria

Death, which threatens us every moment, must infallibly place us within a few years under the dreadful necessity of being forever either annihilated or unhappy. There is nothing more real than this, nothing more terrible...Let us reflect on this, and then say whether it is not beyond doubt that there is no good in this life but the hope of another; that we are happy only in proportions as we draw near it; and that, as there are no more woes for those who have complete assurance of eternity, so there is no more happiness for those who have no insight into it.

> Pascal: *Pensées*

The libretto has by now moved some distance from the details of the day's gospel story and is concerned principally with the central dilemma of faith: how to reconcile the living self with the prospect of its own non-being. The text of this aria is arranged as three verses, each confronting the fear of death. Yet the emotional power of this piece is particular to Bach, for in its fusion of pattern and freedom, of the predictable and the unexpected, and of the melancholy and the encouraging, the setting is a masterpiece of consolation and creativity. There is notable, if understated, mastery in the variety of phrase lengths and the order of entries of strings and continuo, alongside suave transitions of key – often in the muted direction of the subdominant.

As with the opening chorus, the mantra "Lord, if you will" persists throughout: its threefold repetition frames the movement and also recurs between the verses, with their succession of deathbed tableaux. Bach endows the cry of *Herr, wie du willt* with a memorable lyric beauty. He begins as if with a question, for the verbal phrase ends almost in mid-air as the harmonies await a resolution. The answer arrives as a decorative melodic descent - the blessing from above? – passed from one instrument to another and each time coming to rest on a cadence. While these paired elements of human hope and divine response haunt the aria, there are no exact or routine repetitions but a sense of free flow. All that is certain is that the two fragments complete each other. The call to God generates, somewhere in the musical texture, the hoped-for benediction.

Within the overall context, Bach differentiates each of the librettist's verses. The first pants for breath: "Then press, you pains of death, the sighs from my heart, as long as my prayers are acceptable to you". For the second – "Lord, if you will, lay my limbs down in dust and ashes, this most corruptible image of sin" – the visual and the aural image combine as the key sinks into Bb minor, cast adrift from the underlying (C minor) key. The last verse calls for pizzicato strings for the tolling of the funeral bells: "Then strike, bells of death. I follow unafraid; my sorrow is from now on put to rest." Against the clockwork pulse, the vocal line fractures, just as the body must break its connection with the soul. The final, decorated reiterations of *Herr, so du willt* accept the inevitable with melancholy grace.

No 5 Chorale

This closing hymn is the ninth and final verse of *Von Gott will ich nicht lassen* ("I will not leave God") by Ludwig Helmbold (1532-1598). He was an academic, a Lutheran pastor and esteemed poet, born in Mühlhausen, where the young Bach was appointed organist at the

Blasiuskirche in 1707. Helmbold finished his days there as Superintendent – a position in the Lutheran church equivalent in status to a bishop. The hymn as a whole declares perpetual loyalty to God as a bulwark against life's inconsistency and impermanence, not to mention the inevitable sorrows that it brings. The lines here, set in stirring four-part harmony, declare allegiance to the deity: "This is the will of the Father who has created us; his son has inherited the fullness of goodness and grace; God the holy spirit also rules us in faith, leading us to the kingdom of heaven; to him be glory, honour and praise!"

*

Suggested recording: J.S Bach-Stiftung, dir. Rudolf Lutz

Third Sunday after Epiphany

BWV 111: *Was mein Gott will, das g'scheh allzeit*

(Whatever God wills, let that always be)

21 January 1725

Librettist: Unknown

Two miracles of healing are described in the gospel excerpt (Mt. 8:1-13) prescribed for this day. In the first of them, Christ is said to have cured a case of leprosy; and in the second, a servant who is lying paralysed and in great pain is restored to full health. To the theologically minded, such bodily diseases become the surrogate of the spiritual pollution, identified as resistance to faith, that endangers the long-term prospects of the Christian soul.

The text of BWV 111 is based on a hymn by the aristocratic Albrecht Alcibiades, Margrave of Brandenburg-Kulmbach (1522-1557). A perfect illustration of the truth that religious convictions have the flimsiest relationship with personal goodness, the Protestant Albrecht was one of his century's noted warlords. As his career was dedicated to violence and plunder, one wonders how he found the time to write pious verse. Perhaps he delegated the task to a courtier. Or perhaps it was written after a heavy defeat. In this chorale cantata, the first and last of the six movements use verses one and four of the hymn verbatim; for the inner two pairs of aria and recitative, an unknown librettist has paraphrased the rest.

No 1 Chorus

Not all pleasure has to be deferred until the next life. Catchy and vigorous, the musical envelope into which Bach slips the first verse of the chorale brims with tightly patterned energy and optimism. Above the regular steps of the continuo, two oboes engage in a concerto-like dialogue with the violins. The uncomplicated melodic and harmonic vocabulary conveys a simple and robust delight. Even the tread of the bass sometimes loosens into the bounding rhythms of the instruments above. The sparkling style encourages a positive response to the text: "Whatever my God wills, let that always be./His will is the best;/he is ready to help those/who believe steadfastly in him./He helps those who need him, the righteous God,/and punishes no more than necessary:/Whoever trusts God and firmly builds on him,/ God will not forsake".

In the typical manner of a chorale chorus, one of the voices – here the soprano – sings the hymn in slow note values (the *cantus firmus*), set against the greater activity of the other vocal parts. In fact, with the arrival of the chorale, the energy level increases further, thanks to the scurrying accompaniment of the unison violins and viola. At the end of each line of verse, while the last note of the sopranos lingers, the remaining singers repeat the words as if in rousing endorsement. Their solid chordal treatment changes only after the sixth line: "and punishes no more than necessary" (*und züchtigen mit Maßen*). Here, Bach introduces a few bars of stern counterpoint as a gesture towards God's timeless justice. The musical high spirits that sustain the chorus continue to the end with a last repeat (*ritornello*) of the opening material.

No 2 Bass aria

With its choppy partnership of continuo and bass voice, the musical manner is as brisk and unrelenting as the thought: resistance to God's will is impossible, and it is best to yield to a power that is assumed to be for one's benefit. Quoting from the second verse of Albrecht's hymn, the librettist advises: "Do not be terrified, my heart; God is your comfort and confidence and the life of your soul". Using an abrupt motto throughout, Bach sidesteps melodic appeal and variety of tone colour. The curtness relaxes a little for the hymn fragment ("God is your comfort and confidence") and also with the extended, decorative setting of *Seele* – a token of the soul's continuing life, even as the body dies. Though the setting remains consistent throughout, the structure falls into three parts, enclosing a new text in its centre. Here, a rhetorical jab on *Ja* ("Yes") brings another reminder of what cannot be controlled: "what his wise counsel has decided, the world and human might cannot strive against". At this, the vocal line engages in a long and ungainly struggle before the aria ends with more rallying of the self and hope of the life to come.

No 3 Alto recit

It is in any case madness, continues the librettist, to try to evade the divine decree, for nothing escapes the eye of God. Those who are tempted should consider the example of the Old Testament figure of Jonah who plunged into the depths of the sea in a futile attempt to hide: "Oh foolish one, who withdraws from God, and like Jonah flees from God's face: even our thoughts are known to him, and he has counted the hairs of our head" (the latter phrase another reference to the second verse of the chorale). The contours of the vocal line are fiercely emotional, with the "foolish one" (*Törichter*) deliberately discordant against the underlying bass pedal note. Jonah tumbles down in two descending arpeggios, lurching from chord to chord. In contrast, the one who knows what is best for him – "Happy is he who chooses this refuge" – takes a smoother harmonic path that leads him "in faith and trust to look to God's decision and word with hopeful patience".

No 4 Alto/tenor duet

A cheerful collaboration of music and words now leads the believer (in imagination at least) down a willing road to death: "So I step forward bravely, even if God leads me to the grave". The dotted rhythms skip along and the first violin part gives the occasional pirouette, with the key comfortably in G major. The desire to follow alongside God is signalled by the familiar device of canon, i.e. the exact imitation of one voice by the other. The middle part of the lengthy *da capo* design accepts that life's course is pre-ordained, and with that acceptance comes redemption: "God has made a note of my days" – the divine pen moves with a musical scribble on *aufgeschrieben* – "so that when his hand touches me, death's bitterness is driven away". It is not so much the inevitability of death that is the subject of BWV 111, but how one faces it; faith brings liberation from fear.

No 5 Soprano recit

Yet the prospect of terror still looms and the believer must continue to beg for strength: "When death at the end tears my spirit out of my body by force" (*mit Gewalt* – note the piercing ascent of the voice) "then take it, God, in your fatherly hands". The forces of evil, in the form of a clinging to life instead of the beatific renunciation of it, will make a final bid for the soul, and this can only be defeated through the gift of faith: "When devil, death and sin make war against me and my deathbed becomes a battlefield, then help, so that my faith in you may be victorious". Up to this point, the sustained chords of two oboes have remained quietly in the background, but at the final call for "a blessed, wished-for end", they cradle the voice in a slow, rocking melody that lulls all anxiety.

No 6 Chorale

The last verse of the hymn completes BWV 111. It recapitulates the message of the preceding recitative and also returns the listener full circle to the day's gospel reading, with its promise of the miracles worked by faith: "I will ask one thing of you, Lord, and you will not refuse me: when the evil one tempts me, do not let me despair. Help, direct and defend me, to the honour of your name. Whoever desires a thing, it will be granted to him; to that I gladly say 'Amen'".

*

Suggested recording: Concentus Musicus Wien, dir. Nikolaus Harnoncourt

Third Sunday after Epiphany

BWV 72: *Alles nur nach Gottes Willen*

(Everything according to God's will)

27 January 1726

Librettist: Salomon Franck

Nirvana is...liberation. Seen from one side, it appears to be despair – the recognition that life utterly defeats our efforts to control it, that all human striving is no more than a vanishing hand clutching at clouds. Seen from the other side, this despair bursts into joy and creative power, on the principle that to lose one's life is to find it – to find freedom of action unimpeded by self-frustration and the anxiety inherent in trying to save and control the self.

Alan Watts: *The Way of Zen*

Among the cantatas that Bach composed for the third Sunday after Epiphany (the others are BWV 73, BWV 111 and BWV 156), the music of BWV 72 stands out for its verve and exuberance. This is as it should be, for the text, from a collection by the Weimar court poet Salomon Franck, focuses on the purely life-enhancing effects of faith, the practical benefits of which appear in the day's gospel reading (Mt. 8:1-13). It tells the story of two men whose bodily sufferings were healed when they called out to Christ, for he had responded to their perfect trust in him. From this, Franck drew an entirely positive lesson for the here and now. The purpose of his libretto is not to argue, to criticise backsliders or to present fearful visions of death, but to show the value of subjection to the divine will. Faith brings a state of psychological resilience that enables the believer to surf the confusion and instability of life.

Though there are no great dramatic oppositions, Bach gave BWV 72 a vital, iridescent character by means of pulse, energy, and shifting tonal colours. The materials that he works with – whether a given key, his available performing forces or a few small musical phrases – become the playthings of his artistry. Long-acquired expertise (and this is true in general of Bach, as of other exceptionally creative minds) enabled him to express more fully than most the childlike capacity to see the new through the lens of the familiar. From this perspective, the musical treatment of BWV 72 may be said to symbolise the way of faith: the combination of an underlying anchorage with an adaptability to life's fluctuating fortunes.

No 1 Chorus

Franck's starting point is the necessary surrender of control: "All things according to God's will, in happiness and in sadness, in good or evil times". The words instruct; Bach adds the endorphin rush. The setting has certain features in common with the opening chorus of BWV 111 – the cantata that Bach composed for the same day in the previous year. In both cases, the key is A minor, the scoring (in addition to the continuo) is for two oboes and strings, and the style is firm and vigorous. There are, however, some important differences. Apart from the obvious change in pulse (three beats in a bar in the earlier work, four in the later one), there is greater musical complexity in BWV 72 – so much so, that Bach adapted this chorus for the Gloria of his later Mass in G minor. Above all, there is a far more integrated approach to the instrumental and vocal parts.

In BWV 111, the two groups spoke in their own distinct languages, with the chorale inserted into a musically independent context. In the case of BWV 72, however, the realms of verbal and non-verbal meaning become one. The instruments strike up before the voices appear, combining two contrasted but complementary responses to the idea of *alles* ("all"). On the one hand, the oboes, viola and bass, punch out their two-syllable mimicry of the words: firm, strong, admitting of no exceptions. Simultaneously, the violins launch into a rush of brilliant passagework, as if bringing the whole world in their train. The voices enter in a style identical to the instruments but with musical meaning clarified by words: *Alles nur nach Gottes Willen* ("All according to God's will"). As the text continues with its reference to life's joys and sorrows, fluctuations of key illustrate the instability of the mortal lot. The most expressive of these is, perhaps, the G minor darkening of *Traurigkeit* ("sadness") and the subsequent yielding to the subdominant (D minor) key for *so bei gut als böser Zeit* ("in good or evil times").

For a new portion of text – "God's will shall calm me" – Bach takes a further turn toward the subdominant (now G minor). He also brings in an element of formality, with layered fugal entries against the strong reminders of *Alles* in the strings and continuo. A series of suspensions - notes delayed across the beat – slows the vocal pace, while the continuo below falls in a cycle of fifths. Energy levels soon rise with the successive (low to high) entries of "in cloud and sunshine" (*bei Gewölk und Sonnenschein*). A deft key sequence (E minor, B minor and then D major) brings the chorus back to its original A minor declaration of "all according to God's will; though to make his point even clearer, Franck adds: "This shall be my motto".

No 2 Alto recit/arioso

Two short passages of recitative frame a nine-point litany, each beginning with "Lord, if you will" (*Herr, so du willt*) – a phrase taken from the day's gospel reading.

First, though, the libretto presents the model believer: "O blessed is the Christian" (note the initial expressive leap and the lyrical style) "who always submerges his own will in God, no matter what happens, in good times and sorrow". The prayers follow as if in ritual succession, obeying the same basic pulse, yet with differences of melodic shaping and – Bach's constant vigilance against monotony – with transitions of key.

Faith promises the following: everything shall be taken care of; God shall bring contentment; pain shall vanish; the believer shall be spiritually healthy and pure; sorrow shall turn into joy; pasture shall be found amongst thorns; the soul shall one day be blessed; the self shall truly understand the meaning of scripture so as to calm the soul. The final request is for immortality ("Lord, if you will, I shall not die"). The vocal line winds down on *sterb* ("die"), only to resurrect itself on *ich nicht* ("I shall not"). The lyrical style of *arioso* merges into recitative to complete the prayer: "even though life and limb forsake me, as long as your spirit says these words in my heart". The final two chords (the so-called Phrygian cadence) await an answer.

No 3 Alto aria

God has evidently responded – at least, if the music is to be believed, for it transmits the vitality brought about by a renewed surge of faith. Firmly in D minor (which happens to be the subdominant of the opening chorus), the vocal line exudes determination: "With all that I have and am, to Jesus I will leave myself". Yet the most convincing advertisement for the benefits of faith is to be found in the writing for the two violins. Together with the continuo, they make up an exuberant trio sonata whose energy delights the listener. At the same time, tightly controlled repetitions bring a subliminal message of safety. Abandonment of the self to Christ carries no risk.

The next two lines – "Though my weak spirit and mind cannot grasp the plan of the most high" – continue in the same style and key. Some contrast of mood arrives with the resignation to life's uneven journey: "May he lead me ever forward on paths of thorns and roses!" The key changes to G minor (a further move to the subdominant), and the thorns create a few twists for voice and continuo. The activity, though, is unstoppable until a return to the initial text ("With all that I have and am, to Jesus I will leave myself"). There is a wistful pause, for faith's ultimate reward is, as ever, some way off; the diminished harmony hints at death. Yet the movement then finishes as positively as it began.

No 4 Bass recit

Music has demonstrated the mood-enhancing benefits of faith: "So now believe!", exhorts the preacher, "Your Saviour says: 'I will do it'". The bass voice, in Bach generally the vocal persona of Christ, lends its authority to the promise of spiritual help: "He freely stretches out his hand when cross and suffering terrify you, he knows your need, and loosens the fetters of your cross". Christ's concern is tailored to individual need: "He strengthens what is weak" (note the contrast between first the bold leap and then the upward creep of the semitone) "and he will not scorn to stoop and graciously enter the lowly abode of poor hearts". Humility is the way to God.

No 5 Soprano aria

The outcome is a healing self-reassurance: "My Jesus means to do it; he will sweeten your cross. Though your heart lies in many afflictions, it shall nevertheless rest gently and quietly in his arms, provided that it holds firm in faith". A solo oboe is the graceful partner of the strings in the dance-like style of a minuet. Bach's aim is to convey spiritual serenity, which he places in the key of C major – that brighter relative of the A minor with which the cantata began. Such shadows as there are do not greatly darken the surface of the music – as, for instance in the syncopations for the voice at the references to the cross (*Kreuz*).

Similarly, what Bach characterises as the mind's afflictions (*Bekümmernissen*) – which surely include the lurking anxiety over one's end – bring a shift to the minor (E). This remains the key for the long rest (*ruhn*) in the Saviour's arms, accompanied by the steady heartbeat of the continuo; a moment of silence signals the peace of death. The idea of intention is bound up in the German word "*will*", i.e. "wills it". Bach underlines the point with an emphatic high A.

No 6 Chorale

Franck ends with the first verse of the hymn *Was mein Gott will, das g'scheh allzeit* ("Whatever God wills, let that always be"). It had already formed the basis of BWV 111, and the unlikely author of this patient piety was the ferocious Markgraf Albrecht of Brandenburg-Culmbach (1522-1557). A mix of good sense and Panglossian passivity, the text is perhaps a version of "What can't be cured must be endured": "Whatever my God wills, let that always be./His will is the best;/he is ready to help those/who believe steadfastly in him./He helps those who need him, the righteous God,/and punishes no more than necessary:/Whoever trusts God and firmly builds on him,/ God will not forsake". Bach gives it a plain, four-part setting.

*

Suggested recording: J.S. Bach-Stiftung, dir. Rudolf Lutz

Third Sunday after Epiphany

BWV 156: *Ich steh mit einem Fuß im Grabe*

(I stand with one foot in the grave)

Librettist: Christian Friedrich Henrici (Picander)

23 January 1729

To mourn avails not: man is born to bear.
Such is, alas! the gods' severe decree:
They, only they are blest and only free.
Two urns by Jove's high throne have ever stood,
The source of evil one, and one of good;
From thence the cup of mortal man he fills,
Blessings to these, to those distributes ill;
To most he mingles both ...

Iliad Book XXIV, lines 524-530, trans. Alexander Pope

As with the other cantatas for the third Sunday after Epiphany, BWV 156 is linked to the scriptural story (Mt. 8:1-13) of two cases of sickness cured by faith in Christ. Its librettist was Christian Friedrich Henrici (1700-1764), who wrote under the name of Picander. Bach often used his texts, most memorably, perhaps, for his St. Matthew Passion of 1727. BWV 156 is a reflective and philosophical work: part stoic's charter, part plea for God (if he is so minded) to minimise personal suffering and to give strength to endure what lies ahead. Like the leper who placed all confidence in Christ's power to heal, Picander's text becomes a paradigm of perfect trust. If God in his mercy chooses to prolong life and health, well and good; but mortality cannot be escaped because it is (in the Christian view) a product of the endemic sickness of human nature.

The music of BWV 156 reflects the stance of the words: a mix of detachment, renunciation and melancholy rather than desperation. Whether death comes sooner or later, all must be left in God's hands. Hence, perhaps, while expressive of deep feeling, the music of this cantata avoids emotional extremes. The use of the *violone* (today's double bass) rather than the cello gives ballast to the higher timbres of the upper strings and oboe. It is, after all, a weighty subject: for if God's will is accepted in this life, he will grant an eternal refuge to the soul after death. BWV 156 contains no splendid choruses; there are two pairings of aria and recitative, and all four singers join in the final chorale. At the beginning, however, an instrumental prelude establishes the inward-looking mood.

No 1 *Sinfonia*

The title indicates simply an independent piece of music. In this particular case, it may have been an adaptation from an earlier oboe or violin concerto (and destined in fact to be used again in the harpsichord concerto BWV 1056). Whatever its origin, the music is perfectly suited to express the blend of sadness, sweetness and longing with which the Christian soul should ideally contemplate death. A mere twenty bars transmute that entire amalgam of feeling into the slow, elegiac melody of an oboe; the phrases rise and fall in sighs, while strings and continuo pace out the accompanying harmonies.

The emotional effect – the perceived beauty – of the movement derives from a combination of factors, chief of which perhaps involves balanced oppositions. The underlying rhythms could not be steadier, so that against them the decorative solo melody seems a plaintive improvisation. Yet the melody itself has simple foundations. It is initially based on the first four notes of the scale (F major) and then follows a sequence of descending sevenths (used almost two centuries later in the poignant theme of Elgar's Enigma Variations – and exploited to the full in Nimrod).

Despite its brevity – a mere two and a half minutes in duration – the proportions of this prelude are satisfyingly elegant. It is shaped, with seamless and unhurried confidence, in four parts. The first and last of these are almost identical and last for six bars each. Between them are two differing four-bar sections: the first, in G minor, is more emotionally intense in its leaps and chromatic intervals, while the second, gradually moving back to the home key of F major, makes its own melodic impact through its elasticity of rhythm (triplets rather than duplets). Another way to consider the overall structure is to think of it as two halves of ten bars, each built out of six and four bars, i.e. that perennially pleasing ratio of two thirds (which is not to suggest conscious calculation on the composer's part). Bach adjusts the last three bars of the *sinfonia* so that it ends, as if unfinished, with an imperfect cadence.

No 2 Tenor aria/soprano chorale

The human voice now speaks for itself, in a double-layered text. Five lines by Picander are combined with a six-line verse of a chorale by Johann Hermann Schein (1586-1630). He was a noted composer, of much importance for his introduction of Italian styles into Lutheran musical culture, and also one of Bach's predecessors as cantor at Leipzig. Against the background of his personal history, his entire hymn of resignation to God's will is both explicable and heartbreaking; Schein had endured a catalogue of severe ill-health, along with many private tragedies.

The first verse is sung here by the soprano: "Deal with me God, as your goodness decides,/help me in my suffering./What I ask of you, do not refuse./When my soul must depart,/Take it, Lord, in your hands./All is well if the end is well". This declaration of faith is enriched by Picander's simultaneous commentary, sung by the tenor: "I stand with one foot in the grave,/soon the sick body will fall into it,/come dear God when it pleases you,/I have already set my house in order./Only let my end be blessed!". The simplicity of the chorale shines above and through the surrounding texture. Unison upper strings, continuo (with the extra heaviness of the double bass), and the tenor voice form a trio, which Bach weaves together in sombre and elaborate counterpoint.

At the heart of this movement is the fifth line of the chorale – *so mimm sie, Herr, in deine Händ* (*"so take it, Lord, in your hands"*). Schein made it descend over seven notes, and it is this idea that persists in Bach's architecture. The continuo moves down over a seventh with halting, syncopated steps, while the strings above cling to the keynote (F), anticipating the vocal part with its long-held note on *steh* ("stand"). There is a further, more rapid version of the slide down a seventh, which adds rhythmic movement and variety of pace.

If melodic appeal is not part of the remit here (why would it be, given the funereal vision?), Bach rewards the listener with his intricate and concentrated interplay of parts. He also – and this perhaps is a measure of how seriously he regarded this setting – took the trouble to include some dynamic markings: as, for instance, to create soft echo effects. After the chorale has finished, Bach keeps repeating, as if he cannot let go, Picander's final cry of faith: "Only let my end be blessed". The supplicant is then laid gently to rest in F major.

No 3 Bass recit

Christian outlooks on the body and sickness drew on various traditions. The faith absorbed aspects of eastern asceticism, which prized the soul or spirit above the flesh, and Jewish healing traditions were also influential....Hebrew ideas on healing...shared with Egypt and Mesopotamia a religious orientation: disease signified the wrath of God...certain maladies were associated with the Almighty's punishment for sin, including *Zara'ath*, which has usually been translated as leprosy...Such polluting diseases were curable by the Lord alone.

> Roy Porter: *The Greatest Benefit to Mankind*

Ostensibly a conversation with God (though it can equally be regarded as a dialogue with the self), the text falls into three sets of rhetorical oppositions. On the one hand, present circumstances point to divine disapproval. On the other, there is always room for hope. The opening harmonies are as discordant as the emotional state they accompany, but settle eventually in a calm cadence: "My fear and distress, my life and death stand, dear God, in your hands: so would you please turn your gracious eye on me". Picander then makes the connection between the diseases of the inner and outer person: "If, because of my sins" (note the unexpected flattening) "you wish to lay me on my sick bed, my God, then I beg you, let your goodness be greater than your justice". Any hint of presumption quickly vanishes with a return to the state of obedient piety: "Yet if you have planned that my suffering should overcome me, I am ready; let your will be done. Do not spare me but continue; do not let my distress last long" - in other words, the troubled soul looks for the release of death. The final bars settle into a more lyrical *arioso*, as the continuo moves upward at the thought of the heavenly goal: "The longer here, the later there".

No 4 Alto aria

By restoring confidence in God's long-term plan for human good, faith allows the human mind to come to terms with its present lot, however unhappy: "Lord, whatever you will shall please me, for your counsel is best". Music presents this outcome in a – literally – harmonious light. Bach inserts the words into the easy and active pace of a trio sonata for oboe, violin and continuo; in fact, together with the voice it becomes a chamber-music quartet. Its unifying motto consists of a four-note phrase which clearly derives from that essential cry of *Herr, was du wilt* ("Lord, whatever you will"). The key is Bb major, i.e. a turn to the subdominant of the initial F major key; this too brings a hint of acquiescence – in this case, positively cheerful – in the inevitable.

However, on the principle that nothing can be fully savoured without awareness of its opposite, the continuation of the text brings a reminder of what still awaits: "In joy, in suffering, in dying, in beseeching and pleading, let it always happen to me, Lord, as you will". With this, Bach creates a central section of what becomes an overall three-part structure. The vocal setting is correspondingly disturbed, rhythmically and tonally, as the key shifts toward the minor. Awkward syncopations spin out the process of dying (*Sterben*). Even so, the rhythmic momentum continues, reaffirming in musical terms that to submit to God's purpose is the cure for all mental unease.

No 5 Bass recit

This last prayer summarises the point that Picander's text for BWV 156 intends to make. Questions of physical and psychological health are brought together under the umbrella of theology: "And if you will it that I shall no longer be sick, then I shall thank you from the bottom of my heart. Yet grant me also that in my vigorous body my soul too should be without sickness and remain healthy. Take care of this through your spirit and word, for this is my salvation; and when my body and soul fail, then you, God, are my comfort and my heart's portion". Bach's word setting echoes the fervent emotionalism of the plea. What matters is the strength of the inclination to faith – a form of self-healing in the face of life's injuries.

No 6 Chorale

The words are the first verse of the hymn written in 1582 by the learned and much-travelled theologian Caspar Bienemann (1540-1591). For someone caught up, as so many were, in the politico-religious fractures of his time, it was surely reasonable for him to place his trust in the known unknown (if the ways of God are mysterious, those of humans can be even more so): "Lord, ordain things for me as you will, in living and in dying; my desire is only towards you – Lord, let me not perish! Only keep me in your favour, otherwise do as you will; your will is best". This hymn – though set to a different melody – formed the basis of the chorale cantata BWV 73, also for the third Sunday after Epiphany. Here, Bach brings his cantata to an end in C major which, as the dominant key of the F major opening, hints at a hopeful future.

*

Suggested recording: J.S. Bach-Stiftung,
dir. Rudolf Lutz

Fourth Sunday after Epiphany

BWV 81: *Jesus schläft, was soll ich hoffen?*

(Jesus sleeps, what hope do I have?)

Librettist: Unknown

30 January 1724

Rhetorical and dramatic, BWV 81 confronts the believer's recurring and deepest fear: the wavering of faith that threatens the prospect of everlasting life. The day's gospel reading (Mt. 8: 23-27) is taken as an allegory of this inner crisis. According to the story, Christ and his disciples were sailing on the Sea of Galilee when a storm arose. As he slept, his terrified followers called upon him to save them; he woke, reproved their panic, and calmed the wind and waves. Luther's own interpretation, recorded in a sermon of 1517, was that spiritual weakness of this sort is actually a blessing; it leads the soul to cry for help, to which God unfailingly responds. Bach's setting is exceptionally colourful as it translates into the language of music the physical impression of the raging waters – symbolic of devil-inspired turbulence. The narrative moves from dry-mouthed fear, via the internalised voice of Christ, to a final restored confidence. There are no choruses in BWV 81 (other than the final chorale), for the plot depicts two opposing versions of the self: one fearful of death, and the other finding strength to overcome its anxiety.

No 1 Alto aria

Eight bars set the scene. A seasick sway of semitones announces the pitching of the boat, while a pair of recorders, doubling the violins at the octave, wail in sympathy; the key, naturally enough, is in the minor. The continuo line rocks and then descends to the depths. The voice begins its lament: "Jesus sleeps, what hope do I have? Can I not already see, with ashen face, the open chasm of death?" Repeated notes in the bass toll the funereal stillness of *schläft* ("sleeps"), while gasping phrases for the singer act out the terror. Finally, the vocal line stutters into silence, its last hopeless cry followed by a repeat of the opening bars.

No 2 Tenor recit

Although recitative is not as instantly engaging – in purely musical terms, that is – as more extended and lyrical structures, it is nonetheless an authentic and vital part of Bach's sacred cantatas. As with the opera of his time, recitative is crucial to the dramatic shape of the whole. It takes the plot forward and creates the psychological groundwork for the great outbursts of feeling in the arias. Yet to Bach the recitatives were themselves also full of emotional content, for they were part of the project of bringing the human closer to God. Though to recognise all their expressive features requires some understanding of the German text, a listener can, with the general sense to hand, follow the musical gist.

In the case here, the great leaps and twists of the voice, with underlying suggestions of instability in the chords of the seventh, tell an obvious story of the soul's searching. It is full of reproach to the absent one: "Lord, why do you stand so far off?" (note the enormous leap of a minor ninth to show the distance). "Why do you hide yourself at a time of need, when everything threatens me with a wretched end?" (unhappiness seeps through the harmonies). "Ah, is your eye, that otherwise never sleeps, not moved by my need?". The text appeals to biblical precedent: "You did in previous times give a star" (note the top G poised above) "to show the newly converted

Wise Men the right way to travel". Surely no less can be expected by the suffering believer: "Ah, lead me with the light from your eyes, because this path promises nothing but danger". A swooping B minor scale suggests the beam of light falling from heaven, and then the ominous creep of the bass suggests dark and alien territory – a musical no-man's land, full of harmonic threat. An abrupt cadence in G major prepares for the following movement.

No 3 Tenor aria

In Bach's time, a rush of string scales and arpeggios was a standard way of representing the violence of winds and waves; they are no less entertaining for that. The vocal line is tossed about amidst their energy: "The foaming waves of Belial's" (i.e. the devil's) "water redouble their rage". All the same, the voice shows its own defiant power, as in the stream of notes on *verdoppeln* ("redouble"). Identifying the enemy has perhaps transformed earlier weakness into adrenalin-fuelled opposition. Three short *adagio* interludes momentarily check the forward impetus. After these pauses for reflection, the wild waters return – "yet the storming flood seeks to weaken the strength of faith" – bringing a convenient overall symmetry to the musical design.

No 4 Bass arioso

Music, therefore, symbolises man's attempts to make sense out of existence by discovering or imposing order upon it.

Anthony Storr: *Churchill's Black Dog and other Phenomena of the Human Mind*

After chaos, order. Bach's presents the biblical words of Christ in a precisely regulated setting, depicting them in musical terms as a rational antidote to the overwrought imagination: "Why are you afraid, O men of little faith?". Voice and continuo engage in a structured dialogue of imitative counterpoint, with a suggestion of the formality of fugue. Yet the word that stands out is *warum?* ("why?"). Repeated over the rising interval of a fourth, its insistent rhetoric emphasises not so much Christ's rebuke as the lack of reasonable cause for the failure of faith.

No 5 Bass aria

The Saviour calls out to the storm – a fusion of the natural world without and human nature within: "Be still, towering sea! Be silent, storm and wind!". As in the tenor aria, Bach's representation of the scene is stirring and vivid. Strings and continuo together represent the surge and fall of the waves and, for this display of divine power (wizardry, one might say), two oboes replace the earlier soft tones of the recorders. Christ is shown as leader, his commanding persona characterised by fanfare-like calls, heroic leaps and athletic passagework.

The three-part *da capo* design seems particularly appropriate for the image of Christ as guarantor of a regulated universe. In the second portion of text, Christ (in other words, faith) is seen as surrounding his favoured adherents with a defensive enclosure: "May your boundary be set, so that no mishap shall ever injure my chosen child". The *auserwähltes Kind* ("chosen child") is safely positioned in the central (B) section of the aria. While the musical waves can still be heard, they are now clearly subdued. The life of faith, goes the subliminal message, is one of struggle, but God's strength and protection are absolute and unfailing. There is nothing to fear in life or death.

No 6 Alto recit

The same voice that began BWV 81 with the soul's crisis of faith returns with composure regained, thanks to biblical authority: "All is well, my Jesus speaks a word, my helper is awakened; so must the waves' storm, misfortune's night, and all sorrow be gone".

No 7 Chorale

This is the second verse of the hymn *Jesu, meine Freude* ("Jesus, my joy"), written in 1653 by Johann Franck (1618-1677). He was a local official in his native Guben, now on the border of East Germany and Poland, a lawyer by training and writer of poems and hymns. His lines emphasise the sense of threat that is habitual to the religious outlook of the cantata texts (though the fear of death is surely endemic to the human condition). "Under your protection I am free from the storms of all enemies. Let Satan sniff about, let the enemy become angry, Jesus stands by me. Though thunder cracks and lightning flashes, though sin and death terrify me, Jesus will shield me.

*

Suggested recording: Concentus Musicus Wien, dir. Nikolaus Harnoncourt

Fourth Sunday after Epiphany

BWV 14: *Wär Gott nicht mit uns diese Zeit*

(If God were not with us at this time)

Librettist: Unknown

1735

To be chosen in this sense is to be singled out for special purposes, and hence to stand in a unique relation to, the divine. Persons or groups who are chosen are marked off from the multitude, often at first by a divine promise, to enable them to obey and perform God's will. They are required to stand apart, to follow a designated path, which is part of that promise, and determined for them by the deity, but to which they adhere voluntarily. By doing so, they become God's elect, saved and privileged through their obedience to His will and their identification with His plan.

Anthony D. Smith: *Chosen Peoples*

The endpoint of the Epiphany period is set by Ash Wednesday at the start of Lent, and this depends on the date of Easter, which varies from year to year; hence a fourth Sunday after Epiphany is not a regular event. While the earlier cantata for this day, i.e. BWV 8I, was composed in 1724, there was a long gap in time until BWV 14. There are also great differences in the librettist's approach to the theme of threat and in Bach's corresponding manner of setting the text.

The Bible reading for the day (Mt. 8: 23-27) tells of Christ and his disciples sailing on the Sea of Galilee. A storm threatens the boat while Christ is sleeping. His followers panic and wake him; he calms the waves and restores their confidence. To the librettist of BWV 81 this was an allegory of the struggles of the individual mind against the terror of abandonment by God. With BWV 14, however, the orientation seems more towards the survival of the whole group, so that physical and spiritual welfare are inseparable.

In fact, BWV 14 tends far more towards triumph than fear. The text owes its earliest origins to the Old Testament psalm 124, which is a song of thanks to God for victory in battle. In 1524, Luther refashioned it as a three-verse hymn; from this, the librettist of BWV 14 found the materials for a five-movement cantata. He used Luther's first and last verses in their entirety, though freely expanded the sense of the middle one to provide two arias and a recitative.

The tribute to God for deliverance from the enemy was possibly of special significance for Saxony in 1735. Following an international political tussle, the Saxon king Augustus III had, with Russian support, maintained his claim to the throne of Poland. There were further confrontations between the Austrians and the French in the so-called War of the Polish succession, but as the fighting took place in southern Germany and Italy, Saxony itself did not suffer military threat. Nevertheless, the theme of Christians as a beleaguered band under divine protection may well have coincided with contemporary fears and preoccupations – though war has always been an inescapable feature of human affairs.

No 1 Chorus

Like the psalm on which it is based, Luther's hymn looks back to danger overcome and the reliance of the human on divine help: "Were God not with us at this time,/ so should Israel say/were God not with us at this time,/we should have had to despair/we who are such a poor little band/despised by so many of mankind/who all attack us".

The words look to the possibility of a counterfactual: there might (without God) have been an entirely different outcome. This ambivalence is elegantly implied in the vocal counterpoint that precedes each line of the hymn. In every case, the chorale melody is pitted against its inversion. For instance, the tenor first enters with its setting of "Were God not with us at this time", followed by the bass with the same phrase in the opposite direction. Alto and soprano follow in a similar fashion, so that the positive outcome coexists simultaneously with its denial. While the order of voices subsequently varies, there are always two opposing sets: in terms of the direction of pitch, that is, yet all is integrated into a coherent texture. Such technical mastery is, musically speaking, the outstanding feature of the chorus, and is given even more clarity through the reinforcing of the upper voices by the violins and viola. The continuo partially doubles the vocal bass and partially contributes its own independent voice.

The hymn in its complete form arrives simply as melody, strongly presented by two oboes – for the singers' preamble has already, and repeatedly, provided the words. The oboes, therefore, have the function of a *cantus firmus* (i.e. presenting the chorale tune), which is rhythmically distinct in its longer note values standing out against their busier backdrop. As one of Bach's functions was to keep the traditional Lutheran hymns freshly in mind, his solution in this chorus is one of his most original. Along the way, there are, as ever, examples of Bach's sensitivity to text. The "poor little band" (*armes Haüflein*) of the fifth line is full of lingering pathos and, towards the end of the movement, the texture becomes more crowded as a token of the great forces of the enemy "who all attack us". From a structural point of view, this also creates a triumphant climax: the more numerous the foe, the greater the display of divine power.

No 2 Soprano aria

For we see no pleasure can delight us at any time if sorrow goeth not before.

Baldassare Castiglione: *The Courtier*, trans. Hoby

As the notion of God as an entirety escapes definition, the cantata texts instead present the divine being as a collection of recognisable human attributes. A familiar persona, both for the God of the Old Testament and the figure of Christ, is the all-conquering champion who defeats the forces of evil in general, and death in particular. In this three-section aria (though not formally a *da capo*), the horn becomes the hero, leading the string ensemble with military and aristocratic swagger. Again, though, the music implies a certain (and no doubt deliberate) contradiction. The style embodies the kind of stereotypical muscularity that would be attached to an operatic character returning in glory from battle. Yet the vocal line is given to the relatively slender sound of the soprano (in Bach's world, a choirboy) rather than a robust bass.

Equal in musical virtuosity, though not in power, horn and singer exemplify the partnership of the human and the divine. The mortal soul is frail but borrows support from a transcendent grandeur: "Our strength is too weak to withstand our foe". Although the singer imitates the strong manner of the horn, there is a notable mismatch of volume, which is as it should be. While the musical energy thrills, Bach has placed in its path a number of rhythmic obstacles, as, for instance, the syncopations associated with *widerstehen* ("withstand"). As this word ends the first section of the aria, the relevance of the battle become even clearer: rhythmic hindrance in the vocal line is accompanied by a tumbling passage in the bass as a reminder that the loser must fall into the depths of hell.

The second part of the text is full of remembered danger: "If the Almighty had not stood by us, their tyranny would soon have taken our very life". The texture becomes correspondingly more vulnerable, with little input from the horn. Mental agitation at the reminder of threat translates also into a less stable key structure. *Leben* ("life") – i.e., eternal life – is the word that Bach emphasises through extended vocal elaboration. With this, the continuo part is spare and discreet, and a solo violin, rather than the horn, partners the singer. After a short *ritornello*, the text is even more at the forefront, accompanied only by the tumbling figures of the continuo. After a brief reminder of the opening bars of the aria, the voice once again looks admiringly at God's power, and a last instrumental section leaves its own tribute.

No 3 Tenor recit

A paraphrase of the second verse of Luther's hymn forms the text: "Yes, if God had only allowed it we would have perished long ago. They would have ripped us apart in their lust for vengeance, so great is their anger against us". This is followed by the imagery that forms the bridge between Psalm 24 and the day's gospel story: "Their rage would have inundated us like a wild torrent, and no one would have checked their power". The continuo part rises and falls, tossed from one key to another as if by the waves. The vocal line is similarly full of violent leaps and ill-omened intervals – note the diminished fifth on w*ir waren längst* ("we would have long ago [perished]"), *Rachgier* ("lust for vengeance") and *ihre Wut* ("their rage"). Bodily and spiritual preservation become one and the same.

No 4 Bass aria

A refined trio sonata, in the style of a lively gavotte, marks the contrast between the uncontrolled horror of a world subject to the enemy of faith, and the calmer delights of God's orderly rule. It seems that the Almighty is equally at ease in the civil sphere as successful on the battlefield (such all-encompassing benefit is surely the mark of a successful religion). The two oboes that declaimed the *cantus firmus* in the opening chorus now follow each other in the regular steps of a dance. Earlier tempestuousness is set aside; gone, too, is the militaristic sound of the horn: "God, by your protective strength we are set free from our enemies". The central section organises the onslaughts of the attackers into neat key sequences, while only a little murmuring in the continuo hints at their former power: "When they, like wild waves, in fury oppose us, your hands assist us". Rather than triumphalism, Bach suggests the modest joy of those who live gratefully under God's protection.

No 5 Chorale

Luther's third verse closely follows the rest of the psalm: "Praise and thanks be to God, who did not permit their throat to swallow us. Like a bird free of the snake has our soul escaped. the snare is broken in two, and we are free. May the name of the Lord assist us, the God of heaven and earth". More, even, than the freedom of the body, it is the mind's security that brings content.

*

Suggested recording: J.S. Bach-Stiftung,
dir. Rudolf Lutz

February: Prefatory Note

Keeping the faith

The cantatas for February begin with a last glimpse of the sacred child. Three works – BWV 83, BWV 125 and BWV 82 – are an exceptionally profound reminder of the cycle of life. They commemorate the Purification, so called after the Jewish ritual that required a mother to present a male infant at the temple, six weeks after his birth. In the biblical account, an aged man immediately recognises Christ as the coming Saviour of the world, and declares himself content to accept death. It is his sense of fulfilment that is conveyed in Bach's exceptionally moving music.

The rest of the month marks out the weeks before Easter until the penitent season of Lent, when music was not considered appropriate. BWV 44, BWV 92 and BWV 84 are sermons against envy and discontent, while BWV 18, BWV 126 and BWV 181 warn against deviations from orthodox belief. Finally, another four cantatas move to the periphery of Easter. BWV 22, BWV 23 and BWV 127 focus on the central importance of faith, using biblical examples of its miracle-working effects, while BWV 159 takes the listener on an imaginary journey to Jerusalem, watching the Christian soul struggle with its fear of what lies ahead – for Christ, and equally for its own destiny.

One other work has been slipped in. This is BWV 71, Bach's earliest known cantata. While not part of the liturgical year, it demonstrates the close connection between religion and the social order of his world. BWV 71 was composed in honour of a new cohort of elected officials in the city of Mühlhausen; it recognises the inevitability of time and change, in the life of both the community and the individual. In both cases, a benevolent God will ensure a smooth transition from one phase to another.

Purification

BWV 83: *Erfreute Zeit im neuen Bunde*

(Joyous time of the new covenant)

Librettist: Unknown

2 February 1724

Pheres:
You enjoy being alive; do you think your father doesn't?

Admetus:
Dying is not the same thing for an old man

Euripides: Alcestis

Beside the Sundays that were regularly set apart for Christian worship, there were in Bach's working calendar other moments throughout the year – saints' days, for instance, and the commemoration of scripturally significant events – that called for public devotions. The Feast of the Purification (Candlemas) is one of these. Falling on 2 February (which, in 1724, happened to be Wednesday), it marks the ritual presentation of the infant Christ in the temple. The origins of the custom are ancient and appear to be linked to a cultural universal: a sense of awe and fear over childbirth. Its biblical roots lay in the Old Testament book of Leviticus, which decreed that after six weeks a mother should bring a male child to the temple and undergo a symbolic cleansing. It took twice as long after the birth of a female.

Setting aside these anthropological niceties, the texts of the cantatas for the Feast of the Purification turn to a larger vision: the reconciliation of birth and death that is central to the Christian story. According to this, death is not final – at least, not for the believer – but is instead the portal to rebirth. With the arrival of Christ on earth, God was offering forgiveness for human sin, and consequently the promise of immortality. The gospel reading for this day (Lk.2: 22-32) narrates this hope in terms of a personal story. As the Christ child is brought to the temple, an elderly man, Simeon, is inspired to come also in search of the Messiah. He sees the infant and takes him in his arms, recognising him as the sign of a new covenant between God and humanity. Simeon's only wish from now on is to be allowed to take leave of the world in peace; his words are used in the centuries-old evening prayer, *Nunc dimittis*. Other than the final four-part chorale, there are only solo singers in this positive work.

No 1 Alto aria

The music here, and also for the tenor aria (No. 3), seems to have been one of Bach's self-borrowings – from a violin concerto, now lost. Both the style and the harmonic language of this F major movement are bright and open, though perhaps with a touch of ceremony in the rhythmic crispness; the subject matter, after all, is the arrival of God's son. Two horns and two oboes add splendour to the ensemble of strings and continuo. The musical effect is as exultant as the words – "Joyous time of the new covenant, when our faith holds Jesus" – with solo violin and voice matching each other in euphoric energy. Such are the demands on the singer, in fact, that this movement becomes a type of double concerto. While the elaboration of *erfreute* ("joyous") is a standard treatment of the verbal idea, the technical show is more than mere convention. It satisfies the concerto's requirement for brilliance, while celebrating the high spirits when the fear of death is banished.

The structure is a typical three-part *da capo*. For its central section, the libretto moves to the moment of death: "How joyfully at the last hour will we arrange our resting place, the grave!" A key shift from F major to its related D minor fits the seriousness of the thought, and a new quiet (Bach asks for *pianissimo*) surrounds the fading of the body. Horns and oboes fall silent for a little while, and the solo violin sinks to the lowest part of its compass. Yet this must not be the end. Momentum begins to return, along with another allusion to the contradictory coexistence of joy and death; the violin bow dances on the spot (the technique of *bariolage*). A return to the first part of the aria confirms that only happiness awaits.

No 2 Bass aria/recit

As the text alternates the biblical words with the librettist's interpolations, Bach separates the two stylistically while maintaining a unified structure. Simeon speaks with slow calm, in the ritualised manned of an ancient plainchant: "Lord, now let your servant depart in peace, according to your word; for my eyes have seen your Saviour, whom you have prepared for all people". The commentary, on the other hand, adopts the choppier, more speech-like manner of recitative. What binds together these two disparate elements is the recurrence of an upward-flowing canon (i.e. close imitation) between the unison strings above and the continuo below. It signals the ease of the old man's path to death, and by implication invites the listener to follow. Tonality also plays a part, for the transition to the subdominant (Bb major) of the opening movement suits the mood of resignation.

The librettist leaves no room for doubt: "What seems to us as humans terrifying" (note the discordant leap on *schrecklich*) "is our entrance to life". A short canonic interlude leads to the consoling, if not entirely persuasive, assertion that "Death" (a troubled fall of a diminished fifth in the harmonic bass) "means the end of this time of affliction, a pledge given to us by the Lord as a sign that he is kindly disposed and will, after the struggle is over, bring us to peace". The vocal line comes smoothly to rest, blending into another episode of canon before the conclusion that "since the Saviour now is a consolation to our eyes and the heart's refreshment" (a small decoration signals the pleasure), "no wonder that our heart forgets the fear of death". The final bar of recitative merges again with Simeon: "it can say with joy, 'for my eyes have seen your Saviour, whom you have made ready for all people'".

No 3 Tenor aria

This was presumably the last movement of the concerto mentioned above, scored here for strings alone. Liberated from its attachment to the body, the mind flies off on the rapid triplets of the solo violin: "Hurry, heart, full of joy, to step before the throne of grace". The accompanying parts bound forward in staccato quavers, while a rapidly changing harmonic bass pushes onward. As at the beginning of BWV 83, the key is again F major and the structure another *da capo*. Its central section shines the light of the future upon the present: "You shall receive consolation and obtain mercy; yes, in a care-filled time, keep strong in spirit and pray vigorously". This is faith's calling card; assured of good things to come, the believer can confidently face the trials of life now. Although the *kummervoller Zeit* ("care-filled time") produces a chromatic downward slide in the continuo, the troubles of the finite world are soon set aside with the completion of the structure as the music returns to its eager beginning.

No 4 Alto recit

Composer and librettist finish their work with a summary of the tensions surrounding death, and the ultimate assurance of victory: "Yes, though your faith can still only see much darkness, when the night of the grave makes your last hour terrible, you can be sure that you will recognise his bright light in death itself". The D minor key and the doom-laden harmonies embrace the horror, as does the lurching of the vocal line as it contemplates the darkness of the grave; the only musical relief is a climb into D major for *sein helles Licht* ("his bright light").

No 5 Chorale

Luther's hymn, *Mit Fried und Freud ich fahr dahin* ("With peace and joy I travel there"), set to his own melody, is a paraphrase of the day's biblical text. The fourth verse, with its universalist vision, brings BWV 83 to an end: "He is the salvation and blessed light for the Gentiles, to enlighten those who do not know you, and to bring them to pasture, He is for your people Israel the glory, honour, joy and bliss". Death is unavoidable; one hopes to face it with Simeon's fortitude.

*

Suggested recording: J. S. Bach-Stiftung, dir. Rudolf Lutz

Purification

BWV 125: *Mit Fried und Freud ich fahr dahin*

(With peace and joy I travel there)

Librettist: Unknown

2 February 1725

*Nil igitur mors est ad nos neque pertinet hilum,
qandoquidem natura animi mortalis habetur*

(Death, therefore, is nothing to us and does not concern us at all, seeing that the nature of the mind is a mortal possession.)

Lucretius: *On the Nature of Things*

Death – the universal fear – threatens human self-esteem. Conscious of time, the mind projects itself into a future in which it will no longer exist. Is there any significance to the life of the individual, apart from the experience of each moment? Religious belief confronts the question by offering an enlarged model of reality, a new framework of barely conceivable possibilities that would explain everything, if only we could make sense of it. As we cannot, we are urged in the mental world of Bach's sacred cantatas (as in multiple other systems of faith) simply to accept that it is so. The recurring – in fact, the chief – preoccupation of these works is how to confront mortality. If in this respect the Christian beliefs of the cantatas are part of a millennia-old project, this is not to undervalue them, for their version of death as the entrance to new life has consoled the imagination of countless millions. The music of BWV 125 gives an exceptionally moving account of this dream: the fulfilment of a wish that is surely inseparable from consciousness itself.

The inspiration for BWV 125 is the account in Luke's gospel (Lk. 2: 22-32) of the devout old man Simeon. He is described as coming to the temple at Jerusalem when the infant Christ was brought there by his parents, following the ritual requirement of purification after childbirth. Having identified the child as the living embodiment of God, Simeon is overcome by a sense of profound peace and joy and is ready to accept the end of his life. For this chorale cantata, an unknown librettist has based his text on Luther's hymn *Mit Fried und Freud ich fahr dahin* ("With peace and joy I travel there"). Its verses paraphrase Simeon's own words – familiar, in Christian religious practice, in its Latin form of *Nunc Dimittis*. Bach's setting, introspective and powerfully emotional, transforms the experience of one man into a universal accommodation with death. Simeon's insight belongs to everyone; the inner gaze is fixed upon the hope of better things to come.

No 1 Chorus

There are similarities between this movement and the opening chorus of Bach's St. Matthew Passion, composed two years later. They share the same time signature (12/8) and key (E minor), and the mourning sounds of flute and oboe. Yet though both look toward death, BWV 125 aims primarily to reconcile the self with its own fate rather than to grieve at that of another. The bass pedal that features in both works is rooted to the spot at the beginning of the St. Matthew Passion, while in BWV 125 it rocks across the octave, as if pressing forward to its destination; the habitually ascending contours of the instrumental melody suggest an ongoing process. Within this context, the first verse of the hymn appears, line by line, sung as a soprano *cantus firmus* and strengthened by the sound of the horn. Each time, the other voices echo the words in close-set imitation.

Luther's words follows Simeon's: if not always to the letter, then certainly in spirit. He begins: "With peace and joy I travel there/according to God's will/consoled in heart and mind". The fourth line consists of three words only: *sanft und stille* ("peaceful and still"), which Bach turns musically into a dreamlike state of withdrawal. Consciousness ebbs, as the voices fade away above the barely moving notes of the continuo; the key drifts into distant territories, leading to a moment of total quiet. From this, a sudden resurrection of volume and pulse leads to the assertion of faith: "as God has promised me". For the final line – "death has become my sleep" – energy once more subsides. Sinking, chromatic harmonies lead through remote tonal territories; the long, unmoving chord for the lower voices on *Schlaf* ("sleep") speaks for itself. A repeat of the opening bars rounds off the structure, its mood poised between hope and sorrow.

No 2 Alto aria

The approach of death is the supreme test of faith in Christ's power to transcend it: "Even as my eyes falter, I will look to you, my true Saviour". Bach's B minor setting is a supremely poignant lament: painful, yet comforting in its beauty. The texture is relatively spare, with flute and oboe in a sighing duet alongside the voice, and with the dragging footsteps of the continuo (two cellos) below; Bach specifies that the bass should be left unharmonised, i.e. with no chords to soften its outlines. There are again certain parallels with the St. Matthew Passion: in particular *So ist mein Jesus nun gefangen* ("See, my Jesus is now taken"), for soprano and alto, and the heartbreak of the soprano aria *Aus Liebe will mein Heiland sterben* ("For love my Saviour now is dying"). Here, in BWV 125, the two wind instruments advance as one in slowly choreographed movement, until they unfurl to a cadence above. Their elegy recurs throughout the aria, both as an independent *ritornello* and as an accompaniment to the voice.

Two more portions of text project the self further into the process of dying. The spirit must stay resilient: "Although the frame of my body breaks, yet my heart and my hope do not fail". Although the manner of the music is unchanged, key shifts and the play of rhythm keep the listener's attention, as with the emphatic off-beat of "yet" (*doch*) and "not" (*nicht*). Then, following the model of Simeon's trust, the believer looks ahead confidently to divine protection at the last: "My Jesus looks upon me in dying". With the threefold repetition of *Sterben* ("dying"), the vocal line sinks in a symbolic death, while the flute and oboe spiral away into nothing. A silent beat marks the moment, followed by a glimpse into eternity: "and lets no harm come to me". The movement ends full circle with a repeat of the twelve-bar opening ritornello.

No 3 Bass recit

Small flourishes in the upper strings (violins and viola) signal the stirring of life. Their tokens of hope and excitement condition the listener's response to the text, which comprises the second verse of Luther's chorale, interleaved with the librettist's commentary. Bach integrates these two elements into a smooth sequence of recitative and melody – the latter being the hymn in a slightly decorated form. The initial exclamation of: "O wonder, that a heart confronting the tomb hated by the flesh, and also the pain of death, should not be frightened!", leads straight into Luther's declaration that "This is brought about by Christ, the true son of God".

The recitative resumes: "who on the deathbed already delights the spirit with the sweetness of heaven" and is completed by, "and whom you, Lord, have allowed us to see" (note the beatific vocal elaboration). The imagination then projects itself beyond the threshold of the present: "when in the fullness of time faith's arm embraces the salvation of the Lord". The final interplay of chorale and recitative presents faith in Christ as inseparable from faith in God as beneficent universal creator: "and have made it known from the exalted God, the creator of all things, that he is the life and salvation, mankind's consolation and portion, their deliverer from destruction". The chorale's last phrase – "in death and also in dying" – stretches out in torment over the ultimate ordeal for the spirit.

No 4 Tenor/bass duet

Though the recitative ended as if awaiting a resolution in E minor, Bach turns instead – for the first time in BWV 125 – to the major. Music serves the sense of the text by replacing what is sombre with an overwhelming energy and brightness: "An incomprehensible light fills the entire circle of the earth". The duet for tenor and bass brings to mind the later Ascension Day cantata, BWV 11, in which the same two voices (angels?) proclaimed Christ's resurrection. Great flights of vocal coloratura seemingly extend over the world (*den ganzen Kreis der Erden*), equalling the violin parts in their brilliance. In the B section of the *da capo* structure, the voices echo each other in bell-like imitation, evangelising the news: "It rings powerfully on and on, the greatly wished-for word of promise: whoever believes shall be saved". Only the drooping quavers of *höchst erwünscht* ("greatly wished-for") remind the listener that unfulfilled longing is an inescapable partner of faith. A return to the A section sweeps up the listener once more into rapturous certainty: a seeming end to the search for the underlying narrative of life and death.

No 5 Alto recit

As ever in the cantata texts, the dream of heaven triumphs in the face of mortality and evil: "O inexhaustible treasure of goodness bestowed on us humans. For the world that has invited anger and cursing upon itself a seat of grace and a sign of victory has been set up, and every believing spirit is invited into his kingdom of grace".

No 6 Chorale

The last verse of Luther's hymn follows the biblical Simeon in gesturing to a world united by faith in Christ's redemptive power: "He is the salvation and blessed light for the gentiles, to enlighten those who do not know you and to pasture them. He is the praise, honour, joy and gladness of your people Israel". The four-part setting brings in the support of all the instrumentalists, with flute, horn, oboe and violin lending strength to the soprano melody.

Setting aside reservations – and there may be many – over details of dogma, one may argue that BWV 125 answers to a widespread longing, irrespective of creed, to seek refuge in a better world: the thought of it sweetens both present and future. Though the companion of the text, the music, like Simeon, travels to a destination that cannot be limited by words. And, in contrast with the grandiose, not to say murderous, preparations for the afterlife of numerous emperors and tyrants, the Christian approach of BWV 125 asks simply for the mind's acquiescence in what must be.

*

Suggested recording: J.S. Bach-Stiftung,
dir. Rudolf Lutz

Purification

BWV 82: *Ich habe genug*

(I have enough)

Librettist: Unknown

2 February 1727

inde fit ut raro qui se vixisse beatum
dicat et exacto contentus tempore vita
cedat uti conviva satur reperire queamur

(so it is that we can hardly ever find a man who says he has lived a happy life and who, when his time is up, contentedly departs this world like a dinner guest who has had plenty to eat)

Horace: *Satires I*

As with its predecessors for this occasion (BWV 83 and BWV 125), the scriptural reference for BWV 82 is an event described in Luke's gospel ((Lk. 2: 22-32). Following religious custom, the infant Christ had been brought to the temple six weeks after his birth. An aged man, Simeon, had been overwhelmed by the sight of the child, realising instantly that he was to be the Saviour of mankind. Prophesying the newborn's future, he took him in his arms and declared himself happy to depart from life; he knew that this birth signified the reconciliation of the divine with the human and hence death was no longer the cessation of being, but its eternal prolongation in paradise.

Amongst the many cantatas whose artistic vocabulary soars beyond the usual limits of words – including those used to formulate a set of religious beliefs – BWV 82 is one of the greatest. Though the original manuscript sets it for a solo bass voice, evidently it was sung also by soprano and mezzo soprano. The reasons for its wide appeal lie somewhere in the web of relationships between aesthetic satisfaction and emotional capture, and the transference of both into the realm of moral value. The music of BWV 82 conveys a sense of that other-worldly joy that the believer hopes for as life ends: the point of fulfilment at which desire and its realisation momentarily intersect. The mental goal is a semi-mystical altered state of being: a rapturous release from the burden of self, both physical and psychological – an imagined death, in fact.

The libretto presents the words of Simeon and the believer's ideal response to them. It is the music, however, that reveals their meaning in terms of sublime contentment infused with yearning – or perhaps the other way round. Bach achieves this by an interplay of factors that only technical fluency at the service of a generous and humane imagination can fully command: structure, symmetry, the sweet spot of repetition (enough, but not too much), melodic expression, pulse. Not least is the orderly fivefold shape of the work, with its three contrasted arias linked by two recitatives. As the music is so designed as to bring profound pleasure in itself, is there any need for the words? To which the answer must be: without them, would the music exist?

No 1 Bass aria

Now more than ever seems it rich to die,
To cease upon the midnight with no pain.

John Keats: 'Ode to a Nightingale'

Simeon's consciousness of the sacred unites a sense of completion with an unsatisfied hunger for heaven. A perfect faith calls for withdrawal from the mortal self: "I have enough. I have taken the Saviour, the hope of the devout, into my eager arms; I have enough! I have seen him, my faith has pressed Jesus to my heart; now I wish this very day with joy to depart from here. I have enough!" The physical – the embracing and the seeing of the child – proceeds to the inner eye that searches out a transcendent meaning.

There are four main musical elements in this C minor aria, each with its distinct identity and yet all perfectly interwoven. In addition to the singer, the instrumental groups are upper strings, continuo and a solo oboe. From the outset, they speak the musical language of sorrow, with the sighs and murmurs of the two violins, the repeated descending patterns (akin to the funereal ground bass) of the continuo and viola, and the keening of the oboe. Is it death or remaining in this world that it laments?

The melodic lines make full use of the intrinsic poignancy of minor intervals: in particular, the striking phrase that rises and falls over a minor sixth and a minor third (as with *Erbarme dich* in the St. Matthew Passion). Here, rhythm and pitch clearly echo the spoken German of *Ich habe genug* ("I have enough"), and this small fragment becomes the recurring motto of the movement. The most striking feature is, however, the richly expressive, almost improvisatory style of the oboe, as if striving to escape the mundane limits of the scale. In other words, there is an upwelling of energy rather than stillness. Grief there may be, but not stasis.

Against this backdrop of sombre and haunting beauty, the voice at last appears. It picks up the oboe melody but now with words to give focus to what has so far been implied by music alone. Bach unfurls his text, one section at a time, in a spacious design that alternates instrumental passages (*ritornelli*) with those that include the singer. Although the manner and materials remain the same throughout, transitions of key, for instance to G minor and F minor, give a sense of onward travel. There is also a permanent contrast between the slow harmonic pace of the continuo (one chord per bar) and the activity of the parts above: the rocking of the strings and the lavish streams of the oboe.

But the chief business of BWV 82 is to make the imagination soar with Simeon. Bliss at leaving behind the imperfection of the mortal state shines through the vocal heroics of *Freuden* ("joy") before the singer ends with one more firm statement of *Ich habe genug*. The instruments return to complete the great arch of this movement.

No 2 Bass recit

Cantata texts were a teaching tool, and so the librettist provides a response for the listener: "I have enough. My comfort is simply this, that Jesus may be mine and I his very own". To the pious mind, the Saviour is a real presence: "In faith I hold him; thus I too can see with Simeon the joy of that life already". The continuo leads the way and the voice follows its steady footsteps: "Let us go with this man". The spirit is willing, yet the time has not yet come: "Ah! If the Lord would only rescue me from my body's chains! Ah! If my departure were only here, with joy" (a soaring of the vocal line) "I would say to you, world: I have enough!".

No 3 Bass aria

The soul lulls itself to sleep: "Slumber, tired eyes, close gently and blessedly!". In contrast with the first aria, the contours of the music are smoothed and softened. The key is now in the relative major (Eb) of the opening aria, the rhythms are steady, and the melody stepwise. Yet though not as highly coloured as before (no twisting and winding of the oboe), the music is equally eloquent in its profound calm. In fact, the frequent leaning toward the subdominant, as in the leap of the flattened seventh that begins the second bar, tells of submission rather than struggle. Long held notes on *schlummert* ("slumber") and pauses after *zu* (i.e. the closing of the eyes) point to the final sleep that separates life from death.

Structure adds to the sense of completion. Not only is this aria the centre of symmetry of BWV 82, but it embodies a five-part scheme of its own. It is written as a *da capo*, i.e. with two identical parts enclosing a different inner section. However, that section itself subdivides into three. The original lulling melody takes the central place, flanked by two new portions of text. For the first of these, the voice appears alone, without the strings: "World, I will remain no longer here, for I have no part in you that could benefit my soul". The key hovers between major and minor, as it does for the second assertion: "Here, I must reckon with misery, but there, there I shall see sweet peace and quiet rest". The tonal ambivalence of these shifts nudges the listener between the discomfort of the present and the promise of serenity to come. But a taste of the latter arrives as the music returns to the beatific lyricism of its opening.

No 4 Bass recit

Short and dramatic, this recitative conveys the intensity of the believer's eagerness for death: "My God! When will I hear that beautiful word, 'Now'?". The musical rhetoric mirrors the words, so that the question ends on a rising note of impatience. Further appeals are similarly pitched high: "When will I depart in peace and rest both in the sand of the cool earth" (here the voice falls to its depths) "and with you in heaven?". For the final word of parting ("My farewell has been made, world, good night"), the continuo descends two octaves into the longed-for grave.

No 5 Bass aria

Evidently it takes all the energy of the living to convey Christian delight in dying. Though the key is the C minor that began BWV 82, death appears here neither melancholy nor calm, but a dance of joy into the world beyond. The vocal line overflows with happiness: "I rejoice in my death". Even the moment of quiet regret – "Ah, it only it had already come" – is ornamented with trills, and with no loss of rhythmic pace.

However, one further phrase tells of humanity's tragic vision – Christian but not exclusively so: "There I will escape all the affliction that binds me on earth". With his inclusion of a leap of a minor sixth, Bach alludes to the first aria and that great longing to exchange life's mess and misery for a perfect ideal. In a characteristic touch of word painting, *Gebunden* ("binds") is tied over half a dozen or so bars.

The final symmetry of BWV 82 is that it ends, as it began, in an analogous tension between word and music. Whereas in the first aria the music yearned while the text spoke of fulfilment, the final plea of the cantata - "Ah, if only death had already come" - is at odds with the exuberant character of the setting. It speaks of unfinished business, of unattained desire; only the willed hope of a greater good sustains the Christian effort to believe that life has a deeper meaning. Yet the musical message of BWV 82 reaches beyond the confines of creed, age or gender. It brings the greatest of consolations both to those who mourn another's death and those who fear their own: a sense that their anguish is shared and understood.

*

Suggested recordings:
Hans Hotter, Philharmonia Orchestra/Concentus
Musicus Wien, dir. Nikolaus Harnoncourt

John Shirley-Quirk,
Academy of St.-Martin-in-the-Fields,
dir. Neville Marriner

Change of Town Council

BWV 71: *Gott ist mein König*

(God is my king)

Librettist: Unknown

4 February 1708

BWV 71 belongs at the interface of music, religion and social order; it was composed early in Bach's career, when he was organist at the St. Blasius church in Mühlhausen, to mark the election of new town officials. In the mid-thirteenth century, Mühlhausen became an Imperial Free City, enjoying independent rule within the Holy Roman Empire, though by Bach's time its economic importance was overtaken by the trading centre of Leipzig. However, civic pride clearly still flourished, as the parts for BWV 71 were printed at public expense (a significant outlay for a town that had in the previous year suffered a devastating fire); none of Bach's other cantatas was published in his lifetime.

The overriding theme of BWV 71 is the need for continuity and protection. A change in the established order – the danger of stepping over a threshold into the unknown – brings a sense of insecurity and an enhanced dependence on the immovable power of the divine. An alteration in communal life is also mapped onto the individual's adjustment to the passage of time and mental preparation for death. Everything human is finite, whereas God represents the unity that is believed to exist behind the constant fluctuations in the visible scheme of things.

A now-unknown librettist fashioned the text from biblical allusions, a chorale verse, and some original poetry. The format of BWV 71 belongs to an era before

Bach's sacred cantatas began to incorporate the operatic contrasts of recitative (for narrative) and arias (for conveying emotion in large-scale melodic structures). Its movements tend to be more sectional, shifting their manner as the sense of the words requires. In honour of the occasion, Bach was granted a large number of musicians. These included, in addition to his singers: three trumpets and drums, a string group of violins, viola and double bass, two oboes and bassoon, two recorder and cello, and of course the organ continuo. The richness and variety of the instrumentation is matched by the great range of compositional techniques, deployed, as usual, in the service of the words.

No 1 Chorus

The observances in which devoutness finds expression consistently aim to propitiate the deity by extolling his greatness and glory and by professing subservience and fealty. The act of propitiation or of worship is designed to appeal to a sense of status imputed to the inscrutable power that is thus approached.

> Thorstein Veblen: *The Theory of the Leisure Class*

God is at the summit of the political structure and its ultimate endorsement. The librettist begins with an excerpt from Psalm 74 (which may have been a response to the destruction of the temple at Jerusalem around 600 BCE): "God is my king from old, from whom all help on earth comes". The singers join in a great shout – *Gott ist mein König* – which reverberates in space, passing through each instrumental group in turn. Four solo voices continue with *von alters her* ("from old"), in which the prolonged notes of the soprano imply God's extent in time. The tempo becomes a little faster and the style more lyrical as the vocal counterpoint looks to God as the support of the human: "from whom all help on earth comes". For this expression of vulnerability, brass and wind are silent as strings alone double the voices. It forms the centre of the musical design, which is completed with a return to the acclamation of God as universal king.

No 2 Tenor air/soprano chorale

The musical scene changes entirely as the focus moves from God's majesty to the humble retainer who begs to retire: "I am eighty years old; why should your servant burden himself further? I will go back, that I may die in my own city, by the grave of my mother and father". The soft sound of a chamber organ accompanies the heartfelt appeal, and the words are once more from the Old Testament. They recall the aged Barzillai (2 Sam.19: 31-37) who pleads with King David to release him from service. Music adds its own rhetorical emphasis in the repeated questioning of *warum?* ("why?"), which mimics the falling pitch of the spoken German.

At approximately a third of the way through, the soprano voice reveals the soul's deepest wish, expressed in a verse by Johann Heermann (1585-1647): "If I should prolong my life further in this world/taking many a bitter step as I press on into old age/then grant me patience, protect me from sin and disgrace/so that I may wear my grey hair with honour". The lines are from Heermann's *O Gott, du frommer Gott* ("*O God, you righteous God*"), the whole of which is testament to Lutheran values of moral integrity and endurance – moving in itself, even without the knowledge of Heermann's own lifelong misfortunes: he survived much ill health, bereavement, fire and plague.

The insertion of the hymn lends a universal aspect to the particularities of Mühlhausen's election. With easy brilliance, Bach integrates the G major chorale melody into the E minor key of the movement. He also embellishes it to reflect details of the text, such as the rising scale on *höher* ("higher"), the pained semitonal descent on s*auren Tritt* ("bitter step") and the unstable harmonies that accompany the idea of sin and disgrace. Equally, the final section that looks forward to the old man's journey home overflows with decoration in the organ part. In the Lutheran picture of the cantatas, old age brings joy because it leads the believer to God.

No 3 Fugue SATB soli

Another biblical allusion looks to a double blessing: "May your old age be like your youth, and God is with you in all that you do". Bach sets the text as a tightly constructed fugue, in which the constant invention of the part writing is contained with a fixed harmonic framework. Unusually, the entries of the subject on which the fugue is based remain in the same key of E minor throughout – change and continuity are part of the same picture. There is also a theological purpose in Bach's treatment of *alles* ("all"). Appearing first as a short, flowing phrase, it dominates the texture towards the end. The whole of life must be permeated with the presence of God. Fugue, with its continuous stream of voices that promise renewal without monotony, and seemingly endless possibilities from one small beginning, is perhaps a brief musical intimation of the infinite.

No 4 Bass arioso

Psalm 74 is again the reference point for the text: "Day and night are yours. You make both sun and stars run in their appointed course. You set the borders of every land". The connection of divine power to the functioning of the cosmos and thence to political order could not be clearer. In fact, the musical structure encloses the organisation of the human world within the great scheme of the universe. The outer sections, containing simply "Day and night", proceed with slow majesty (*Lente*) and commanding vocal leaps. Two groups of instruments – oboes and bassoon, and recorders and cello – echo and respond to each other, with their distinct colours suggesting the contrast between the presence and then the withdrawal of light. Similarly, pitch becomes a musico-visual metaphor for the bright and the dark: *Tag und Nacht* ("Day and night") are an octave's distance apart.

A change of pulse (four beats rather than a slow three) differentiates the central section, aesthetically and also conceptually – for the divinity, though boundless himself, ordains boundaries for the material world, whether planetary or human. Although the musical manner remains formal – especially so in the ceremonious vocal line – the rhythms become more animated, for God is at work guiding the hand of the map maker, so to speak. More important: by acquiescing in the status quo, believers are showing themselves at one with the mind of the ruler above.

No 5 Alto air

A further conflation of biblical sources continues the image of God as guarantor of limits (Zeus, the ruler of the Greek gods, had the same function), and hence the maintainer of peace on earth. Contrasts of style look, on the one hand, to the all-conquering power of the creator, and then to the stability that this ensures. Three trumpets and drums speak the language of military force – "Through mighty power" – and then fall silent as the voice calmly lists the especial benefits that this brings: "You maintain our borders; here peace must shine when murder and the storm of war arises everywhere. Though crown and sceptre shake" (note the illustrative tremble on *bebt*) "you have ensured salvation through mighty power". Salvation (*Heil*) combines the temporal and the eternal; the believer sees in the God-granted stability of Mühlhausen a token of the world to come, free of all dissension.

No 6 Chorus

Hic Hecuba et natae nequiquam altaria circum
praecipites atra ceu tempestate columbae
condensae et divum amplexae simulacra sedebant.

(Here Hecuba and her daughters, like doves driven headlong by a dark storm, sat huddled close together uselessly around the altar, clutching at the statues of the gods.)

Virgil: Aeneid Book 2, 515-517

Yet the present world is full of threats, against which weak humans cannot defend themselves without God's protection: "We ask that you would not give the enemy the soul of your turtle doves" (another excerpt from Psalm 74). The German *du wollest* conveys a hint of "You wouldn't, would you?" This chorus is marked *Affettuoso e larghetto* ("expressive and quite slow"), for Bach intends the maximum pathos. The doves rustle their wings in the constant murmuring of the cello part and coo in the trills and rising semitones of the instrumental parts. Meanwhile, the organ treads delicately below and the voices are set close together as if in communal defence; there are no adventurous leaps. The high range of the vocal bass contributes to the impression of weakness and as the movement advances, the overall pitch tends to rise as if in desperate entreaty. In a final moment of understated drama, all the voices subside into a monotone appeal, as if in the ancient style of plainchant.

No 7 Arioso, Chorus and soloists

The full instrumental panoply of the opening of BWV 71 returns to send off the newly elected officials. Two poetic stanzas ask God to underwrite the incoming regime, requesting first that: "This new government, in all it does, crown with blessings! Peace, calm and prosperity must constantly attend it." Each section of text receives its own treatment, as in the dance-like sway for "crown with blessings".

The Joseph in question is the Old Testament figure who was sold by his brothers into slavery, prospered in Egypt, and became the benefactor of his people. The rootedness of the text of BWV in the world of the ancient Israelites is particularly apposite. Their struggles to survive, with God and faith intact, amidst surrounding hostility mirror the sense of threat that features so often in the religious mentality of the cantatas. It is not surprising if this, rather than the life to come, is at the forefront of BWV 71, whose concern is the perpetuation of the social order under duly appointed authority.

A long fugal section, beginning with a solo quartet and gradually including the great mass of voices and instruments, is the musical symbol (compare the third movement earlier) of Joseph's – and hence the community's – endlessly renewed prosperity. The tenor part rings out *beständig* ("steadfast") before the final clamour of *Glück, Heil und großer Sieg* ("Good fortune, salvation and victory!"). At the end, violins, oboes and recorders die away in turn, echoing through space to reach the ear of God.

*

Suggested recording: Concerto Stella Matutina, dir. Alfredo Bernardini

Septuagesima

BWV 144: *Nimm, was dein ist, und gehe hin*

(Take what is yours, and go away)

Librettist: Unknown

6 February 1724

> the desire of bettering our condition…comes with us from the womb and never leaves us till we go into the grave. In the whole interval which separates those two moments, there is scarce perhaps a single instance, in which any man is so perfectly and completely satisfied with his situation, as to be without any wish of alteration or improvement of any kind.
>
> Adam Smith: *The Wealth of Nations*

Promethean discontent has no place in the outlook of Bach's sacred cantatas. Or rather, dissatisfaction tends to be directed toward the self's own failings and not those of one's surroundings. God's method of allocating good things must be trusted; social justice and human ideas of fairness are not a priority, for endurance of the given is part of the duty of faith. BWV 144 gives a musically illustrated lecture on the subject. The text takes its cue from the day's gospel reading of the parable of the vineyard (Mt. 20: 1-16). This describes the successive hiring of labourers throughout the day, when all are offered the same pay, irrespective of the work's starting point. Those who have toiled for hours protest when the newcomers receive the identical reward, but the master has no sympathy with their position. He is merely honouring the contract that he made with each individual.

No 1 Chorus

The awe-inspiring abstraction of God (unlike the figure of Christ) is rarely a personal presence in the cantatas. Here, Bach takes a brisk and concise fugue as the musical vehicle for the divine voice. The curt words of dismissal – "Take what is yours and go away" – form the entire text of the movement and are contained within the short fugue subject; the counter-subject that follows focuses on the last two words: "go away" (*gehe hin*). Strings and oboes double the voices, so that the contrapuntal texture is unadorned, though the continuo line is partly independent of the others.

Neither decorative charm nor aggressive rhetoric is needed; the asymmetry of power between master and man imposes no obligation on the former to justify his actions. Similarly – we are meant to understand – humankind can make no claim on God, so vast is the gulf between them. Complaining merely estranges the believer from the divine, something that the insistent repetition of *gehe hin* makes clear. The firmly controlled fugal structure, with its short episodes, frequent entries of the subject and counter-subject, and lack of inclination for tonal adventure (it rarely strays from the tonic key), is all laconic strength.

No 2 Alto aria

Preaching obedience, this miniature sermon makes the connection between the biblical parable and the present difficulties of life: "Do not grumble, dear Christian, when things do not go as you wish". The key remains the E minor of the preceding fugue, the instrumental texture is close-knit, and the pitch low-lying. A back-and-forth shift of semitones whines in discontent, while repeated quavers rumble in the background. The sixteen bars that precede the entry of the voice divide into two sections, with the second inverting the melody of the first. This compositional trick both gives musical variety but at the same time carries the implied message that things are not necessarily as they seem – one's standpoint may change. A touch of syncopation, i.e. rhythmic hindrance, illustrates *wenn was nicht nach Wunsch geschicht* ("when things do not go as you wish").

The *da capo* form of the aria fulfils its expressive purpose by offering in its central section a marked contrast of mood. As the text becomes more encouraging, so the key changes to the relative (G) major: "Instead, be content with what God has allotted to you; he knows what you need". This rapidly moves further in a positive tonal direction (i.e. to D major), though a repeat of the text brings a more sombre A minor. Further syncopations for "he knows what you need" (*er weiß, was dir nützlich ist*) perhaps suggest that a few obstacles along the way are part of God's plan to test the soul. A return to the A section completes the homily.

No 3 Chorale

A simply sung hymn contains the essence of BWV 144: that one should live in a state of acceptance of God's will. It is the first verse of a great Lutheran favourite, by the devout poet and teacher Samuel Rodigast (1649-1708). The words were written in 1676, possibly to console a dying friend: "What God does is done well, his will is always just; whatever he decides for me, I will submit quietly to him. He is my God, who knows well how to sustain me in distress; therefore I will just allow him to rule". The plain four-part setting, free of chromaticism, mirrors the willed simplicity of the outlook.

No 4 Tenor recit

Pious resignation, the librettist adds, is not merely virtuous, but it also coincides with self-interest, for it leads to psychological wellbeing: "Where contentment rules and takes the helm, there a person is happy with what God ordains". The harmonic language is clear and straightforward, until murky chords of the seventh accompany a different scenario: "On the other hand, where discontent has its say, grief and sorrow arise, and the heart will not be at peace". The pace steadies at the end for an allusion to Rodigast's hymn: "and people do not remember that whatever God does is well done".

No 5 Soprano aria

What does contentment sound like? In this case, a gently paced (*andante*) lyrical duet for oboe d'amore and the soprano voice: "Contentment is a treasure in this life, which can give pleasure in the greatest sadness. For it lets itself in everything be pleased with what God has arranged". The German word *Genügsamkeit* carries with it the idea of a modest satisfaction in what one has. It occurs sixteen times in the course of this short aria, and its associated musical phrase even more often; the desirable life is happy in its repetition. Bach does not look for the tragic possibilities of his B minor key, but rather to all that is steady and sober. There is a great deal of patterning which, in this brief context, sounds (as it is meant to), more sweetly compliant than tedious.

No 6 Chorale

It is surely no accident that almost every religion promises its adherents that they – and they alone – are the "chosen of god", guaranteed salvation no matter what, assured that the almighty (or whatever form the gods take) will assist them through their current difficulties if the right rituals and prayers are performed. This undoubtedly introduces a profound sense of comfort in the face of adversity.

> Robin Dunbar: *The Human Story*

The concluding hymn was written by the Markgraf Albrecht of Brandenburg-Culmbach (1522-1557), whose warlike character one would not immediately associate with meekness and resignation. Ostensibly humble, it basks in God's especial concern for his followers: "Whatever my God wills, let that be done always. His will is the best; he is prepared to help all those who believe in him steadfastly. He helps us out of trouble, this righteous God, and he punishes us justly. Whoever trusts God and builds firmly on him will not be forsaken". The harmonisation ends with an extended and oddly ambiguous cadence, as if the goal of unalloyed content must remain out of reach.

*

Suggested recording: J.S. Bach-Stiftung, dir. Rudolf Lutz

Septuagesima

BWV 92: *Ich hab in Gottes Herz und Sinn*

(I have in God's heart and mind)

Librettist: Unknown

28 January 1725

What the old man does is always right.

Hans Christian Andersen

The twelve-verse chorale on which BWV 92 is based was written by the Lutheran divine Paul Gerhardt (1607-1676). Its message is that one should regard everything that life inflicts as the will of God and submit to it always. Although there is no direct reference to the day's biblical reading (Mt.20: 1-16) – the story of the vineyard owner who granted the same reward to all his labourers, irrespective of the hours that they had worked – the connection is clear. The divine plan surpasses all human understanding, and the believer must take it on trust that even the most testing events are meant for some underlying benefit.

 Given the length of the hymn and its consistently austere tone, the librettist, and more especially the composer, had to supply contrasts of mood that would keep the listener engaged. The purpose of a cantata was to bring emotional immediacy to familiar theological concepts: to present them in an artistic format that would bring enjoyment and novelty to well-worn lessons. In fact, BWV 92 follows the chorale closely, using five of its verses verbatim, though with frequent additions by the librettist. The texts of the remaining four movements are a freer exploration of the general message that suffering is a necessary prelude to eternal salvation. Bach's challenge was to honour the chorale while adding musical colour to the lengthy script. Inventive as ever, he responded with energy and drama, rewarding piety with pleasure.

No 1 Chorus

A believer is eminently a person who knows how to obey and accept chastisement with a good grace.

> Thorstein Veblen: *The Theory of the Leisure Classes*

Gerhardt's first verse introduces the (seemingly male) Christian manifesto: "I have to God's heart and mind surrendered my own heart and mind. What seems bad is my gain; death itself is life for me. I am a son of him who has ascended the throne of heaven. Though he strike me and impose a cross, yet his heart remains well disposed". While the hymn may appear an odd mix of humility, pride and denial of instinct, Bach places it within a musical context of gentle, slightly melancholy resignation. The key is B minor and the instrumental ensemble consists of two mellow-toned oboes d'amore along with the usual strings and continuo. From them, he weaves a constantly varying texture, alternating wind and strings in the manner of a dance-like, graceful concerto movement. The easy flow of melody and rhythm is at times checked by tied notes that seem to hold their breath before the next beat, as if held back from their goal. A few bars later, the violin rises steadily upward, accompanied by an ascending sequence in the oboes; all finally converge on the keynote.

And so, when the voices finally enter with the chorale, the emotional ground is already prepared: if there is a sense of travel, there is also tranquillity and smoothness. The small buoyant phrase that began the movement becomes its constantly recurring motto, exchanged amongst the three lower voices supporting the soprano *cantus firmus* which leads in each line of the hymn. These are separated by more instrumental episodes in the style of the beginning. Though the key palette is limited (the B minor tonic, its dominant of F sharp minor, plus its own related A major), the constant interplay of parts and the ebb and flow of texture animate the surface of the music. All the instruments and voices come together to acknowledge Christ's arrival on the throne of heaven, while life's cross is signalled by a brief tonal uncertainty. The concluding bars repeat the introductory *ritornello*: a little subdued in spirit but full of charm.

No 2 Bass chorale and recit

The foundation of the text here is the second verse of the hymn, but its words also generate lengthy observations by the librettist – as if he were thinking aloud, looking for evidence in support of his beliefs. Hence Bach switches between two different styles. The chorale (now in E minor) is always introduced in the continuo by a decorated version of its initial melody, while the librettist's insertions appear in the speech-like manner of recitative.

The chorale begins: "It" (i.e God's love) "can never fail me". This inspires an apocalyptic vision: "It must happen soon, as the faithful witness himself says, that with creaks and horrible cracks the mountains and the hills will fall; but my Saviour does not let me down". A rapid collapse in the continuo accompanies the jagged vocal line. For the second line of the chorale, which proclaims "My father must love me", Bach decorates the melody with a tender prolongation of *lieben* ("love"). The proof of God's care lies in the sacrificial death of Christ:

"In Jesus's red blood I am written on his hand; he does protect me".

The hymn continues: "Even if he should cast me into the sea", at which the continuo churns below to intimate that drowning signifies the loss of faith that condemns the soul to hell. Another aside follows: "The Lord lives in great waters; he has himself given me my life; therefore I will not drown, even if the waves should seize me and their rage rush with me into the abyss". The chorale then calmly resumes: "He is just testing me" – as with the Old Testament figure of Jonah, who tried to flee God by jumping into the sea – "To see if I will think of Jonah, or whether, with Peter" (i.e. the New Testament apostle), "I will turn my mind to him. He will make me strong in faith and he will watch over my soul". Next is a rapid-fire exchange between hymn and response: "And make my spirit, which always falters and weakens, accustomed to his goodness, which nothing equals in steadfastness, and stand firm".

Thought of the indestructible divine brings a cry of: "My foot shall, until my last days, firmly ground itself upon this rock". The last few bars again increase the pace of the dialogue between chorale and commentary: "if I stand firm and let myself be fixed in rock-like faith, then surely his hand, which he already extends to me from heaven, will at the proper time raise me up again". There are aural images of God's hand reaching down and the final lifting of the gaze to the world above. Through musical means, Bach has created a bridge between the simple faith embodied in the chorale, and the theological rhetoric of the recitative. Belief sustains itself in multiple ways.

No 3 Tenor aria

Full-throttle music drama takes centre stage as the text, based on the fourth verse of the hymn, contrasts the devastation awaiting those without God's protection with the security enjoyed by the faithful. Skittering ascents in the first violin, and the disconnected tumbling of the continuo, project the violence to come. The vocal line is shrill and rhythmically distraught: "See, see! How everything tears, breaks and falls that God's strong arm does not hold". The subject matter and its setting are reminiscent of the tenor aria of BWV 81 ("Jesus sleeps, how can I hope?"), depicting the storm on the Sea of Galilee.

In both cases, the turbulence lessens as the spotlight moves to Christian fortitude: "But see how firm and immovably glorious is the one enclosed by our champion and his might". Although the form of this aria is not a strict *da capo*, it contains a central section which makes yet more demands on the singer: "Let Satan rage, storm and crash; the powerful God will make us invincible". The violence of the setting is in proportion to that perpetual fear of the weakening of faith by the imagined forces of evil.

No 4 Alto chorale

In another contrast of mood, Bach slips the fifth verse of the chorale into the harmonious envelope of a trio sonata for two oboes and continuo: "In addition, he has wisdom and understanding beyond all measure; time, place and hour are known to him – when to act and when to leave alone. He knows when joy and when suffering will serve us, his children; and what he does is all good, even if it seems to bring sorrow." The mood is serene, though the key is in the minor (F sharp). Brief musical hints of pain at the reference to suffering and sorrow are barely noticeable within the tranquil and orderly context.

No 5 Tenor recit

As in the earlier recitative, the text offers guidance and comfort. The words are loosely based on Gerhardt's eighth verse: "We no longer need to worry and fearfully consider the needs of flesh and blood as before, because we are in God's care". Christ's endurance is the model: "I think of this, how Jesus did not fear his thousandfold suffering; he regarded it as a source of everlasting joy." Given the premise, the conclusion is clear: "And for you, my Christian, your fear and torment, your bitter cross and pain, will through Jesus become salvation and sweetness. Trust God's graciousness and note what is needed". The lecture ends with a repeated call for "Patience! Patience!", and a downwards droop of semitones.

No 6 Bass aria

An effortful partnership of voice and continuo – a technical showpiece for both – tells how the trials of life are sent to ripen the spirit: "The blustering of raw winds ensures that we find a full harvest of corn". Unrelenting passagework acts out, through musical metaphor, a life buffeted by the winds of circumstance. Yet the energy is palpable, and the key has changed to D major – at least, in the outer sections of the *da capo* structure. Its central part returns to B minor for the tough lesson that an endless grind is for the good of the soul: "The cross's tempest produces fruit in a Christian. Therefore let us surrender all our life to our wise ruler. Kiss his son's hand and honour his faithful discipline". The opening section of the aria then returns to give more assurance that all is for the best.

No 7 Chorale/SATB recit

The tenth verse of Gerhardt's hymn appears in a slightly elaborated four-part setting, while solo voices in turn guide the listener through the orderly surrender of the spirit. The first two lines of the chorale, "Ah now, my God, so now I fall confidently into your hands", receive an approving nod from the bass: "Thus speaks the spirit that has entrusted itself to God, when in faith its praises the Saviour's brotherly disposition and God's faithfulness". "Take me", the chorale continues, "and make of me what you will, until my final end", to which the tenor adds: "I know for certain that I shall be unfailingly blessed when my distress and my affliction are thus ended by you".

This is the all-important Christian nexus that links sorrow now with the joy to come, confidence in which gives enormous psychological uplift – assuming the mental construct of a beneficent supreme power. The chorale underlines the point – "As you well know that through it my spirit gains benefit" – and the alto observes that Christian contentment frustrates the devil: "so that already on this earth, to Satan's annoyance, your heavenly kingdom shows inside me". The conclusion of the chorale verse is that as a result of such acquiescence, "your honour may ever more and more be exalted". The soprano voice ends with the soul's desire to praise: "Thus can my heart, in accordance with your will, O my Jesus, blessedly calm itself, and I can with muted strings prepare a new song for the Prince of Peace".

No 8 Soprano aria

Bach accordingly softens the sound of the string instruments by instructing them to play *pizzicato* throughout i.e. plucked rather than sustained, as with the gentle strumming of a guitar. Their quartet, standing alone without the chordal filling of the organ, lightly accompanies the voice and a solo oboe. The intended effect is sweet and ingenuous, and the rhythm sedately dancelike, as befits the happy soul: "To my shepherd I will remain faithful. If he wishes to fill the cup of my cross, I shall rest completely in his will – he stands by me in my suffering". Small deviations from the D major key allow for the darker side of life, but faith is unruffled: "After weeping, Jesus's sun will shine again. To my shepherd I will remain faithful. I live for Jesus, who shall rule". Death – always the main issue – is to be of little consequence: "Rejoice, heart, you can now go cold through dying; Jesus has done enough". The voice floats to a serene: "Amen: Father, accept me into heaven".

No 9 Chorale

BWV 92 ends with the twelfth and last verse of Gerhardt's hymn, scored in four-part harmony: "Should I then also travel on the way of death and its dark streets – well then, I step on the road and path that your eyes direct me to. You are my shepherd, who will bring all things to such an end that one day, within your hall, I may honour you forever".

Separating the domains of the person and the political, BWV 92 follows a route that leads both to resignation and optimism: stoically realistic, yet with dreams of a transformative unknown. Typical of the cantata texts in general, it attempts to mitigate the fear of death by absorbing it into a larger edifice of the hopeful imagination. Like many concepts, it may seem to rest on thin air, but its effects are practical enough if it loosens the grip of the mind's deepest fears.

*

Suggested recording: J.S. Bach-Stiftung, dir Rudolf Lutz

Septuagesima

BWV 84: *Ich bin vergnügt mit meinem Glücke*

(I am content with my lot)

Librettist: Unknown

9 February 1727

In societies where most of us need storage lockers more than we need nanotech miracle boxes, we need to declare that we have enough stuff.

Bill McKibben: *Enough*

The theme of BWV 84 is a sense of gratitude for life that would suit the interests neither of big business nor of a social justice campaigner. It is a response to the day's scriptural allegory of the labourers in a vineyard (Mt.20: 1-16) who complained that they had not been fairly treated. Those who had worked long hours received no more pay than those who came later. Their grievance was dismissed by the owner, who had promised the same amount to all. The intended lesson is that believers should be happy with what God has allotted them and not compare themselves with others, for the divine purpose cannot be grasped by the human mind. The mood of BWV 84 is personal and intimate, using only a solo soprano voice, along with an ensemble of string, continuo and oboe. It is also one of the shorter cantatas, comprising two arias with linked recitatives, plus a final chorale. With no need to express and then resolve inner conflicts, its message is consistent in its bright-eyed and humble piety; the vivacity of the music counteracts what might otherwise seem a cloying catalogue of contentment.

No 1 Soprano aria

As with certain other religions – eastern or western – Christianity embodies a tension between material and presumed spiritual values. The opposition between the two appears constantly in the texts of Bach's sacred cantatas, never more so than in BWV 84. This is where music plays its part, for the pleasure it gives is real and yet unquantifiable in material terms. Like other forms of art, it can act as a surrogate for spiritual riches; hence this aria, with its elaborately ornamented lines for the solo oboe and voice, expresses inner abundance in a language that soars above the text: "I am content with my lot which the dear God has granted me".

There are many occasions when Bach uses the timbre of the oboe as an expression of human feeling. An obvious example is the opening aria of BWV 82, *Ich habe genug*. In that particular case, the listener's response is conditioned from the outset by the oboe's poignant rising interval of the minor sixth, followed by a sinuous lament. Here, in BWV 84, the melodic and rhythmic contours are different: full of sprung energy and lavish with trills, while the pulse suggests an elegant dance. Such is the independent importance of the oboe that this movement could be part of a concerto – yet with the voice as co-soloist, as the two elements match each other in virtuosic challenge.

At the same times, there is an impression of innocence in the light tread of the other parts and the relative simplicity of the underlying harmonies. The remainder of the text arrives in the central part of Bach's structure: "If I am not to have great riches, then I thank him for small gifts and am not even worthy of them". Some modest, i.e. neither unexpected nor startling, changes of key give tonal variety, but the style, along with the sentiments, remains the same. Delight in the given maps on to the outpouring of oboe and voice. The repeated thanks for the "small gifts" (*kleine Gaben*) turn into a melodic cornucopia. Bach completes the aria with a slightly modified repeat of its opening, leading it to rest in the security of the E minor tonic key.

No 2 Soprano recit

Use every man after his desert, and who should 'scape whipping?

Shakespeare: *Hamlet*

Another foundational tenet of Christianity is the moral unworthiness of all humankind in the face of God, which precludes all sense of entitlement: "God indeed owes me nothing, and when he gives me something, he shows that he loves me. I can earn nothing from him, for what I do is my duty". Virtue signalling is out of the question: "Yes! however good my deeds seem to be, I have still accomplished nothing righteous". The train of thought leads to a corrective of discontent: "Yet human nature is so impatient that it often becomes unhappy when the dear God has not given it an overflow of things. Has he not for such a long time fed and clothed us for nothing, and will he not one day lift us blessedly into his glory? It is enough for me that I need not go hungry to bed". Faith sets a low bar.

No 3 Soprano aria

Then happy low, lie down!

Shakespeare: *Henry IV Part II*

There is an uncomplicated directness in this musical celebration of the simple life: "I eat with gladness my scanty bread and sincerely do not grudge my neighbour what is his". The protagonists, other than the singer, are a solo violin (scraping away like a folk fiddler) and again the oboe, though now without ornamentation. The vocal line – remembering that in Bach's time it would have been a boy soprano – is similarly disarming, with little jumps for joy. The key is G major, which is to say, the brighter side of the E minor of the opening aria, though this reappears in the more introspective inner portion: "A calm conscience, a joyful spirit, a grateful heart that glorifies and praises, increases blessing and sweetens need". Always attentive to the words, Bach picks out *Not* ("need") for a touch of chromatic melancholy, *ruhig* ("calm") for a long, still note, and *fröhlicher* ("joyful") for a little melodic extravagance. After a slight pause, the upbeat energy of the opening resumes. Is it poverty that is invigorating, or the freedom from envy?

No 4 Soprano recit

The slow, quiet background of the strings tells the listener that here is the heart of the matter. All endurance in this life is for the sake of a reward out of reach in the present: "In the sweat of my brow I will meantime take my bread, and when the course of my life, my life's evening, comes to an end, God will dole out my pennies to me as sure as heaven stands". The ideal of the afterlife is the greatest longing of existence, its touchstone of value: "Oh! If I have this gift and payment of grace, then I need nothing further". A cadence in F sharp minor awaits the conclusion of the cantata.

No 5 Chorale

The words are by the aristocratic Ämilie-Juliane of Schwarzburg-Rudolfstadt (1637-1706), a noted female hymn writer. While one imagines that she would not have lacked the basics of life, neither can one assume that she knew nothing of suffering. The search for meaning knows no barriers of class or creed: "I live meanwhile contented in you and die without any grief; I am satisfied with how God ordains things. I believe it and of it I am certain: through your grace and Christ's blood, you will make my ending good". The conflict in the cantatas is always between two types of symbolic goods: those that signify visible status in the world, and those that answer to the need for an invisible and eternal standard of value. The flesh and blood human must balance their respective claims.

*

Suggested recording: Concentus Musicus Wien, dir. Nikolaus Harnoncourt

Sexagesima

BWV 18: *Gleichwie der Regen und Schnee vom Himmel fällt*

(Just as the rain and snow come down from heaven)

Librettist: Erdmann Neumeister

February 1713

In 1700, the deeply conservative Lutheran pastor Erdmann Neumeister published an innovative volume of libretti for church cantatas, recasting in poetic form the private meditations associated with his preaching. Later, he began to include biblical extracts amongst his verses, creating scripts that offered a range of possibilities for the exploration of faith in music. The text of BWV 18, from a collection produced by Neumeister in 1711, contains a typical variety, bringing together references to the Old and New Testaments, the Lutheran litany (a set of appeals to God), and Neumeister's own explanatory comments; it concludes with a chorale.

The gospel reading for the day (Lk. 8:4-15) is Christ's parable of the sower, which imagines God's word as a seed that is nurtured by the human spirit – provided that its growth is not choked by opposing influences. The importance of the biblical word to Lutheranism cannot be overstated. The right – the need – of the individual to engage personally with scripture, without the gatekeeping authority of the Catholic Church, was a founding principle of the Protestant Reformation. While Protestantism lost no time in developing its own orthodoxies, the maxim of sola scriptura (scripture alone) remained a rallying cry. As Neumeister's primary concern was to unfold the implications of the day's gospel excerpt, the music of BWV 18 is exceptionally detailed in its response to the text: in particular, its expanses of recitative portray the terrors and threats surrounding the Christian community as it seeks protection in the revealed word of God.

No 1 Sinfonia

Perhaps to restore the balance between the roles of the verbal and the musical, Bach begins with an instrumental piece. BWV 18 dates from Bach's time (1708-1717) at the court of Weimar, where he had access to the scores of Italian string concerti. This opening movement, combining the lyrical flow of Corelli (1653-1713) with the neat structure typical of Vivaldi (1678-1741), is a stylised evocation of the scene of the parable. The fall of rain and snow, and the stirrings of new life, are represented in turn by a sequence of descending fifths and an imitative outgrowth of one upper part from another. The key is G minor and the timbres are unusually dark – four violas, bassoon, cello and double bass – though when the cantata appeared subsequently in Leipzig, Bach added two recorders to brighten the effect. With his alternations of falling, pattering, and growth, Bach builds a structure that is knit together by the repeated unison motto of the beginning. The central section passes the musical tokens of rain, snow and germination from one group to another, combing and recombining in a way that, despite the introverted sound quality, suits the idea of nature's creativity. God's world is both orderly and life-giving.

No 2 Bass recit

The picture of God the sower appeared originally in the Old Testament Book of Isaiah (Is.55: 10-11), which Neumeister quotes at length: "Just as the rain and snow fall from heaven, and do not return to it but water the earth, making it fruitful and fertile, so that it gives seed for sowing and bread for eating: so shall my word be, that goes from my mouth. It shall not return to me empty, but it shall do what pleases me and succeed in the purpose for which I sent it". Bach transmits the speech with the authority of the bass voice, accompanied by the deep tones of bassoon and double bass, in addition to the organ continuo.

The text is presented as four musically differentiated sections, alternating rhythmic freedom with passages that are regularly paced. It begins with visual imagery, as the pitch of the vocal line falls along with the rain and snow. Then, at the thought of a productive land, the rhythm steadies and the key turns to the major. The reference to God's word again uses the more naturalistic style of recitative, though embellished with trills as a measure of its status. Finally, with the fulfilment of the divine purpose, the movement ends with a dignified pulse, while settling back in G minor.

No 3 Tenor/bass recits, litany for soprano and chorus

In essence, this verbally detailed movement consists of the fourfold reiteration of the Lutheran litany, preceded each time by Neumeister's dramatic commentary. His purpose is clear: not to let the familiarity of the ritual prayer dull the mind to its significance. What is at stake is the protection of a group bound together in faith. Their shared outlook rests on the biblical word as the source of revealed truth; it is the token of both individual and communal identity, and subject to external threats.

With his changes of tempo and key, and exceptionally vivid word painting, Bach gives musical colour to the hopes, terrors and warnings of the preacher. First, softly sustained chords from the accompanying violas establish a mood of intimate reflection. The prayer for tenor voice is set calmly in Eb major: "My God, here is my heart. I open it to you in Jesus's name; scatter your seeds in it as if on good ground. My God, here is my heart: let it bring fruit a hundred times over. Oh Lord, Lord, help! O Lord, let it succeed well!" At this point, the music enters another world of urgent, imploring need. The pace quickens, the volume increases, and the key changes to the minor for the appearance of the litany. It is sung antiphonally, split between the soprano chant – "May you grant your spirit and power to the Word" – and an answering choral cry of "Hear us, dear Lord God!".

With a return to the thoughtful style of the beginning, the bass voice considers the first obstacle to the reception of the sacred Word: that pervasive force of evil that Christian belief characterises as the devil. The key remains in the minor and the setting becomes chromatically twisted: "But forbid, faithful father, that either I or any Christian should be perverted by the devil's deceit. His mind is entirely set on robbing us" (note the agitated length of *berauben*) "of your word, with the blessing that it brings". Another furious interpolation of the litany cries out to "Tread Satan under our feet".

The next menace, identified by the tenor, is the oppression that causes some to falter in their loyalty: "Ah, many deny word and faith, and fall away like rotten fruit when they have to suffer persecution" (Bach subjects *Verfolgung* to musical torture) "then they fall into eternal grief for the sake of avoiding a temporary pain". The litany points the finger at the known enemies – genuinely the case, in the history of Lutheranism: "And from the Turk's and the Pope's cruel murder and blasphemies, rages and storms, preserve us like a father". The continuo storms below.

Much the longest time, verbally and musically, is spent on the threat of self-indulgence, of succumbing to the demands of the flesh and material goods. The bass fulminates: "Another cares only for his belly, while completely forgetting his soul" (an existing portrait shows Neumeister as a well-nourished individual); "Mammon also has taken hold of many hearts, so that the Word can gain no power. How many souls are the prisoners of sensuality? So greatly does the world lead them astray! The world, which for them takes the place of heaven, from which they have strayed" (the setting of *irregehen* wanders into the distance). The final part of the litany completes the movement: "All those who have erred and gone astray, bring back. Hear us, dear Lord God".

No 4 Soprano aria

After so much mental tumult, the Christian soul assures itself of its commitment to divine truth: "My soul's treasure is God's Word. All other treasures are just nets spun by the world and Satan to ensnare base souls". Bach's setting is correspondingly smooth, with the four violas in flowing unison, predictable rhythmic patterns, and a solidly Eb major tonality. There is a little more vocal animation for the waving off of temptation: "Away with them all, away, away!", but not so as to create dissonance. Having moved for the moment to the relative (C) minor, the key returns at last to its sanctuary in the major; faith is immovable.

No 5 Chorale

This is the eighth verse of a hymn by Lazarus Spengler (1479-1534): "I pray, O Lord, from the depth of my heart, that you will not take from me your holy word. Then I will not be ashamed of my sin and guilt, for in your graciousness I place all my trust. Whoever firmly relies on it will not see death". Spengler was an early and devoted follower of Luther and, like him, excommunicated by the Pope in 1521. The conflicts of belief between Catholic and Protestant that were alluded to in the litany threatened life's prospects both in this world and the next. What creature other than the human will kill for the sake of ideology?

*

Suggested recording: Ricercar Consort, dir. Philippe Pierlot

Sexagesima

BWV 126: *Erhalt uns, Herr, bei deinem Wort*

(Keep us, Lord, in your Word)

Librettist: Unknown

4 February 1725

> God has ordained two governments: the spiritual, by which the Holy spirit produces Christians and righteous people under Christ; and the temporal, which restrains the un-Christian and wicked so that – no thanks to them – they are obliged to keep still and to maintain an outward peace.
>
> Martin Luther: *LW 45:91*

Most societies have their sacred or quasi-sacred texts that their members huddle around for security. Psychological protection and physical protection are interdependent; a shared mental framework becomes a fraternal bond, a badge of common identity and source of stability, both individual and communal. Conformity in thought brings practical benefits (if also risks).

    A central theme of Bach's cantatas is therefore the need to stand firm with what is believed to be the truth of God, as revealed in scripture. Yet as the Bible is a collection of diverse texts, there has always been space for different interpretations, often promoted with violent intensity. With its multiple possibilities, Christian lore can seem more like the I Ching, the ancient Chinese book of divination, than the precise code of Hammurabi. Luther, of course, had his own strong views on the message of personal salvation promised by the New Testament account of Christ. He insisted on the right of each individual to engage directly with God without the mediation of a priestly caste, and at the same time took his cue from St. Paul in connecting obedience to the divine Word with social order. The final reckoning of merits and demerits was for the life to come.

The subject of BWV 126, as with its predecessors for this day (BWV 18 and BWV 181), is the primary importance of God's Word. Musically highly coloured, its anchorage lies in a hymn written by Luther in 1541. The cantata text is haunted by a sense of danger – a familiar theme in the cantatas – and calls on God as warlike defender of his people. There are allusions to both of the day's gospel readings: the parable of the sowing of God's Word in the human soul along with the obstacles that it may meet (Lk. 8:4-15), and the assertion in Paul's second letter to the Corinthians (2 Cor.11:19- 12:9) that divine grace works through human weakness. The admission of helplessness is both a necessary and sufficient condition of God's blessing. This in turn confers more than spiritual goods. A realm in which citizens are united in their devotion to God's word may also – so Luther imagined – hope for benevolent rulers, peace and good government.

No 1 Chorus

Luther saw the antichrist as being at work in the papacy because that which had been added to the gospel had adulterated its purity.

Bernhard Lohse: *Martin Luther*, trans. Robert C. Schultz

Both the struggles out of which the reformed church had emerged two centuries earlier, and the Turkish military might that had once menaced Christian Europe, clearly lingered in the eighteenth-century religious memory. Luther's chorale still resonated: "Keep us in your word, Lord, and steer us clear of the murderous intentions of the Pope and the Turks, who wish to overthrow Jesus Christ, your Son, from his throne". Taut and brilliant, the setting of the old hymn arms itself with the trumpet above the ensemble of oboes, strings and continuo. Fanfare-like cries of *Erhalt* ("Keep us") in the lower voices propel onward the first line of the soprano melody. In the succeeding lines, references to the enemy's wickedness seethe with semiquavers below. Yet the endless upbeat energy points to victory.

No 2 Tenor aria

The text – "Send down your power, Lord of Lords, mighty God" – derives from Luther's second verse. Bach begins with the musico-visual representation of flow from above: two oboes, accompanied by the continuo, pour out a stream of lyrical descending phrases. The voice follows in the same style, though becoming more crisply rhetorical for a rising sequence of salutes to the Almighty: *Herr der Herren, starker Gott* ("Lord of Lords, mighty God"). A shift to the dominant key leads to a contrasted central section with its three further lines: "to make your Church rejoice/and the foe's bitter mockery/in an instant to dispel". The vocal part suddenly changes character, bounding and cascading in a display of virtuosity as if with uncontrollable joy (to stay within the beat is a genuine challenge for the singer). A similar, though even more strenuous scattering of notes – surely a deliberate nod to the parable of the sower – has the derisive opponents tossed away to the four winds. A modified version of the opening of the aria completes the design.

No 3 Alto/tenor recit and chorale

Every hymn was part of a sacred tradition: at once an illustration of an aspect of faith and a way to unite the communal voice. Particular reverence would no doubt have surrounded the hymns ascribed to Luther himself;

Bach's setting here of the third verse of the chorale is one of his most inventive.

The librettist had interleaved the lines of the hymn with his own reflections. This – a familiar situation – required Bach to differentiate the separate elements while giving a coherent shape to the whole. In such cases, the obvious solution was to present the asides in the freer style of recitative, while leaving the lines of the chorale in their original form. Here, Bach gives additional variety by alternating the sections of recitative and hymn between alto and tenor. He emphasises the chorale further by presenting it in a slow (*adagio*) tempo, by embellishing its melody, and by combining it in a duet with the other voice; the words are identical, but the melodic lines are independent.

The extra portions of text underline the fear that haunts the Lutheran consciousness; without divine aid, humanity is vulnerable. The alto voice begins: "Mankind's favour and might are of little use if you do not protect this poor little band of ours"; in response, the chorale looks to the defender as "God, Holy Spirit, dear comforter". Next, the tenor takes up the baton of recitative with a generalised accusation of wrong think: "You know that the persecuted city of God has its worst enemy within itself, through the danger of false brethren". The chorale then prays for unity – "Give your people one mind on earth" – and the alto adds: "That we, members of Christ's body, may be one in faith, united in life".

This leads to an exposure of the deepest terror – that of death – in Luther's plea to: "Stand by us in our last hour of need!". In the image of God as gatekeeper to, and enabler of, immortality lies the consoling strength of Christian belief: that is, provided that the mind keeps itself on the path of faith, for it contains its own power of self-destruction, generally projected on to the devil. In the final portion of recitative, the tenor voice identifies the evil influence that would at the end of life deny the hope of heaven: "The last enemy then breaks in on us and would remove the comfort from our hearts; yet let yourself be known then as our helper." The two voices then combine in the supreme prayer: "Lead us into life out of death!"

No 4 Bass aria

For [Luther] the world was a combat zone where the forces of darkness and light battled each other for creation, including the souls of human beings.

Richard Marius: *Martin Luther*

With the aural symbols of power – heroic vocal leaps, crashing descents and furious arpeggios – it appears that the mind has conquered its demons, though it ascribes the victory to the Almighty: "Cast to the ground this pompous pride! Frustrate its plans!" The unrelenting pace and punch, without a trace of lyrical charm, suggests a battle to the limits, with the continuo part engaged in a game of musical snakes and ladders: alternately crashing down and then climbing laboriously up. Roaring, striding, assertive, the vocal line embodies all that the feeble human cannot achieve unaid but may exult in vicariously. In the central section of the *da capo* structure, Bach increases the sense of drama with yet more spectacular demands on the voice to match the extravagant rhetoric of the text: "Let the abyss suddenly devour it; curb the raging of the enemy's might, never let its desires succeed!" Doubt has been crushed.

No 5 Tenor recit

All that remained for the librettist was to summarise the lesson of BWV 126: that a transcendent source of truth exists; that humans may – in fact should – gain access to it through biblical texts; and that its function is to protect and unify those who believe in it. In contrast with the emotionalism of the preceding aria, the style is straightforwardly speech like, making its points one by one: "Thus your Word and truth will be revealed and presented in the highest splendour – that you watch over your Church and make the teachings of the holy Word fruitful with blessing". The ending, though, is part statement, part expression of hope: "And if you would turn to us as helper, then in peace we will be granted an overflow of blessing".

No 6 Chorale

Two hymns were spliced together in a majestic four-part setting to make a weighty conclusion. The first is Luther's prayer for peace (inspired by the Latin *Dona nobis pacem*): "Grant us peace graciously, Lord God, for our times; there is indeed no other who could fight for us than you, our God alone". The second is by Luther's younger contemporary, the musician Johann Walter (1496-1570). It gives voice to a longing that most can understand: "Grant our princes and all in authority peace and good government, that we under them may lead a peaceable and quiet life in all godliness and honour. Amen". The rule of law – arguably one of the conditions for human flourishing – has often been thought to need divine endorsement. Which god, and what his (or her) preferences are imagined to be, is another question.

*

Suggested recording: English Baroque Soloists, dir. John Eliot Gardiner

Sexagesima

BWV 181: *Leichtgesinnter Flattergeister*

(Empty headed, fluttering souls)

Librettist: Unknown

13 February 1724

> Endowed with unbelievable cleverness, mankind sometimes takes the bad direction, sometimes the good.
>
> Sophocles: *Antigone*

This is the second cantata (the first was BWV 18) inspired by the parable of God as sower of truth in the human heart (Lk. 8:4-15). Sometimes, according to the allegory, it fails to take root, either as birds devour the seed (the malice of the devil), or from the stoniness of the soil (the mind's indifference), or because thorns choke the new growth (the lure of the flesh and the world). The librettist lists these various scenarios, which Bach duly illustrates with pictorial flair. Nonetheless, whatever the proximate cause, the result for those who turn their back on faith will always be the same: eternal doom in hell. After the lesson has been spelled out in a succession of solo arias and recitatives, BWV 181 ends in a large-scale, triumphant chorus, exulting in the comfort that God's word brings, and praying for its continuation.

No 1 Bass aria

In the biblical account, the birds are the symbol of the devil's trickery. The librettist of BWV 181 likewise portrays those who allow themselves to be deprived of spiritual nourishment as feeble-brained collaborators:

"Empty-headed fluttering souls rob themselves of the Word's power. Belial" (i.e. Satan) "and his children seek to block it so that it brings no benefit". Deliberately disjointed, the music revels in the conflation of ideas: sound picture and mental concept unite in the ungainly phrases, staccato peckings and squawks which ridicule the unbeliever. Yet the cries of "Belial" caution the listener that this is more than comedy, for the forces of evil are at work: descending scales in the continuo lead the imagination to the world below. Possibly because the chief business of this aria is its pictorial effect, the structure is relatively simple. Its two main elements - the mockery aimed at the unbelievers and the shouts of warning appear, with small changes of key, in ABAB alternation. The backdrop of musical satire remains the same throughout.

No 2 Alto recit

In turn indignant and sorrowful, this sermon turns on those shallow beings who deliver themselves into Satan's power: "O unhappy state of perverted souls, who are, as it were, the seed at the wayside! And who could describe Satan's cunning when he steals the Word from the heart whose understanding is too blind to perceive or believe its harm?". The harmonies are deliberately unstable, lurching from one chord of the seventh to another. Yet as the text goes on to mingle outrage with hints of concern for the sinner's welfare, the angular contours of recitative soften to the more melodic style of *arioso*: "They must have hearts of stone to wickedly resist and make light of their own salvation; they will one day go to their ruin".

Repeated notes in the voice and continuo parts hint at obstinacy, until an eventual collapse in pitch points toward the descent to hell. Finally, and with typical circular logic, the bible (faith in which is the point at issue) is mined for examples of the miraculous power of the divine: "Christ's final word causes the rocks themselves to split as the angel's hand moves the gravestone; yes, and the rod of Moses brings water out of a mountain". The stone of the sepulchre rolls down majestically in the arpeggios of the continuo, and a lyrical descent in the vocal line paints the stream of water. One last appeal (to the potential backsliders in the congregation?) is tinged with harmonic pathos: "Would you, O heart, be even harder than these?"

No 3 Tenor aria

The literature of Hell boasts famous villains, but most of the damned are ordinary people like you and me, each judged to be deserving of eternal punishment for their own private sins.

> Scott G. Bruce: *The Penguin Book of Hell*

Only the vocal and the continuo parts of this movement have survived; modern performers are left to devise a suitable addition, possibly with a solo violin or the organ. But the lesson of the text is clear enough: "The infinite numbers of harmful thorns – concern for sensual pleasure and increasing one's wealth – will feed the fire of hell's torment throughout eternity". From the time signature (3/8) and the light, detached tread of the continuo, it seems that the route to the world below will be speedy. The word setting is once more full of pictorial associations, as with the great spread of *zumehren* ("increase"); the fire (*Feuer*) that burns over several bars; the lingering over *Ewigkeit* ("eternity"); and the melodic twists of *Qual* ("torment"). All the same, the energy has its charm, as if the frivolous ones are dancing their way into the clutches of Satan.

No 4 Soprano recit

After a succession of minor keys, the sudden brightness of D major points the way to those who offer their souls as fertile ground for God's Word. Spiritual cultivation cannot be left until the last moment: "By these things the Word's strength is choked, and the noble seed lies useless in someone who does not prepare his spirit and heart in good time". A life of obedience to God promises happiness now and forever: "so our heart may taste the sweetness which this Word reveals to us, the powers of this life and its future".

No 5 Chorus

After the stick, the carrot. The warnings disappear as music and text celebrate the great benefits of faith: "Grant us, O highest, at all times our heart's comfort: your Holy Word". A trumpet arrives to crown the entire ensemble of flute, oboe, strings and four voices. Half march, half vigorous dance, the rhythm, along with the straightforward major tonality, sweeps the listener along in its path. It is one of the anomalies of the religious culture of the cantatas that the pleasure of music – with the instinctive bodily response that it generates – escapes the general stricture against indulging the senses. The festive style is equally applicable to secular and sacred, for divine glory can only be imagined as a projection of visible pomp.

What counts especially is the architectural design. Bach offers an artistic analogy of the cosmos that God's rule represents – a world of order and consequently abundance. The overall structure of the movement is a three-part *da capo*, in which the repeated outer sections, like nesting dolls, contain their own triple symmetry. They are made up of two identical instrumental *ritornelli* which enclose a richly inventive fugal word setting.

Technically accomplished as ever (using three countersubjects), Bach highlights the concept of time (*Zeiten*), holding it fast in the soprano, bass and then alto parts against the surrounding activity; God's Word stands for ever.

The central section of the chorus brings the remainder of the text and a more intimate manner, for this is the soul's pledge of openness to the divine Word: "You alone, through your almighty hand, can prepare in our hearts a good and fertile soil". Soprano and alto, now accompanied only by the continuo, weave an elaborate duet of homage. As a return to the opening splendour perhaps confirms, while God may speak in words, the human – Bach at least – responds with music.

*

Suggested recording: Bach Collegium Japan, dir. Masaaki Suzuki

Quinquagesima

BWV 22: *Jesus nahm zu sich die Zwölfe*

(Jesus gathered the twelve to him)

Librettist: Unknown

7 February 1723

From 1717 to 1723, Bach was director of music at the court of Cöthen. It was a good position; he was well paid and enjoyed the respect and encouragements of Leopold, his music-loving prince. As the official form of worship at the court was Calvinist (too austere for music), Bach's duties did not as a rule include the performance of church cantatas; his function was to provide other types of musical entertainment.

An initial period of creative and personal satisfaction was brought to an end first by the sudden death (in Bach's absence) of his wife Maria Barbara in 1720, and then by the reduction in princely support for the musical activities of the court. In the latter half of 1720, Bach had already considered a move to Hamburg, and two years later he applied for the post of Cantor at the Thomaskirche in Leipzig. For the audition, he brought two cantatas, one to be performed before and the other after the sermon; BWV 22 was the first of these, and BWV 23 the second.

7 February was the Sunday before the beginning of Lent: the six weeks when the devout mind prepares itself through fasting and meditation for the solemn remembrance of Christ's crucifixion. at Easter time. In one of the scriptural readings for the day (Lk.18:31-43), Christ calls together his twelve disciples for the final journey to Jerusalem. He talks of his approaching death, but they cannot understand. With this in mind, the

librettist created a script that brings the listener directly to the biblical scene: first as onlooker and then absorbed in the role of disciple, though now no longer ignorant.

At issue is the centrality of suffering in life. The Christian attitude is not merely to regard it as unavoidable, but to make a virtue out of necessity. Each life should be a symbolic journey to the cross, rejecting the comforts of the physical self for the sake of everlasting spiritual benefits. With relatively modest forces – strings, oboe, and a choir large enough to contrast solo voices with the group – Bach refashions the sermon as a personal drama of the soul that first watches and then takes its place alongside the self-sacrificing Saviour.

No 1 Arioso/chorus

The words are from the day's gospel reading: "Jesus gathered the twelve to him and said, 'Behold, we are going up to Jerusalem and all that is written of the Son of Man will be completed'; but they understood nothing and did not know what he meant". The music converts the text into a compressed piece of theatre. Six bars for instruments alone predict the coming events: the steadily upward journeying of strings and oboes leads to falls of a sixth and the droop of a semitone, while the continuo proceeds in a sequence of descending scales over a seventh.

From these three motivic elements, Bach weaves the backdrop to the first section of his text. A few words from the narrator – the characteristic tenor sound of the evangelist – introduce the scene: "Jesus gathered the twelve to him and said". This flows immediately into the voice of Christ – sung, as usual, by the bass – with his call for attention: *Sehet* ("See"). He continues in a lyrically ornate style that pays homage both to his high status and the critical importance of his message: "we are going up to Jerusalem and all that is written of the Son of Man will be completed". All the while, oboe, strings and continuo add their lamenting commentary.

Having ended the first, repeated presentation of Christ's words with a move to the subdominant key (a hint perhaps of yielding to the divine will), Bach takes up the text again with even more embellishment. Nothing, however, can dispel the disciples' ignorance. Their perplexed chatter is captured in a rapid choral fugue which integrates expressive purpose Bach's technical expertise. Four solo voices lead the way, with the fugal entries adrift from the usual tonic/dominant alternation. One of the countersubjects, with its abruptly syncopated *was das*, suggests a puzzled: "What's that?". With the gradual entry of all the voices and instruments, the volume grows until it reaches a climax in a shrill chromatic ascent for the sopranos – so that the movement ends, as it began, in G minor.

No 2 Alto aria

Unlike the disciples, the believer does know the significance of what is to come and pledges the self's readiness to follow in the steps of Christ: "My Jesus, draw me to you; I am prepared, I will depart from here and go to your agony in Jerusalem". The setting flows willingly enough: solo oboe and voice partner each other in a sedately dance-like trio sonata – yet the (C) minor key, the swoops and sighs of the oboe melody especially, and the halting syncopations resist lightheartedness. Similarly, the tonality wavers between major and minor, for instance darkening for sudden dramatic effect on *Leiden* ("agony").

The personal relevance of the crucifixion becomes clear in the brief central section of the aria: "It is a blessing for me if I can fully understand the importance of this time of suffering and dying: that it brings consolation". A four-fold repetition of *wohl mir* ("it is a blessing for me") underlines the perennial paradox: that what is terrible in human terms will yet bring about the supreme good. Just as Christ's death on the cross enabled his resurrection, so it has also brought the prospect of immortality to all who believe in his miracle-working divinity. Having made this connection, the pious soul again resolves to follow Jesus to the end; the final *Leiden* becomes a musically tortured preparation for a perfect cadence in C minor, after which the oboe ritornello then completes its solitary journey.

No 3 Bass recit

Sharing the vocal identity of Christ (i.e. the bass voice), the believer explains to himself – and hence to the surrounding audience – the full implications of following the path to Jerusalem. Only those who sever the connection of the soul to the body, seeking happiness in the world beyond rather than the lures of the present, are truly able to follow in the Saviour's path. String chords shimmer above as the theology unwinds.

It begins with a plea that is also a declaration of intent: "My Jesus, draw me, then I will run" (the notes sprint along the stave) "for flesh and blood, like your disciples, simply cannot understand what is meant. It yearns for the world and the greatest crowd". The human dilemma is the wish to share in the coming glory without the sacrifices that it entails: "Both they and my physical being wish, when they see you transfigured, to build a secure fortress of Tabor's mount" (the librettist's reference is to the radiant vision of Christ that was said to have appeared on Mount Tabor to the favoured disciples Peter, James and John).

The harmonies then move out of their comfort zone to paint the scene of horror: "but they look away from Golgotha, so full of suffering and your humiliation";

at the latter word (*Niedrigkeit*) Bach has the outline of the chord collapse in on itself. Only the extinguishing of all immediate desire will do: "Ah! crucify in me – in my corrupted breast – above all this world and all forbidden pleasure". Only through perfect detachment from the body can the cross, as promise of a transcendent afterlife, be understood: "Then I will grasp your meaning perfectly and go to Jerusalem with a thousand joys". Three final melodic bars in the major (Bb) key show the sense of release from the physical being and consequent identity with Christ.

No 4 Tenor aria

It is a commonplace that religious people seem, in general at least, to be happier than those who lack religious belief. Indeed, there is good empirical evidence to support this...One reason must be that they feel they have greater control over the circumstances that beset them – God will look after them, whatever happens.

> Robin Dunbar: *The Human Story*

A constant irony of Bach's sacred cantatas is that the happiness of the spiritual self is expressed through the sensuous pleasure given by music. Very often in fact (as here), it is the rhythm of the dance that seems best to convey the joy of union with heaven, even if – in fact probably because – it is conditional on self-denial: "My all in all, my everlasting good, improve my heart, change my disposition; strike everything down that blocks the renunciation of the flesh!". The style is all lightness, with skipping ornaments in the first violin part. The key naturally is in the major: the Bb that concluded the recitative and which is a tonal transformation of the G minor of the opening chorus. Bach's design is in three parts, with the text of the central section looking ahead to the eternal rest that death will bring: "Yet when I am spiritually mortified, then draw me towards you into peace". The pause that ends the three-bar lingering on *Friede* ("peace") leaves thought suspended in the realm beyond. Similarly, in the modified repeat of the first part of the aria, the soul's everlasting good (*ewiges Gut*) stretches into the symbolic eternity of eight bars, while the voice at last echoes the brilliance of the violin.

No 5 Chorale

The lines are from a hymn (see also BWV 96) by Elisabeth Kreutziger. Leaving the convent and fleeing to Wittenberg, she became part of Luther's circle and, in her all too brief life (1500-1535), a noted poet. Music and words combine here in that merging of concepts of life and death that is rooted in Christian belief and is especially marked in Bach's Lutheran texts. At the heart of it is a certain disgust at being human: the self must in some sense will its own destruction so that it may live forever free of the body. In this project, it calls upon the help of the deity that the religious imagination creates: "Mortify us with your goodness, awaken us through your grace; destroy the old human nature, so that the new may prosper on this earth, and so that our mind and all our desires and thoughts may be directed towards you." Bach inserts this willed annihilation into a context of endless movement with a flowing descant for oboe and violin in unison. Music, as ever, is the template for the life to come.

*

Suggested recording: The Monteverdi Choir,
dir. John Eliot Gardiner

Quinquagesima

BWV 23: *Du Wahrer Gott und Davids Sohn*

(You, the true God and David's son)

Librettist: Unknown

7 February 1723

When Bach came from Cöthen to Leipzig to audition for the post of cantor at the Thomaskirche, he brought with him two cantatas for different points in the church service. BWV 22 took place before the sermon, while BWV 23 prepared the mind for the ritual of the Eucharist – the performative union of the human with Christ through the consumption of consecrated wafer and wine. In its original form, BWV 23 consisted of three movements (duet, recitative and chorus) but for the occasion, Bach added a setting of the German version of the Agnus Dei – the prayer for mercy that belongs at the end of the Mass. He also lowered the key of the cantata and replaced the oboes with the deeper sound of the oboe d'amore. Subsequently, Bach used both versions at different times; this account refers to the C minor setting.

The theme of BWV 23 is true knowledge, understood as the inner vision of faith. Its starting point is an episode from the day's gospel reading (Lk. 18:31-43). Conscious of his approaching death, Christ is travelling to Jerusalem, accompanied by his disciples who fail to see what lies ahead. On the way, they meet a blind beggar who calls out, "Jesus, Son of David, have mercy on me". Thanks to his perception of Christ as the Messiah, the man's sight is miraculously restored. The story exists in a slightly different version in Matthew's gospel (Mt. 20:29-34), which features two men. Presumably this is what Bach had in mind for the imploring duet of the first movement. BWV 23 is also, as it was meant to be, a showcase of the composer's talents: an astonishing fusion of skill and imagination.

Soprano/alto duet

How does this profoundly emotional movement achieve its effect, and in what way do the words enhance it? As always, there are multiple factors. The starting point is a notably slow tempo (*molto'adagio*), which already inclines the listener to thoughtfulness, and the plaintive timbre of two oboes. The melodic lines hover on the spot, as if powerless to advance; the triplet motto that is a distinguishing feature of the movement moves back and forth before plunging down – and then continues its tortuous path.

From this material, Bach crafts a large-scale structure, consistent in mood but with much surface variety. The oboes and the continuo form a trio which passes the melancholy theme from one to another, copying and combining in ever-changing patterns. The voices join the texture in a similarly imitative fashion, though their overall pace is slower and independent of the instruments. They too move mostly in small, semitonal steps – confined rather than confident – even if the larger outline of their phrases can extend over a minor sixth: that unfailing musical sign of yearning.

Alongside the inventive part writing there is an inherent restlessness in Bach's pushing at the boundaries of his tonal system. Not to destroy it, for that would remove the source of tension, but to test its possibilities. In this respect, the minor key (whether in its harmonic or melodic form) invites all sort of ambiguities, of hints and flickers of new directions. Within the overarching tonal context there are possibilities of slippage, of the insecure and the unknown. The interplay of all these aspects intrigues and disturbs the listener, consciously or not.

With the arrival of the voices, the text anchors the so far undefined – though nonetheless powerful – impression of pathos to a particular scenario: the blind beggars who implored Christ to restore their sight. They in turn become the representatives of the general human plight, floundering in ignorance. Words and music reciprocate and enlarge each other's meaning: "You, the true God and David's Son, who from distant eternity have already seen in every detail my grief and my body's torment, have pity on me". Chromatic sighs and sobs, slow to reach harmonic resolution, lift the anguish into a realm of poignant beauty.

Yet any plea carries with it the hope of a favorable answer and so, after a returning instrumental passage (*ritornello*), a change to the major signposts the possibility of a miracle: "and through your wondrous hand that has averted so much evil, let help and comfort likewise come to me". This comparatively bright interlude acts as the centre of the entire design, which Bach completes with a modified repeat of the beginning; this time the alto voice, not the soprano, leads the canonic imitation. He evidently took infinite pains with this setting, to impress his future employers of course, but also (one imagines) to give it the emotional depth that his own faith demanded.

No 2 Tenor recit

Again, both text and music are multi-layered. The opening cry – "Ah, do not pass by!" – brings a startling change of harmony and a clear reference to the day's biblical story. Yet the intended lesson is far more general: a reminder of the universal need for the divine healing of the soul. The librettist, steeped in biblical learning, brings in references to other passages of scripture: "You, the salvation of all people, came to serve the sick and not the healthy. Therefore I too can share in your almighty power; I look to you from these paths where they wanted to lay me in my blindness". Bach takes his usual care over the verbal meaning – as, for instance, in the groan of a diminished chord on *Kranken* ("sick") – but the instrumental context is equally significant. Violin 2 and viola fill in the underlying harmonies, while violin 1 and the two oboes quietly (*pianissimo*) intone the melody of Luther's German version of the *Agnus Dei*: the ancient supplication for mercy and peace. The vocal line curves at the last in lyrical embrace of the Saviour: "I cling to you and will not let you go without your blessing". A cadence in the major (Eb) looks ahead to the next movement.

No 3 Chorus

As this chorus was first envisaged as the ending of BWV 23, its position in the church service would have been just before the taking of communion. Hence the urgent, syncopated rhythms that push forward in expectation: "All eyes wait, Lord, Almighty God, upon you!". This becomes the refrain both of the communal voice and the instrumental ensemble. Between these solidly scored passages, the vocal ensemble reduces to solo tenor and bass and the instrumental group is correspondingly pared down. The solo pair clearly recall the tale in Matthew's gospel of the two blind beggars; their words – "and my eyes particularly" – emphasise the personal nature of faith. Did Bach's listeners notice that this was set as a canon at the fourth?

The remainder of the text appears similarly, section by section, interspersed with the full chorus, each time showing Bach's expertise. He flows easily between imitative counterpoint and soft euphony for: "grant them strength and light and do not leave them forever in darkness"; but is back to canon (this time at the interval of a seventh) for: "In future, your beckoning alone shall be the beloved centre of all that my eyes undertake". The longest treatment is reserved for the last: "Until one day in death you decide to close them again". It begins as a canon at the second but gains ornamentation – and a long emphasis on *Tod* ("death") – appropriate to its centrality in the Christian picture. This is the purpose and rationale of faith: the promise of eternal union with the divine after death.

No 4 Chorale

The sense of guilt towards the divinity has continued to grow for several thousands of years, and always in the same proportion as the concept and sense of god has grown and risen into the heights...The arrival of the Christian God, as the uttermost example of godliness so far realised on earth, has brought with it the phenomenon of the uttermost sense of guilt.

> Nietzsche: *On the Genealogy of Morals*, trans. Douglas Smith

Bach's decision to finish BWV 23 with the entirety of Luther's 1528 hymn, *Christe, du Lamm Gottes* (i.e. his German version of the *Agnus dei*), gives a magnificent balance to the whole, as he revisits the weight and complexity of the opening chorus. Each of the three verses receives a different treatment. The first – "Christ, lamb of God who bears the sins of the world, have mercy on us!" – is majestic in tempo and style. Instrumental and vocal parts go their separate ways. The voices advance in slow, measured footsteps, while the oboes above cry out in small, beseeching phrases; the musical surroundings of the hymn are lavish with the chromaticism that indicates suffering. They point to the imminent crucifixion and the human failing that (in the Christian view) was its cause.

While the words of the second verse are an exact repeat of the first, here they are presented quite differently. The pulse becomes more animated (*andante* replaces the previous *adagio*), and the key even hints at the relative major (Bb), though it soon settles back into G minor. With another assured contrapuntal touch, Bach presents the chorale melody as a three-part canon between sopranos, oboes, and first violin, while the lower voices weave their own separate commentary. The third verse ends in hope: "Christ, lamb of God who bears the sins of the word, give us your peace. Amen." Here, the sopranos, strengthened by the violin, sing the hymn above the bustle of the other voices. The oboes meanwhile add an energetic, syncopated descant that propels its way through the fervent, prolonged and elaborate "Amen".

Though the final chord of C looks back to the key of the opening chorus, in a sense completing the tonal circle, the effect is of being suspended in mid-air, as if still waiting for the fulfilment of the soul's desire. Such a state is possibly intrinsic to the human condition. Bach's world saw it through the lens of religious belief; others may view the same truth from a different angle. Listening to the music is better than arguing.

*

Suggested recording: The Monteverdi Choir, dir. John Eliot Gardiner

Quinquagesima

BWV 127: *Herr Jesu Christ, wahr' Mensch und Gott*

(Lord Jesus Christ, true man and God)

Librettist: Unknown

11 February 1725

Has anyone noticed the extent to which a true religious life (which includes its favourite work of microscopic self-examination, along with that state of gentle calm called 'prayer', the ongoing preparation for 'the coming of God') is dependent on external leisure, by which I mean that time-honoured, guilt-free ancestral leisure that is not entirely different from an aristocrat's feeling that work *desecrates* – that it debases soul and body?

Nietzsche: *Beyond Good and Evil*, trans. Marion Faber

Death – the universally unwanted outcome of life – is the focal point of Christian religious belief, for it is viewed as the transition to eternity. The paradigm and proof of this possibility is held to be the figure of Jesus Christ, embodiment of the human and divine, who acquiesced in his own crucifixion (a fate that exemplifies the human talent for cruelty). He then, according to scripture, survived this to resume his transcendental existence.

The story brings with it the promise of the same miracle for all who wish to follow the example of Christ by practising a detachment from the usual concerns of the bodily self and a readiness at any moment to leave it. From the evidence of the cantata texts, which continually revisit the subject, the lesson was difficult to absorb. To be sure, stories of Hell and damnation had been preached to terrifying effect for centuries past and to come, but we may never know how many had the mental space or inclination to ponder their eternal destiny when there was a living to be made and the need to care for home and family – especially when technology gave little help.

The gospel reading for this Sunday (Lk. 18: 31-43) tells of Christ's last journey to Jerusalem, conscious of his approaching end. With this in mind, the librettist of BWV 127 built his text around a hymn for the dying, written by the theologian and Wittenberg professor Paul Eber (1511-1569). Its first and last verses frame the cantata, with the remainder paraphrased to make a sequence of recitative, aria, and a long, dramatic recitative. BWV 127 brings a quasi-cinematic projection of the moment of death, the peace of the grave, and the terror of Judgement Day. The Christian survives the cataclysm, for faith ensures that Christ will fulfil his promise.

No 1 Chorus

A chorale chorus both serves and expands the hymn on which it is based. Paul Eber's first verse inspires a rich musical setting that unites three ideas: the recognition of Christ's divinity, an awareness of his suffering, and the human need for his intervention. Bach alludes to all of these in the opening instrumental bars. Two recorders wail above in dotted rhythms that continue throughout the movement, passed back and forth to the oboes and at times the violins. If crisply performed, they suggest the scourging motif that appears, for instance, in the alto recitative, No. 60, of the St. Matthew Passion.

This coexists with an equally persistent phrase, announced at the outset by the oboes. It comprises the first eight notes of the chorale melody which, as a constant, wordless reminder of "Lord Jesus Christ, true man and God" is the foundational acknowledgement of

Christ's identity as God. As such, it also recalls the episode from the day's scriptural reading in which a blind beggar had called out for the restoration of his sight. The third symbolic strand is part of Luther's version of the ancient *Agnus Dei*, i.e. *Christe, du Lamm Gottes* ("Christ, lamb of God"). Its slow-paced melody in the first violin acts as a foil to the activity of the wind instruments above, while an initial tonic pedal in the continuo provides anchorage.

The implicit meaning of the music is fully revealed with the arrival of Eber's hymn. Bach presents it in the usual way of a chorale chorus, with each line separated by instrumental passages. The words echo the *Agnus dei*: "Lord Jesus Christ, true man and God/who suffered torment, fear and scorn/and finally died for me on the cross/and won for me your Father's favour/I pray through your bitter suffering/that you would be merciful to me, a sinner". The sopranos maintain the melody – there was presumable a number of them to cut through the surrounding texture – as the other voices repeat the words in independent counterpoint. All the while, the rhythmic mantra associated with "Lord Jesus Christ" recurs again and again, as a unifying feature and call to attention. Chromatically inflected sighs evoke the saviour's suffering, and the final call for mercy brings back the original *Agnus dei* in the strings. The voices in turn repeat the last words ("that you would be merciful to me a sinner") while Bach steers the music back to the F major of its opening.

No 2 Tenor recit

There can be no shrinking from the horror of the last moments: "When my whole being is overcome by a state of terror, and when the cold sweat of death moisten my stiffening limbs, when my tongue speaks only in sighs, and my heart breaks". The musical language is gloomy, with a diminished seventh on *Todesschweiz* ("death-sweat"), gasps for breath on S*eufzer* ("sighs"), and the choked outline of *dieses Herze bricht* ("this heart breaks". Yet the picture eventually brightens: "it is enough that faith knows that Jesus stands by me there, who with patience" (note the subdued harmony on *Geduld*) "goes to his own agony and leads me on the same hard road and prepares my rest for me". The last two bars relax into the more melodic style of *arioso*, leading once again to a cadence in F major.

No 3 Soprano aria

Luther (after he had ditched his belief in Purgatory around 1530) openly affirmed soul-sleep: that was one of the reasons that he encouraged the siting of new cemeteries outside the noisy bustle of town, so that the sleep of the dead could be properly and decorously symbolised.

Diarmaid MacCulloch: *Reformation*

This is the emotional heart of BWV 127, intended to soften and soothe the fear of the grave. Death will bring a time of quiet until the moment of personal resurrection: "My soul will rest in the hands of Jesus, when earth covers this body". The structure is a long-breathed da *capo*; the style is both calm and elegiac; the scoring is ethereal. Above a light *pizzicato* bass, two recorders become the gentle tolling of bells, while the sound of the oboe reaches out in yearning for the afterlife. Voice and solo instrument combine in a duet of ornate lyrical beauty; the decoration is integral to the entire meaning.

The result – both melancholy and consoling – is pure song, set against relatively unchanging harmonies. It is the musical persona of the sleeping soul which lies still, even as the pulse of existence continues. Given such an ideal vision, the living self becomes impatient for death. The central part of the aria urges: "Ah, call me soon, you funeral bells; I am not terrified of dying because my Jesus shall waken me again". The vocal line separates into breathless fragments and the upper strings, previously silent, add their own rapid *pizzicato* in imitation of the bells. The A section returns the listener to the cool of the grave, where the soul awaits its resurrection.

No 4 Bass recit

In this moment of high drama, Judgement Day is revealed as the test of the authenticity of faith and of the validity of Christ's promise of eternal life. Bringing theological abstraction to life, one singer acts both for the believer's anxieties and the divine response. The trumpet rings out, summoning humanity to judgement as the world shakes and trembles in a stylised musical apocalypse. The craggy contours of the vocal line echo the scene of destruction: "When one day the trumpets sound, and when the edifice of the world, along with the heavenly cosmos, shatters into pieces, then think on me, my God, with favour". Sighs and glides, however, soften the outline as the text becomes more fearful: "when your servant appears one day before the judgement, where my thoughts accuse each other, so you, Jesus will speak in my defence and offer words of comfort to my soul".

The figure of Christ responds in a more measured tempo, with a blend of biblical quotation, parts of Eber's hymn, and the librettist's own additions. The classic preamble – "Truly I say to you" – is set to the motto that dominated the opening chorus of the cantata. In other words, Bach links these words to that elemental profession of faith – "Lord Jesus Christ, true man and God" – without which there can be no salvation after death. From here onward, the recitative continues as a series of contrasts between a world in violent collapse and the security promised by Christ. Each has its own style and tempo: trumpet and flickering arpeggios in the strings for one; the continuo alone for the other.

The first alternation is between: "Though heaven and earth pass away in flames, so shall a believer nevertheless eternally stand", followed by: "He will not come into judgement and shall not taste everlasting death. Only hold to me, my child." More agitation arrives for: "I break, with strong and helping hand, death's powerful, tight noose". At the ending – and this must have been Bach's choice – the earlier words of Christ are repeated: "Truly I say to you, though heaven and earth pass away in flames, so shall a believer nevertheless eternally stand". This enables the final, prolonged *stehen* ("stand") to hold its own against the surrounding tumult.

No 5 Chorale

Paul Eber's last verse completes BWV 127: "Ah, Lord, forgive all our guilt;/help us to wait with patience/until our little hour come near,/and may our faith be ever bolder/to trust your Word firmly/until we fall blessedly asleep". Yet the harmonisation of that last line is troubling.

*

Suggested recording: Collegium Vocale Gent,
dir. Philippe Herreweghe

Quinquagesima

BWV 159: *Sehet, wir gehen hinauf gen Jerusalem*

(See, we are going up to Jerusalem)

Librettist: Picander (Christian Friedrich Henrici)

27 February 1729

The latest of four cantatas written for this Sunday in the Church year, just before the penitential season of Lent, BWV 159 is both more personal and possibly more mystical than its predecessors. As before, it is a response to the day's gospel reading (Lk. 18: 31-43). In it, Christ prepares to confront his death as he embarks on his last journey to Jerusalem – yet his disciples are baffled when he tells them that he is about to complete his earthly mission. Picander, the librettist of BWV 159, unfolds the relevance of this biblical episode to the believer, opening up the process of self-discovery by which the soul confronts its ambivalence towards the crucifixion. A double weight of guilt oppresses human consciousness: from that innate weakness that led at the beginning of time to the fall from paradise, and from awareness that God in mortal form has endured suffering and death for the sake of the unworthy, sinful self.

If agonising to contemplate in another, the coming crucifixion is also a symbol and harbinger of the believer's own death: the ultimate test of faith's resolve. The intense inner drama of BWV 159 places the listener by the side of the self-sacrificing Saviour, helpless to offer anything in return but a lifelong dedication to the ideal of reunion with Christ in heaven. In keeping with the psychological intimacy, there is no chorus. Four solo voices enact Christ and the changing reactions of the human soul: from surprise to shame, the pledging of loyalty, and the penitence that the thought of the crucifixion demands; the quartet unites for the final chorale. A solo oboe joins the string ensemble in the last aria of reconciliation and understanding. Here, with Bach's use of inversion, music becomes philosophy. In this aural universe, reality bends back on itself; the given and its contrary are part of the same truth.

Bass arioso/alto recit

For this exercise in biblical interpretation, the librettist uses the beginning of Christ's speech to his disciples – "See, we are going up to Jerusalem" – and, stage by stage, unpicks its theological content. As usual, Bach allots the role of the Saviour to the bass voice, while the alto takes the part of the soul. Style demarcates the divine from the human. The bass passages are lyrical in manner (*arioso*), rhythmically and tonally firm, and associated with a steadily rising phrase in the continuo, which ends in a fall of a seventh. In contrast, the freer style of recitative gives the soul's emotional reaction, as it moves from respectful interest to horror and agitation.

First, the call for attention: *Sehet* ("See"). A prolonged vocal flourish lets us know that an important message is on its way, and the soul obediently takes note: "Come, my mind, look, where is your Jesus going?". The answer, "We are going up", is acted out in the ascending path of the continuo and the voice. Harmonic calm then shatters as the soul recoils in guilt and confusion: "O difficult path! Up? O monstrous mountain to which my sins point! How bitter your climb will be!" An awkwardly chromatic bass line whirls the unhappy mind through a succession of keys before Christ's completion of his message: "to Jerusalem".

Bach then offers the complete sentence, again with the imitative partnership of voice and continuo. Yet there is an ambiguity in the music: after repeating its upward phrase three times, the continuo presents it a further three times in inversion. Thus to climb and then to fall (i.e. go to Jerusalem and die) is transformed into descent followed by rising up (i.e. death and resurrection). The mind now confronts its greatest difficulty, asking if Christ must really die: "Ah, do not go! Your cross is already prepared for you, where you must bleed to death; here they seek whips, there they fasten together rods; bonds await you. Do not go there!" Again, Bach gives a deliberate impression of harmonic floundering but allows the key to settle (in F minor – the subdominant) for the need to accept Christ's fate: But if you were to stay back, then I myself would be forced to go – not to Jerusalem, but ah, alas, down to hell". There is no alternative: without the victimhood of the divine, the human soul faces its own destruction.

No 2 Alto aria/soprano chorale

The rising patterns for the continuo in the previous movement – the musical illustration of "up" – are adapted here into a smooth, almost dance-like, motion. The alto voice begins in the same way, in illustration of the words: "I will follow after you, through spitting and shame". However, Picander also included for this movement a verse by the great Lutheran hymnodist, Paul Gerhardt (1607-1676): it was part of his much-performed Easter hymn *O Haupt voll Blut und Wunden* ("O head covered in blood and wounds"). Bach adds it to the texture of alto and continuo as a soprano *cantus firmus*: "I will stand beside you here, do not despise me!" Though a written text must only deliver one line at a time, music may present two (or more) simultaneously. In this way, there is a reciprocal gain: the hymn becomes even more immediately personal, and Picander's words draw on the pre-existing emotional weight of the chorale.

From a structural point of view, it means also that the chorale appears more ample, for it is sustained by the larger format of the aria, which is built from repeated and expressive word settings. For instance, while the hymn continues with: "I will not go from you/ until your heart breaks", the alto line is full of musical imagery as vivid and extended as its text is brief: "At the cross I will still embrace you". *Am Kreuz* ("At the cross") begins with the rising minor sixth that evokes all manner of distress, while *umfangen* ("embrace") takes a tenacious, clinging path. The remainder of the hymn leads, line by line, to the final tragedy: "When your head will turn pale/in the last stroke of death/even then I will embrace you/in my arm and lap". The alto comment is again verbally concise – "and when you must finally depart, you shall find your grave in me" – but Bach's treatment of it leads the listener's thoughts to the very moment of death. The rhythmic flow begins to falter, and the vocal line eventually sinks, as if into the tomb. Yet the continuo maintains its steady path until the end, satisfying the demands of form and the need to show Christian fortitude.

No 3 Tenor recit

Her happiness, like that of most of us, was ever in the future – never reached but always coming.

Anthony Trollope: *The Way We Live Now*

Until the last moment, the believer must spend his life mourning quietly for Jesus and rejecting attachment to the body: "Now I will grieve for you, my Jesus, in my own little corner; let the world continue to feed on the poison" (note the accusatory cry on *Gift*) "of sensual pleasure". There can be no true happiness until, after death, one is face to face with the resurrected Christ: "I will feast on my tears and will not yearn for any joy until that day when I gaze upon you in your glory, when I have been redeemed through you; then I will find refreshment in you". A simple chordal accompaniment sustains the singer, for here words take precedence over music: this is the lesson that all are meant to live by. After dwelling in life's minor keys, the movement ends with a Bb major glimpse of the awaiting heaven.

No 4 Bass aria

The death-wish so often expressed in the cantatas should not be taken at face value. It is nothing less than the longing for life on better terms than the present: an escape from all types of suffering that afflict the physical state. The dream is human and widespread: as appealing as it is unrealisable. It is this very ambivalence – between hope and the knowledge that it cannot as yet be satisfied – that is beautifully embodied in this aria. Not only that: the subtlety of the setting suggests that all certainty is open ended, for contradictions are part of the whole.

The first phrase of the text – *Es ist vollbracht* ("It is accomplished") – speaks Christ's last words on the cross. Bach interpreted this musically in terms of a two-stage melodic fragment (note its yielding gesture towards the subdominant key), so that the second part is an inverted image of the first. In a sense, therefore, they complete each other, yet though the whole begins and ends on the same note (Bb), the underlying harmonies lead away to the relative minor. The effect is of a paradoxically unfinished finality. A solo oboe, plangent and expressive, introduces this motto in the opening eight bars against a quietly shimmering background of string chords; the continuo below moves with ritual slowness.

With the entry of the voice, the full text – to which Bach has already primed his listeners' solemn response – unfurls: "It is accomplished, suffering is over; from our sinful fall we have been made righteous in God". In Christian thinking, this is the deep truth of the death-story of the crucifixion: it validates the dream of paradise that otherwise would be blocked to the mortal self, subject as it is to time and change. The imperfect and the perishable may at the last be transmuted into their opposite. Small sighs from oboe and violin add to the longing.

After an instrumental interlude, the remainder of the text brings a new musical impetus, as if to create a central section: "Now I will hurry to give thanks to my Jesus". The voice runs along with the thought, as do the accompanying instruments. A firm vocal arpeggio dismisses all that is transitory: "World, good night!"

No 5 Chorale

The German hymnodist and preacher, Paul Stockmann (1603-1636), produced an impassioned thirty-four verse account of the trial and crucifixion of Christ, and the grief, guilt and hope that it brought to the believer. Its penultimate stanza ends BWV 159: "Jesus, your suffering brings joy for me; your wounds, crown and scorn are my heart's pasture". Recalling, as imagination and honesty oblige us to, the circumstances of those times, so afflicted by war and plague (the cause of Stockmann's early death), one imagines that the figure of the suffering Saviour would have been all too recognisable. That the mind can still make of this a transformative vision is, perhaps, the real marvel.

*

Suggested recording: Academy of St.-Martin-in-the-Fields, dir. Neville Marriner

March: Prefatory Note

Birth, Death and Resurrection

There are only four cantata accounts in this section, for the weeks close to Easter were dominated by reflections on the crucifixion of Christ. This reminder of the human capacity for violence, and indifference to suffering, called for a penitential plainness in forms of worship, so that cantatas were not routinely performed. The great musical events of this period were reserved for Good Friday. These were the Passions: settings of the New Testament accounts of the trial and death of the human figure of Jesus. Dramatic and of towering intensity, Bach's two surviving examples are based on St. John's and St. Matthew's gospels respectively. They are not included in this book.

However, there were also reasons to celebrate. The first of these is the Annunciation on 25 March. For believers, it is fundamental to the story of Christ's divinity. It marks the occasion when, according to scripture, an angelic messenger arrived to inform the young woman Mary that she was to be the mother of God's son – conceived by purely spiritual means. BWV 182 and BWV 1, composed more than ten years apart, combine a sense of joy with the erotic mysticism that features from time to time in the text and music of the cantatas.

The remaining two works are for Easter Day itself, with Christ triumphant over the powers of darkness and death. BWV 4, a very early cantata, is remarkable for its adherence throughout to the words of a hymn by Luther. BWV 31 spills over with exultant energy – enough and to spare to conduct the self, in its imagination, to its own ultimate resurrection in the life to come.

Palm Sunday/Annunciation

BWV 182: *Himmelskönig sei willkommen*

(King of Heaven, welcome)

Librettist: probably Salomon Franck

25 March 1714

When Bach was promoted to concertmaster at the court of Weimar, he was required to perform an original work in the castle church each month; BWV 182 was the first that he produced in his new position. The occasion was Palm Sunday, which commemorates the final entry of Christ into Jerusalem before his arrest and death. It was not usual to mark this day with elaborate music, as it marked the beginning of Holy Week, ending with the death of Christ. However, when, as in 1714, Palm Sunday coincided with the date of the Annunciation, an exception was made.

BWV 182 thus serves a dual function, and both converge on the imperative to yield in faith to God. The Annunciation (Lk. 1:26-38) tells of the angel Gabriel's message to the Virgin Mary that she was to be inseminated by the Holy Spirit so as to give birth to God in human form; though perturbed by this (as one would be), her response was to bow to the divine will. An analogous scene of welcome and obeisance is described in the reading for Palm Sunday (Mt. 21:1-9), when a crowd of followers spread branches and garments in Christ's path.

The text is most likely by Salomon Franck, the Weimar court poet. It grafts together elements of the two religious festivals, presenting Christ's birth and crucifixion as facets of one truth – that God sacrificed his own life to save mortals from death – rather than as separate episodes in the religious story. In turn, believers must submit in absolute devotion to the figure of Christ, which brings with it the need to accept suffering. Bach's emotionally vivid setting combines the personal and the communal, the immediately welcoming, and the longer vision of tragedy and joy. The scoring is intimate and adopts the older fashion of including two violas. Above the strings and continuo are a solo violin and a recorder, whose part originally had to be written in a different key to fit the needs of tuning – though this was reconfigured for later performances in Leipzig.

No 1 Sonata

Here, the term *sonata* simply refers (as with *sinfonia*) to an introductory instrumental piece. Its function is to establish a mood appropriate to the subject of the cantata. The music is both refined and stately. Dotted rhythms suggest the formal arrival of royalty (an aural symbol borrowed from the French overture) – yet without obvious pomp, for this is the stealing of the Holy Spirit into the human heart (or, in the supposed case of the Virgin Mary, the body). Violin and recorder join in an elegant imitative duet above the light-textured accompaniment of the violas and cello. The sounds are delicate, but the patterns – both melodic and harmonic – are securely controlled. The last few bars convey gathering anticipation: after a sustained string chord, the bass instruments join take up the rhythmic energy of the recorder and violin, propelling the music to its conclusion and the listener's mind toward the next scene.

No 2 Chorus

Communal and private emotions mingle in the cross currents of the two religious festivals. The Annunciation initially concerns one person, whose joy is shared in retrospect by the whole Church; conversely, the universal acclamation of Christ's entry into Jerusalem is made up of many individuals. Counterpoint in general (the interweaving of separate parts) and fugue in particular (a separating out of identical voices in succession) is an ideal way to unite the two types of identity. The structure of the chorus is the three-part *da capo*. Its outer section divides the text into two independent fugal settings. First is the cry of: "King of Heaven, welcome". The layering of entries, from soprano down to bass, combined with the gradual accumulation of instruments, suggests the gathering eagerness of the crowd.

The next phrase – "let us also be your Zion" (i.e. Jerusalem) – is a further fugue, though this time with the parts in ascending order from bass to soprano, until all the voices join in chordal solidarity for the whole text. The central part of the chorus is more intimate: "Come within! You have captured our heart". The words echo the eroticism of the Old Testament Song of Solomon, linking present and past by making Christ the fulfilment of ancient human longing. The key changes to the minor and the vocal lines crowd upon each other. Long pedal notes in the continuo add to the sense of urgent waiting. The cries of welcome resume and the music merges seamlessly into a repeat of the opening.

No 3 Bass recit

In contrast with Bach's later cantatas, with their regular alternation of recitative and aria, this is the only recitative movement in BWV 182. Again, the librettist looked to an Old Testament text (Psalm 40: 7-8), projecting on to it the voice of Christ: "See, I come; it is written of me in the book; I gladly do your will, my God". An initial speech-like spontaneity soon settles into a calm, regular rhythm. The ascending phrases of the continuo end always in a fall of a seventh, as if pointing to the inevitable death.

No 4 Bass aria

The bass voice now takes on the role of the believer: "What strong love that drove you, great Son of God, from your throne of glory, that you offered yourself as a sacrifice for the salvation of the world and pledged yourself with blood". The setting is dignified, as befits its divine subject, with an unshakeable rhythmic pace and an orderly alternation of instrumental and vocal episodes. While the melodic material remains essentially the same throughout, different colourations of key mark out the enormity of Christ's self-sacrifice, as with the chromatic twists for *daß du dich mit Blut verschrieben* ("that you pledged yourself with blood"). A deft return to the opening key allows the aria to finish as it began.

No 5 Alto aria

Images and ideas from Palm Sunday and the Annunciation feed upon each other in this deeply emotional aria, which exploits the expressive possibilities of the (E) minor key. Believers are urged to prostrate themselves before Christ, like the garments that were strewn before him: "Lay yourselves down before the Saviour, O hearts that are Christian!" The swooning of the recorder, (sole accompaniment of the voice, other than the continuo) conveys the physical act, and this in turn is a metaphor for the mental submission that faith demands. The vocal line follows suit, with its obeisances on *leget* ("lay down").

The centre of the *da capo* structure brings a slightly more animated tempo – *andante* instead of the previous *largo* – as its text makes the link between Palm Sunday and the Annunciation: "Wear an unblemished garment of your faith to meet him; let body, life and possessions now be consecrated to the King". Clean clothing ("Sunday best") is a symbol of both outer and inner purity and links the believer to the figure of the Virgin Mary as a vessel of the Holy Spirit. Caressing thirds and sixths between recorder and voice suggest the quasi-erotic pleasure of the self's union with its spiritual ideal. The entire aria, in fact, is nothing but the song of the lovesick soul – a mystic aspiration to the divine that featured in some pietistic strands of Lutheranism.

No 6 Tenor aria

In a contrast of style, the individual (no longer the communal "us" of the opening chorus) cries out for help in following the hard path of faith. Life is identified, military style, with battle under its divine leader: "Jesus, through weal and woe, let me also go with you. Though the world cries only 'Crucify!', still do not let me flee, Lord, from the banner of your cross. I shall find here both crown and palms". Instead of a soldier's plunder, the prize is eternal life, which can only be gained by imitating Christ in the willingness to deny the flesh and welcome the moment of death. Bach's approach to the text matches the toughness of its vision. A strenuous cello solo accompanies the voice, whose part is marked by sudden stops and abrupt rhetoric. Urgent calls of *Herr* ("Lord") clutch at the Saviour, while a twisted setting of *Kreuzige!* ("Crucify!") denotes not only the pain of the sufferer but perhaps also the inner deformation that calls for the death of the innocent. The climax arrives with a lingering high G on *Weh* ("woe"); after a dramatic pause, a doubly emphasised *mich* ("me") points to the desperate personal need to endure to the end.

No 7 Chorale

Belief is not merely an epiphenomenon of human communities but also the way diverse cultures give meaning to the world and what lies beyond, both natural and supernatural, spiritual and mystical. Human societies in the past have all displayed some form of cosmological explanation, and many still do.

Richard Overy: *Why War?*

This hymn, written in 1633 by Paul Stockman (1603-1636) – see also the closing chorale of BWV 159 – summarises the meaning of the approaching crucifixion, i.e. its transformation of weakness and pain into transcendental benefit. Rapture and horror are interdependent: "Jesus, your Passion is pure joy for me;/your wounds, crown and are my heart's pasture./My soul walks on roses when I remember that because of this/ a place in heaven is given to us". In Bach's contrapuntally saturated setting, words and music are in perfect equilibrium. Instrumental colour does not attract attention away from the words, for the role of the instruments is to double the vocal lines. Yet the finely-honed musical skill is a pleasure on its own terms. Before and alongside the slow soprano melody, the imitative interplay of the lower parts is full of life and variety, making space also for an expanded treatment of *Freude* ("joy") and *Weide* ("pasture") to highlight the positive message of the crucifixion. The chorale unfolds as a series of ebbing and flowing, with each line gradually increasing in strength until the final, hovering climax – a glimpse toward the life to come.

No 8 Chorus

The recorder becomes the piper leading a dance of delight: "So let us enter that Salem of joy" (i.e.

Jerusalem), "accompanying the king in love and sorrow" (a brief shadow of the minor key on *Leiden*). Again, the structure is *da capo*, with the remainder of the text in the centre: "He goes before us and opens the way". A series of modulations – a tonal journey – mirrors the words, and long pedal notes in the bass stretch into an imagined future. The repeat of the first part of this movement returns to the celebration. spirit of its opening. To the believer, both the Annunciation and Palm Sunday are part of the same narrative: that the birth and death of Christ brought liberation from death.

*

Suggested recording: Bach Collegium Japan, dir. Masaaki Suzuki

Annunciation

BWV 1: *Wie schön leuchtet der Morgenstern*

(How beautifully shines the morning star)

Librettist: Unknown

25 March 1725

During Lent – the penitent weeks before Easter – there is one event at least to lift the spirits of the faithful. BWV 1 celebrates the Annunciation, the supposed arrival of the heavenly messenger, the angel Gabriel, to inform a young woman (Mary) that she was to be the mother of God in human form (Lk. 1:26-38). Although promised in marriage to a man (Joseph), she was to be impregnated by the Holy Spirit. As this was the precondition of the birth of Christ, the Annunciation prompts a moment of festivity. It is a welcome reminder of God's greatest gift to mankind: the possibility of the forgiveness of sin and consequent power to annul death.

With its libretto based on a hymn by Philipp Nicolai, BWV 1 is a chorale cantata. It begins and ends with Nicolai's first and seven verses, while the essentials of verses two to six are paraphrased to create the texts of two pairs of recitative and aria. Noted in his lifetime as pastor, writer and composer, Philipp Nicolai (1556-1608) remains a revered figure in the history of the Lutheran Church. The language of his hymn is full of Baroque ripeness, with its profuse endearments and metaphors of flowers and jewels to address the figure of Christ. Bach's librettist has pruned out this imagery, though keeping the general sense of that mystic union of flesh and spirit that faith represents for the devout believer. The setting is appropriately – and tirelessly – positive in its intimations of divine majesty and the great joy that this brings to the human spirit: a joy that demands to be expressed in music.

No 1 Chorus

Nicolai's first verse pays homage to multiple impressions of the future redeemer: the princely child who ushers in the new yet represents continuity with an ancient past; humanity's mighty king; and the tender lover of each individual soul: "How beautifully shines the morning star/ full of grace and truth from the Lord/ the sweet root of Jesse!" (the reference is to the father of king David, believed to be the distant ancestor of Christ). "You son of David from Jacob's stock/ my king and my bridegroom/ you have taken possession of my heart./ Lovely, kindly/ beautiful and glorious, great and honourable, rich in gifts,/ highly and most splendidly exalted."

As one might expect, Bach responds to these words with music of exceptional brilliance and grandeur, using the format of an instrumental concerto to enclose the hymn. In addition to the usual group of upper strings and continuo, there are three pairs of soloists: horns, deep-toned oboes *da caccia* (their curved shape mimicked a horn), and violins. Such variety of tone colour, coupled with the dance-like sway of the rhythm, gives instant pleasure to the listener. Along with this, however, it seems that Bach is acutely aware of the layers of theology embedded in the hymn; the music and the message permeate each other.

A central paradox of the incarnation is that the immeasurable divine adopted a notably humble identity on earth. Hence, amidst the sophisticated inventiveness of the *concerto grosso*, there are nods to pastoral simplicity in the frequent use of a drone-like rocking bass pedal, the untroubled harmonic language, and perhaps also the rustic-sounding duet for the oboes. This in turn blends with the horns, with their regal, space-filling sound to signal God's magnificence. The two violins complete the trilogy of soloists; their gleaming passage work (as with the recorder in the first movement of BWV 96) suggests the radiance of the star. It is possible also that Bach's choice of three groups of soloists alludes to the Trinitarian nature of God – Father, Son and Holy Spirit.

The overall design of the movement alternates instrumental sections with elaborate settings of each line of the chorale. The opening *ritornello* sets the scene. It starts with a violin phrase derived from the hymn melody – that first leap of a fifth – and then, above the harmonic foundation of the continuo and the full body of the strings (*ripieno*), the three solo groups combine in homage to Christ's coming. Towards the end of this section, a descending sequential figure for all the strings implies the arrival from above of the divine presence: time is spun out in a moment of free fall before the completion of a long-delayed cadence and the eventual arrival of the chorale. The slow-moving soprano melody, reinforced by the horn, leads the way; the other voices interweave below, again beginning with the leap that recalls the hymn.

For the next line ("full of grace and truth from the Lord"), the lower voices precede the sopranos, with the tenor and alto lines anticipating the chorale in urgent, halved note values; following this, the third line ("the sweet root of Jesse") is treated in a similar manner to the first. After a repeat of the introductory *ritornello*, lines four to six of the hymn are set on the model of the first three lines. Although the tonality is firmly anchored to its key of F major, the incessant energy and interplay of parts prevents any sense of monotony.

However, the next long interlude does allow Bach to venture into the relative (D) minor before settling back into the tonic for the final expressions of adulation and awe. These begin with the block harmonies of "Lovely, kindly", but incorporate more movement for the succeeding lines – note the driving energy of the vocal bass as it unites with the continuo. For the last phrase of the text, basses, tenors and altos reach up in succession until they are rewarded by the final descending octave of the chorale melody. The music ends as it began, with a last appearance of its rich and ceremonious opening.

No 2 Tenor recit

An especially comforting aspect of the cantata texts is the sense that not only is the individual life of particular interest to the all-seeing mind of God, but that one's personal existence forms part of the large, continuous span of past and present. The birth of Christ represents the elevation of God's chosen ones, and also links them to the ancient narrative contained in the biblical Old Testament: "True God and Mary's son, king of the chosen ones, how sweet" (note the aching leap of a minor seventh) "to us is this life-giving word, according to which the earliest fathers already counted years as days, and that Gabriel joyfully promised there in Bethlehem". The remainder of the recitative plays out as a series of exclamations of wonder that Christ's coming brings the assurance of immortality: "O sweetness, O bread of heaven, which neither grave, danger nor death can snatch out of our hearts". Yet the harmonies shift to the minor, for the believer's mind can never be entirely free of its deepest instinctual fears.

No 3 Soprano aria

The librettist of BWV 1 toned down the erotic style of Nicolai's hymn, with its "heart sick and smouldering and wounded with love", and self-declaration as the bride of Christ. Nevertheless, the trope here is much the same: "Fill, you heavenly divine flames, the breast of the believer who longs for you!" Bach's musical version is warm and lyrical while avoiding the extremes of passion. The format is an intimate, yet decorous trio sonata for voice, the expressive sound of an oboe da caccia, and a continuo part that moves with a delicate, pizzicato tread. Yet although spiritual love is untroubled by the restless hunger of chromaticism, a sense of longing is implicit in the shaping of the melody. It begins with a succession of rising phrases and is characterised throughout by upward leaps and flowing syllabic settings. A neat tripartite design encloses a central section in which both language and music gain in intensity: "Our souls feel the most powerful urges of the most burning love and taste on earth the delight of heaven". The key moves to G minor and the oboe pours out the holy spirit in continuous cascades. After this, the two lovers – human and divine – return to the safe embrace of Bb major; they are, as ever, in perfect harmony.

No 4 Bass recit

In grüner Landschaft Sommerflor,
Bei kühlem Wasser, Schilf und Rohr,
Schau, wie das Knäblein Sündelos
Frei spielet auf der Jungfrau Schoß!
Und dort im Walde wonnesam,
Ach grünet schon des Kreuzes Stamm!

(In a green summer landscape, full of flowers, by cool water, reed and sedge, Soo how the little child, innocent and free, plays on the virgin's lap! And there, in the beautiful wood, alas, the stem for the cross already grows.)

Eduard Mörike

Christianity posits a dual self: the soul capable of eternal life, and the perishable mortal identity that lives out its time in the world of appearances. The previous aria used the soprano (in Bach's time always a boy) for the voice of the soul, but in this recitative the outer being speaks with the robust sound of the bass: "Worldly splendour, and the light that my body sees, leave my soul unmoved; a light of joy" (the vocal line springs into life) "has come to me from God". The token of this transforming light is the symbolic consumption of the body and blood of Christ in the Eucharist – which is to say: even at the Annunciation, the believer's thoughts move on to the crucified God: "for a perfect goodness, the Saviour's body and blood, is there to give us refreshment". This physical act, in an analogy with the penetration of Mary by the Holy Spirit, restores the presence of God to the body, and hence inspires heartfelt gratitude: "and so the overflowing blessing which was decreed for us from eternity, and which our faith takes in to itself, must move us to thanks and praise".

No 5 Tenor aria

Music becomes the perfect medium for honouring God. It acts upon mind and body alike, but its sound can neither be seen nor touched. voices and instruments are summoned to demonstrate commitment to an other-worldly ideal: "Our mouth and the sound of strings shall, for ever and ever, prepare for you thanksgiving and sacrifice". Bach returns to the *concerto grosso* style of the opening movement, but now with a lightness in the string and continuo parts that recalls the mood of the soprano aria (No 3). He also gives precise instructions for varying the dynamics, for this is a special occasion. The earthiness of oboes and horns is set aside in favour of the more ethereal sounds of two solo violinists, and a tenor part that strains the singer's endurance to its limits. The central section of the *da capo* structure is exceptionally demanding for the voice. In calling upon an unending supply of musical worship – "Heart and senses are raised lifelong in singing, great king, to your praise" – the singer practices what he preaches, taxing lungs and larynx to the utmost. To lose the whole self in the best that human art can devise is to enjoy a sense of sacred possession.

No 6 Chorale

A splendid and heroic setting of Nicolai's final verse ends this cantata. Bach arranges the voices in solid four-part harmony, adding to them the weight of all the instruments: "How glad my heart is that my treasure is the Alpha and Omega, the beginning and the end. He will indeed to his glory take my up to paradise, for which I clap my hands. Amen! Amen! Come, you crown of joy, do not delay, I wait for you with longing". The horns bring their especial glamour and power to the whole with a rousing, independent descant: God is processing through the universe, drawing all into the divine embrace.

*

Suggested recording: J.S. Bach-Stiftung, dir. Rudolf Lutz

Easter Day

BWV 4: *Christ lag in Todesbanden*

(Christ lay in the fetters of death)

Libretto: Martin Luther's chorale

Uncertain – perhaps as early as 1707

Amongst Bach's sacred cantatas, BWV 4 is unusual in using an entire chorale verbatim. It is one of the reasons – along with the musical style – for ascribing it to an early period in Bach's career, before the development of the cantata libretto as an independent literary genre; the shift began in the early part of the eighteenth century. Even when, in Bach's later years, a chorale might provide the foundation of a cantata, the original verses would be to some extent recast so that they could be adapted to the more modern format of arias and recitatives. In BWV 4, however, the words, dating from 1524, are Martin Luther's own.

    Luther combined theological learning with an intense desire to communicate his beliefs to others. His linguistic abilities enabled him to express his religious vision in an accessible style; thus *Christ lag in Todesbanden* turns the essentials of Easter – Christ's death and resurrection – into a simple and direct narrative. With the words and melody of the hymn as his foundation, Bach presented a series of musical scenarios that take the listener past the stillness of the grave into the epic struggle in the underworld and finally victory over death.

    As with the language, there is nothing exceptional about Bach's raw materials: four vocal lines, a string ensemble of two violins and two violas, plus organ continuo, and a melody that restricts him to the key of E minor. Working within these parameters, he achieved an astonishing variety, alternating choruses with duets and solos and absorbing each final Alleluia! into the prevailing mood of the movement. The result is a display of a rare theatrical imagination directed to one purpose: to breathe life into what he, along with Luther, considered to be the essential truth of his faith.

No 1 Sinfonia

In the Lutheran musical tradition, the events of Good Friday, i.e. the trial and execution of Christ, were narrated fully in settings of the gospel accounts – as with Bach's Passions according to St. Matthew and St. John. BWV 4 begins at the point when the crucified Christ is the prisoner of death. Its short prelude is a musical exploration of the bounded: tethered to its key chord of E minor, yet able to rise and fall within its limits. It is dominated at first by falling semitones in the first violin: part of music's vocabulary of sorrow, and here borrowed from the beginning of the chorale melody. From this emerges a series of rising phrases that reach a climax of lamentation before collapsing on to the final cadence.

No 1 Chorus (Verse 1)

The sopranos launch immediately into the chorale: "Christ lay in the fetters of death, given for our sins". Despite the solemnity of the message, the tempo is upbeat (*allegro*), as is the energy of the interwoven voices below, as they repeatedly echo the words. The two violins animate the whole with their perpetual motion. For the remainder of the text, Bach gives each line first to the lower voices, as if in conversation, before the entry of the slower-paced soprano hymn: "He is risen again and has brought us life; for this we should be joyful" (note the outpouring on *fröhlich*) "praise God and be thankful to him and sing Alleluia". The cries of "Alleluia" separate out as bursts of laughter and merge into an accelerated final section with more of the same. Time seems to stand still as the voices continue to celebrate and praise. Easter is a moment of euphoria for the promised escape from death.

No 2 Soprano/alto duet (Verse 2)

This is Luther's retelling of the old story of the expulsion from paradise: "There was no one who could master death, amongst all humankind. Our sin caused that; no innocence was to be found. For that reason death came so soon and gained power over us, held us captive in his kingdom. Alleluia!" As with the opening *Sinfonia*, Bach exploits the expressive potential of that first drooping semitone of the chorale melody. It colours the tale of human shame with its deep melancholy, intensified by the deliberately prolonged discords between the two voices. There are no communal festivities here, only a bare, elegiac lament accompanied by the repetitive patterns of the organ continuo. Even the final Alleluia becomes a series of wailing suspensions. Music and text inform us that, without Christ, humanity must cower in penitence and fear.

No 4 Tenor solo (Verse 3)

German Christians, for instance, looked forward on Easter morning to a good time celebrating Christ's harrowing of hell – his cosmic hooliganism when he triumphantly descended to the Devil's kingdom after dying on the Cross.

> Diarmaid MacCulloch: *Reformation*

Help is at hand: "Jesus Christ, God's Son, has come in our place and has removed out sin and with it has taken away death and all its claim and power. Now only death's outward from remains; it has lost its sting. Alleluia". Unison violins in perpetual athletic motion embody the divine hero's unconquerable strength in battle. There is a wonderful moment of drama when the champion despatches the monster with a few double-stopped sword thrusts, whereupon a snaky collapse in the continuo shows the enemy slithering to his death. He then slowly (*adagio*) fades away. The violins then resume their pace, and the singer combines with them in a brilliant Alleluia.

No 5 Chorus (Verse 4)

In this central movement, the onlookers appear to comment on the epic battle: "That was a wondrous war waged between life and death. Life gained the victory and swallowed death. Scripture has proclaimed how one death devoured the other and made a mockery of it". Bach brings a change of colour and texture, using the organ alone to support the rush of vocal counterpoint. He also gives the chorale melody as a *cantus firmus* to the alto line, surrounded on all sides by the commentary of the others. The devil that has been overcome is the same creature who robbed the first humans of eternal life; now their descendants may crow in spiky musical contempt (*ein Spott*, i.e. "a mockery"). The chorus ends with each voice engrossed in its own rejoicing yet blending into the universal cry of "Alleluia".

No 6 Bass solo (Verse 4)

The trope of decline and rebirth or renovation involves ritual that must be precisely observed, often in the form of human sacrifice or blood offerings to appease the gods and ensure their continued protection.

Richard Overy: *Why War?*

The physical and the spiritual confront each other in Luther's earthy imagery: "Here is the proper Easter lamb which God demanded, roasted in hot love on the spit of the Cross". With one act of perfect self-sacrifice, Christ has made himself the blood offering that reconciles the Creator with a flawed race of humans (the relationship of eater to eaten is complex, to say the least. Christ, whose death "swallowed up death", is now apparently a lamb kebab). Bach brings back the strings and adapts the hymn melody to a triple pulse, embellishing it and giving an imitative descant to the first violin. The continuo takes on its own expressive role, beginning with funereal descending semitones. At *Kreuzes* ("cross"), the melody writhes in symbolic torment against the harmonic backdrop of a diminished seventh chord.

After its sombre beginning, the contours of the music turn upward for the positive message of the text: "Its" (i.e. the lamb's) "blood marks our door, our faith displays it to death, and so the destroyer can harm us no more". Two theatrical gestures signal the opposition of life and death. A great plunge in pitch on *Tode* ("death") illustrates the abyss which threatened humanity before its redemption; Bach follows this with an upward leap to a heroically sustained high note to proclaim liberation from the destroyer (*der Würger*). The fourfold rhetoric of *nicht* ("not") finally waves him away. The final Alleluia is hearty and muscular, ending with a great vocal stride over two octaves.

No 7 Soprano/tenor duet (Verse 6)

Another transformation of the chorale turns it into a relaxed dance above the skipping rhythms of the continuo which, following the alternating patterns of BWV 4, is once again the sole accompaniment of the voices. All can, indeed must, now be happy: "So we celebrate the high feast with joyful hearts and the bliss which the Lord allows to shine through us; he is himself the sun, which through the brightness of his grace lights up our hearts completely; sin's night has vanished". The singers' swaying triplets continue into the Alleluia. Bach loved to give his cantatas a positive ending.

No 8 Chorale (Verse 7)

The emperor his father published an edict, commanding all his subjects, upon great penalties, to break the smaller end of their eggs. The people so highly resented this law, that our histories tell, there have been six rebellions raised on that account...It is computed that eleven thousand persons have at several times suffered death, rather than submit to break their eggs at the smaller end.

Jonathan Swift: *Gulliver's Travels*

Luther's hymn culminates in an allusion to the consecrated wafer that symbolises the sacrificial body in the ritual of the Eucharist: "We eat, and we live truly on the real Easter bread. The old sourdough does not contain the word of grace. Christ wants to be our food and feed the soul alone. Faith would live on nothing else. Alleluia!".

The words require some explanation. During Christianity's first millennium, one of the causes of dissension between its Eastern and Western branches had been the exact nature of the communion bread. The Orthodox Church favoured ordinary risen bread, considering it important to distinguish between Christian practice and the unleavened bread of the Jewish Passover. Luther, however, was at one with the Catholic Church (despite other points of difference) in maintaining the tradition of unleavened bread.

Accordingly, in this verse the rejected *Sauerteig* (natural sourdough) stands for the legalistic Old

Testament covenant with God, which must give way to the new covenant promised by Christ's crucifixion, and which grants salvation through faith alone. The old yeast dough must be replaced by the purity of unleavened bread, sign of God's grace and the true food of the soul. This is the *Osterfladen* (flat Easter bread) referred to in the hymn. Bach's setting at least needs little comment. It is a four-part harmonisation, with voices doubled by instruments, and the endpoint of the cantata's lesson on the meaning of Easter.

*

Suggested recording: The Monteverdi Choir, dir. John Eliot Gardiner

Easter Day

BWV 31: *Der Himmel lacht! Die Erde jubilieret!*

(The heavens laugh! The earth rejoices!)

Librettist: Salomon Franck

1715, though with later revisions

Utnapishtim said: 'There is no permanence. Do we build a house to stand for ever, do we seal a contract to hold for all time? Do brothers divide an inheritance to keep forever, does the flood-time of rivers endure? It is only the nymph of the dragonfly who sheds her larva and sees the sun in his glory. From the days of old there is no permanence'.

The Epic of Gilgamesh, trans. N.K. Sanders

Death and rebirth in the cycle of nature have inspired numerous myths across time and culture. If, for instance, the tale of the resurrection of the Egyptian God Osiris dates back several millennia, that is not to discount the power of the Christian re-telling, but only to confirm its deep roots in the human resistance to mortality. Easter, therefore, is the central event in the Church year as through the person of the risen Christ it holds out the promise of eternity for all. The particular character of the Christian version derives from the attitude to life that it promotes: a view of existence that sees the present always in terms of one's other-worldly destiny. To reject the appeal of the bodily now in favour of the hope of heaven was – at least in the Lutheran faith of the cantata texts – the condition both of true virtue and of the deepest joy.

BWV 31 combines pageantry and reflection. Its libretto is by the prolific Weimar poet and official Salomon Franck (1659-1725), and Bach's orchestral forces are sumptuous: three trumpets, drums, four oboes, bassoon, five string parts, cellos, double bass and organ continuo. With great acclaim of the Almighty, the music presents Christ as the warrior leader whose heroic example all must aspire to follow. Yet as the text moves to the inner battle awaiting the human in its personal struggle with sin and death, so the loud, public quality of the opening movements gives way to quieter meditation. The musical language of the cantata as a whole is relatively untroubled, with little harmonic disruption, for it carries a message of confidence and hope.

No 1 Sonata

Grandeur, energy, splendour: these are the hallmarks of a prelude that pays homage in sound to the risen God. Its style is that of the instrumental concerto, with distinct groups of instruments – brass, woodwind, strings – separating out and then recombining in a jam session of joy. It begins and ends with a great six-bar fanfare for all the players in unison, underlined by a pounding drumbeat. Out of this emerge imitative figures for the trumpets, passed in turn to the oboes, strings and an active continuo contingent below. The result is a quasi-martial display of pure triumph: victory over death. While the musical material stays the same, Bach creates variety by steering the underlying key along a cycle of fifths, driving onward until the final assertion of power.

No 2 Chorus

Whether or not the Venerable Bede was right to suppose that the word "Easter" derives from the name (Eostre) of the Germanic goddess of springtime, the truth is that this festival, at the heart of Christian belief, coincides with the regeneration of the natural world. Franck's text here –

"The heavens laugh! The earth, and all that she carries in her bosom, rejoices" – seems to agree. A five-part chorus (two sopranos), otherwise virtually unknown in Bach's sacred cantatas, joins the large orchestral ensemble. The initial solidity of *Der Himmel* ("The heavens") instantly dissolves into an overspill of laughter, imitated by the voices in turn. Similarly, *jubilieret* ("rejoices") takes on the same character of irrepressible happiness, punctuated as before by the acclamation of trumpets and drums. It goes without saying that the interweaving and accumulation of the parts displays Bach's peerless skill.

The next portion of text – "The Creator lives! the Highest triumphs and is free from the snare of death" – is set similarly, with the vocal elaboration now on *lebt* ("lives") and *triumphieret* ("triumphs"). After this, however, a sudden change of gear, conceptually and hence musically, looks to the central mystery: "He who chose the grave for his rest, the most holy one, cannot decay". The tempo slows to *adagio*, the keys change to the minor (A, followed by D), and the vocal lines linger over the thought. Yet this, i.e. the imperishable nature of the divine, is the real cause of celebration, and so the initial pace resumes for a dazzling fugal confirmation that "the most holy one cannot decay". As fugue itself relies on thematic renewal, it is a perfect metaphor for the process of resurrection.

No 3 Bass recit

The spotlight moves to the individual as he turns from the festive crowd, humming to himself (see how the initial phrase echoes what has gone before) and considering what the resurrection means to him personally: "The wished-for day! Be happy again, my soul". The music slips from recitative to a more flowery *arioso*, with voice and continuo following each other's lyrical path. From this, the librettist unwinds the theological argument that if Christ overcame death, then his human acolytes may do the same. Bach sets all this as a spontaneous process of thought, with its stops and starts and pausing for reflection. A slow tempo (*adagio*) looks to human blame for the Saviour's sacrifice: "The A and O, the first and the last" (note the drop of a seventh) "whom our heavy guilt placed in death's dungeon" – and then gains pace (*allegro*) for the happy outcome: "has now been snatched out of distress".

An analogous sequence follows. First, the slow marvelling of: "The Lord was dead, and look, he lives again!"; next, a calm, melodious, flow of voice and continuo for the lesson to be drawn: "If our head lives, so shall his limbs". The final images lead the listener from the horror of the crucifixion to the glorious living Christ: "The Lord holds in his hand the keys of death and hell. He whose garment was splashed blood red in his bitter suffering will today clothe himself with finery and honour". A ninth tempo change (*andante*) in a mere thirty bars brings the movement to a smooth and stately conclusion.

No 4 Bass aria

Enter the victorious figure of Christ: "Prince of life, mighty warrior, highly praised Son of God". Stiff and formal, the dotted rhythms speak of majesty. The tone colours are equally unbending, as cello, double bass and organ unite in a display of strength; no other instruments are invited. Bach gives the same ramrod posture to the voice part, though leaving room for a prolonged setting of *Lebens* ("life") and *höchsten* ("highly"). A change of key, though not of style, arrives with the continuation of the text: "Does what previously bound you" (note the tied, i.e. "bound" notes to illustrate *gebunden*) "now become your finery and jewel? Must your purple wounds become bright rays of light?". Such an elevation of suffering is, of course, a mainstay of the Christian outlook, and the lesson ends with a repeat of the opening salutation to the resurrected God.

No 5 Tenor recit

From now on, BWV 31 moves toward preparation for the fate that all must in time confront. The words of this recitative rouse the listener to a better way of being: "So rise up spiritually with Christ, you whose soul is devoted to God! Set out on the new course in life! Up! (the voice rises with the rhetoric) "From your dead works! Let your Saviour live in you and be the lifelong object of your thoughts!" All of this corresponds to Luther's focus on the inner, rather than the outer self. Actions could never be enough for divine favour; a perpetual striving for faith was the only route to eternal life. The librettist backs up his preaching with allusions to John's gospel (Ch. 15): "The vine that blooms now will bear no dead fruit! The tree of life makes its branches live". There is nothing to fear: "A Christian flees" (with a rush of an F major scale) "hurrying from the grave. He leaves the stone, he leaves the garment of sin behind and chooses to be alive with Christ".

No 6 Tenor aria

Compliant harmony and melody in the key of G major become the musical tokens of spiritual renewal: "Adam must decay in us if we are to recover the new man who is created in God's image". Strings alone accompany the inclination to faith, for the modest status of the human could not aspire to the triumphalism of trumpets and drums; the rocking motion of the first violin part decorates the simple outlines of its melody. Against this easy background, the singer completes his message: "You must be resurrected in the spirit and leave the graves of sin if you are a limb of Christ". The key moves gently to the relative (E) minor, not so much to indicate a shadow as to bring tonal variety to the structure. The aria ends with a restatement of its opening bars.

No 7 Soprano recit

From the beginning, BWV 31 has gradually narrowed its focus, moving from the pageantry of the first two movements to reach at last the inner core of the self. The soprano, as so often, takes the part of the soul: "As the head naturally draws its limb with it, so nothing can separate me from Jesus". Faith enables endurance, for it leans on the hope of a better world in the hereafter: "If I must suffer with Christ" (the diminished seventh harmony on *leiden* acknowledges the pain) "so I will also after this time rise again with Christ to honour and splendour". The voice ascends to C major and, along with the continuo, proceeds in fanfare-like steps to its imagined apotheosis: "and see God in my flesh!".

No 8 Soprano aria

What greater test of faith could there be than the immediate longing to depart from life?: "Final hour, descend upon me and close my eyes!" Only the key of C major links this intimate setting to the brilliance that launched BWV 31. Instead of their previous vigour, cello and double bass give quiet support, either *pizzicato* or in long pedal notes as if anticipating the stillness of death. The expressive timbre of a solo oboe d'amore partners the soul's desire; there is no drama here, merely the unbroken poetry of longing, all the more affecting for its understated manner. Bach is particular about the alternations of loud and soft that enhance the emotional effect.

A repeated motto for both voice and instrument sinks down with the sighing duplets that characterise the whole aria. Yet the phrases soar upward as the soul turns to its vision of the resurrected Christ: "Let me see Jesus's light of joy and look upon his bright light! Let me be like the angels!" Within the texture of voice, oboe and continuo, Bach adapts the melody to the triple pulse of the aria, making sure that its presence is felt by giving it to violins and violas in unison and presenting it, line by line, in the style of a *cantus firmus*. As with so much of Bach's sacred music, this movement embodies a puzzle: how can it be easy to renounce a life that contains the consolation of such art? Presumably the music will be even better in heaven.

No 9 Chorale

The final thoughts of BWV 31 arrive in the form of a verse by Nikolaus Herman (1500-1561). An early supporter of the Reformation, he shared Luther's fervent belief in Christ's redemptive power. His hymn prepares the mind for its end: "Then I go forth to Jesus Christ with outstretched arms; then I fall asleep and rest well; no man can wake me, for Jesus Christ, God's son, who will open heaven's door, will lead me to life everlasting". While the four vocal parts are doubled by strings and oboes, a soaring descant for first violin and trumpet conducts the believer to heaven.

*

Suggested recording: Bach Collegium Japan, dir. Masaaki Suzuki

A Note on Translations

In preparing my own translations of the libretti of the cantatas, I have consulted both Melvin P. Unger's Handbook and the versions by Richard D.P. Jones in his translation of Alfred Dürr's guide to the cantatas (details of both are in the bibliography). The German is quite straightforward, even if the theological concepts are particular to the time and place. I have aimed to be literal rather than literary; any errors are mine.

Sources and Select Bibliography

The essential source is, of course, the *Neue Bach-Ausgabe*: the authoritative edition of the cantata scores, published by Bärenreiter and edited by the great Bach scholar Alfred Dürr. His complete musicological guide to all of Bach's cantatas, sacred and secular, is similarly invaluable, as is Melvin P. Unger's compendium of all the texts, with detailed theological references: for details of both these volumes, see below. Amongst online sources for the complete texts of the hymns that are a constant presence in the cantatas, the Bach-Cantatas website is particularly useful.

As this present book places musical and textual analysis within a further context of ideas and cultural history, it would be impossible to list each separate stimulus for the connections made; but of the myriad writers and thinkers who have helped give me a wider picture, I can at least thank the following:

Armstrong, Karen. *The Bible: The Biography*. London: Atlantic, 2007
Bauman, Zygmunt. *Liquid Modernity*. London: Polity Press, 2000
Beattie, Tina. *The New Atheists: the twilight of reasons and the war on religion*. London: Baron, Longman & Todd, 2007
Bell, Catherine M. *Ritual Theory, Ritual Practice*. Oxford: Oxford University Press, 2009
Benson, Ophelia and Jeremy Stangroom. *Why Truth Matters*. London: Continuum, 2006
Berkhoff, Louis. *The History of Christian Doctrines*. London: Banner of Truth Trust, 1969
Berlin, Isaiah. *Four Essays on Liberty*. Oxford: Oxford University Press, 1969
Boudon, Raymond. *The Poverty of Relativism*. Oxford: Bardwell Press, 2005
Bukofzer, Manfred. *Music in the Baroque Era*. New York: J.M. Dent, 1947

Burkert, Walter. *Homo Necans*. Trans. Peter Bing. Berkeley: University of California Press, 1983
Burleigh, Michael. *Sacred Causes*. London: HarperPress, 2006
Burton, Robert. *The Anatomy of Melancholy*. New York: New York Review of Books, 2001
Butt, John, ed. *The Cambridge Companion to Bach*: Cambridge: Cambridge University Press, 1997
Calvino, Italo. *Why Read the Classics?* Trans. Martín McLaughlin. London: Vintage, 2000
Carey, John. *What Good are the Arts?* London: Faber and Faber, 2005
Chadwick, Henry. *The Early Church*. London: Hodder & Stoughton, 1968
––, *East and West*. Oxford: Oxford University Press, 2003
Chafe, Eric C. *Analysing Bach Cantatas*. New York; Oxford: Oxford University Press, 2000
Clark, Christopher M. *Iron Kingdom: the rise and downfall of Prussia*. London: Penguin, 2007
Cohn, Norman. *The Pursuit of the Millennium*. London: Pimlico, 1993
Conquest, Robert. *Reflections on a Ravaged Century*. London: John Murray, 1999
Cooke, Deryck. *The Language of Music*. Oxford: Oxford University Press, 1959
Daniell, David. *William Tyndale*. New Haven, Connecticut: Yale, 2001
David, Hans and Arthur Mendel. *The Bach Reader*. New York: W.W. Norton & Company, 1998
De Waal, Frans. *Our Inner Ape*. London: Granta, 2005
Desmet, Mattias. *The Psychology of Totalitarianism*. London: Chelsea Green, 2022
Dixon, Norman F. *Our Own Worst Enemy*. London: Futura, 1988
Douglas, Mary. *Leviticus as Literature*. Oxford: Oxford University Press, 1999
––, *Natural Symbols*. London: Routledge, 2003
Draaisma, Douwe. *Why Life Speeds Up as you Get Older*. Trans. Arnold and Erica Pomerans. Cambridge:

Cambridge University Press, 2006
Dunbar, Robin. *The Human Story*. London: Faber, 2004
Dupuy, Jean-Pierre. *The Mechanisation of the Mind.* Trans. M.B. DeBevoise. Princeton: Princeton University Press, 2000
Dürr, Alfred. *The Cantatas of J.S. Bach: with their librettos in German-English parallel text*. Revised and translated by Richard D.P. Jones. Oxford: Oxford University Press, 2005
Edelman, Gerald M. *The Remembered Present: a biological theory of consciousness*. New York: Basic Books, 1989
Edwards, David L. *Christianity: the first two thousand years*. London: Cassell, 1998
Edwards, Paul. *Heidegger's Confusions*. Amherst, New York: Prometheus Books, 2004
Gardner, Howard. *Frames of Mind: the theory of multiple intelligences*. London: Fontana Press, 1993
Geertz, Clifford. *The Interpretations of Cultures: selected essays*. London: Fontana Press, 1993
Gellner, Ernest. *Conditions of Liberty: Civil Society and its Rivals*. London: Penguin, 1996
Ginsborg, Paul. *The Politics of Everyday Life*. New Haven, Connecticut: Yale University Press, 2005
Gould, Stephen Jay. *Rocks of Ages: science and religious in the fullness of life*. London: Vintage, 2002
Graham, Angus C. *Disputers of the Tao: philosophical argument in ancient China*. La Salle, Illinois: Open Court, 1989
Gray, John. *Black Mass: Apocalyptic Religion and the Death of Utopia*. London: Penguin, 2008
——, *Two Faces of Liberalism*. London: Polity Press, 2000
——, *Heresies*. London: Granta, 2004
——, *Straw Dogs*. London: Granta 2002
Green, Arthur. *A Guide to the Zohar*. Stanford: Stanford University Press, 2004
Haidt, Jonathan. *The Righteous Mind*. London: Penguin, 2012
Hampson, Norman. *The Enlightenment*. Harmondsworth:

Penguin, 1976

Hay, David. *Something There*. London, Darton, Longman & Todd, 2006

Hempton, David. *The religion of the People: Methodism and Popular Religion, c. 1750-1900*. London: Routledge, 1996

Howard, Michael. *Liberation or Catastrophe: Soundings in the History of the 20th century*. London: Hambledon Continuum, 2007

Hudson, Liam. *The Cult of the Fact*. London: Cape, 1976

Huizinga, Johan. *Homo Ludens*. London: Routledge & Kegan Paul, 1949

Hume, David. *Of Superstition and Enthusiasm. The Scottish Moralists on Human Nature and Society*, ed. Louis Schneider. Chicago: University of Chicago Press, 1967

Jaynes, Julian. *The Origin of Consciousness in the Breakdown of the Bicameral Mind*. Harmondsworth: Penguin, 1982

Johnson, Samuel. *The History of Rasselas, Prince of Abyssinia*. Oxford: Oxford University Press World Classics, 1988

Jourdain, Robert. *Music, The Brain, and Ecstasy: How Music Captures Our Imagination*. New York; London: Harper Perennial, 1997

Kahl, Joachim. *The Misery of Christianity; or A Plea for a Humanity without God*. Trans. N.D. Smith. Harmondsworth: Penguin 1971

Karant-Nunn, Susan C. *The Reformation of Ritual: An Interpretation of Early Modern Germany*. London: Routledge, 1997

Kekes, John. *The Roots of Evil*. Ithaca, New York: Cornell University Press, 2005

Kevorkian, Tanya. 'The Reception of the Cantatas during Leipzig Church Services, 1700-1750'. *Early Music* 30.1 (February 2002): 26-44

Kingdon, Jonathan. *Self-Made Man and his Undoing*. London: Simon and Schuster, 1993

James, William. *The Varieties of Religious Experience*.

London: Longman's Green & Co, 1922
Lane Fox, Robin. *The Unauthorised Version*. London: Viking, 1991
Lang, Paul Henry. *Music in Western Civilization*. New York: W.W. Norton & Company, 1941
Lasch, Christopher. *The Minimal Self*. New York: W.W. Norton & Company, 1984
Lohse, Bernhard. *Martin Luther: an introduction to his life and work*. Edinburgh: Clark, 1987
MacCulloch, Diarmaid. *Reformation: Europe's House Divided, 1490-1700*. London: Allen Lane, 2003
Machiavelli, Niccolò. *Discourses on Livy*. Trans. Bondanella. Oxford : Oxford University Press, 1997
Marius, Richard. *Martin Luther: the Christian between God and death*. Cambridge, Massachusetts. London: Belknap, 1999
– –, *Thomas More*. London: Phoenix Giant, 1999
McGilchrist, Iain. *The Master and his Emissary*. New Haven, Connecticut: Yale University Press, 2009
Melanchthon, Philipp and Johannes Cochlaeus. *Luther's Lives: two contemporary accounts of Martin Luther*. Trans. and annotated by Elizabeth Vandiver, Ralph Keen and Thomas D. Frazer. Manchester: Manchester University Press, 2002.
Miller, Geoffrey. *Must-Have: the hidden instincts behind everything we buy*. London: Vintage Books, 2010.
Mishra, Pankaj. *An End to Suffering: the Buddha in the World*. London: Picador, 2001
Mithen, Steven J. *The Singing Neanderthals: the Origins of Music, Language, Mind and Body*. London: Weidenfeld, 2005
Monod, Jacques: *Chance and Necessity*. Trans. Austrian Wainhouse. London: Collins, 1972
Scott Bruce, ed. *The Penguin Book of Hell*. London: Penguin, 1967
Nurser, John. *For All Peoples and All Nations*. Georgetown: Georgetown University Press, 2005
Obermann, Heiko A. *Luther: Man between God and the Devil*. Trans. Eileen Walliser-Schwarzbart. New

Haven Connecticut: Yale University Press, 2006

Ozment, Steven. *A Mighty Fortress*. London: Granta ooks, 2005

Palmer, Martin. *The Elements of Taoism*. London, Element Books, 1991

Patel, Aniruddh D. *Music, Language, and the Brain*. New York; Oxford: Oxford University Press, 2008

Pelikan, Jaroslav. *Spirit versus Structure: Luther and the institutions of the Church*. London: Collins, 1968

Popper, Karl R. *The Open Society and its Enemies*. London: Routledge, 2003

Porter, Roy. *The Greatest Benefit to Mankind*. London: Fontana Press, 1999

Postman, Neil. *Building a Bridge to the 18th Century*. New York: Random House, 1999

Riches, John K. *The Bible: a very short introduction*. Oxford: Oxford University Press, 2000

Runciman, David. *The Politics of Good Intentions*. Princeton: Princeton University Press, 2006

Sacks, Oliver W. *Musicophilia: tales of music and the brain*. London: Picador, 2007

Sandall, Roger. *The Culture Cult: designer tribalism and other essays*. Boulder, Colorado; Oxford: Westview, 2001

Scott, Susan, and Christopher Duncan. *Return of the Black Death: the world's greatest serial killer*. Chichester: Wiley, 2004

Sen, Amartya. *Identity and Violence: the illusion of destiny*. London: Penguin, 2007

Sen, K.M, *Hinduism*. London: Pelican Books, 1961

Sennett, Richard. *Respect: the formation of character in a world of inequality*. London: Allen Lane, 2003

Smith, Anthony D. *Chosen Peoples; sacred sources of national identity*. Oxford: Oxford University Press, 2003

Steiner, George. *After Babel: aspects of language and translation*. Oxford: Oxford University Press, 1975

Storr, Anthony. *Music and the Mind*. London: Harper Collins, 1997

Stoye, John. *The Siege of Vienna*. Edinburgh: Birlinn, 2006
Stringer, Martin D. *A Sociological History of Christian Worship*. Cambridge: Cambridge University Press, 2005
Sutton, John L. *The King's Honor and the King's Cardinal: The War of the Polish Succession*. Lexington: The University Press of Kentucky, 1980
Toulmin, Stephen. *Return to Reason*. Cambridge, Massachusetts; London: Harvard University Press, 2001
Unger, Melvin P. *Handbook to Bach's Sacred Cantata Texts*. London: Scarecrow, 1996
Vermès, Géza. *The Resurrection*. London: Penguin, 2008
Wallin, Nils L., Björn Merker, and Steven Brown, eds. *The Origins of Music*. Cambridge, Massachusetts; London: MIT Press, 2000
Watts, Alan W. *The Way of Zen*. London: Ariana, 1999.
Weber, Max. *The Protestant Ethic and the spirit of Capitalism*, trans. Stephen Kalberg. Chicago; London: Fitzroy Dearborn, 2001
Webster, Richard: *Why Freud was Wrong: Sin, Science and Psychoanalysis*. London: HarperCollins, 1996
Wedgwood, Cicely V. *The Thirty Years War*. London: Pimlico, 1992
Weiskrantz, Lawrence, ed. *Thought Without Language*. Oxford: Calendar, 1988
Winkler, Heinrich A. *Germany: The Long Road West, vol. 1*. Trans Alexander J. Sager. Oxford: Oxford University Press, 2006
Winter, Ernst F., trans. and ed. *Discourse on Free will by Erasmus and Luther*. New York: Ungar, 1961
Wolff, Christoph. *Bach: essays on his life and music*. Cambridge, Massachusetts; London: Harvard University Press, 1991
--, ed. *The World of the Bach Cantatas: Johann Sebastian Bach's early sacred cantatas*. New York; London: W.W. Norton & Company, 1997
Young, John Z. *Programs of the Brain*. Oxford: Oxford University Press, 1978

Zimbardo, Philip G. *The Lucifer Effect: how good people turn evil.* London: Rider, 2009

Zuckerkandl, Victor. *Sound and Symbol; music and the external world.* Trans. Willard R. Trask. London: Routledge, 1956

Acknowledgements

Any book is the product of innumerable influences. It would be impossible to list all those, living or dead, who have opened up new ideas to me and enlarged my sense of life's paradoxical mix of richness and difficulty, the complex and the would-be simple. Some of these influences will be evident from references and epigraphs within this book. While writing this guide to Bach's sacred music and its context of thought, I have been given endless encouragement and practical support by my family. The memory of William Lovell is always with me.

My ideas and writing have been enriched by conversations with my daughter Julia Lovell, my son-in-law Robert Macfarlane, and my son Stephen Lovell. Their breadth of historical understanding and their literary judgement have been a constant stimulus and source of advice. I am grateful to them for so many far-reaching exchanges on history and culture and for helpful comments on my work. I would also like to thank Tony Watts for his consistent faith in the value of this project and the many discussions we have shared over the music and wider meaning of the Bach cantatas. His immense love of music and his perceptive comments on performance have been an invaluable support in the years since I first envisaged this book, as a continuation of a lecture course on the cantatas.

I owe a great debt to Rob and to Julia, for they have spared much time from their already packed lives to make possible the publication of this book. I can only thank them for their expertise, generosity and kindness. My guide to the cantatas is dedicated to them, with love.

Index of Cantatas in order of BWV Number

BWV 1: *Wie schön leuchtet der Morgenstern*	354
BWV 3: *Ach Gott, wie manches Herzeleid*	214
BWV 4: *Christ lag in Todesbanden*	361
BWV 13: *Meine Seufzer, meine Tränen*	220
BWV 14: *Wär Gott nicht mit uns diese Zeit*	255
BWV 16: *Herr Gott, dich loben wir*	154
BWV 18: *Gleichwie der Regen und Schnee vom Himmel fällt*	305
BWV 22: *Jesus nahm zu sich die Zwölfe*	322
BWV 23: *Du wahrer Gott und Davids Sohn*	328
BWV 28: *Gottlob! nun geht das Jahr zu Ende*	128
BWV 31: *Der Himmel lacht! Die Erde jubilieret!*	368
BWV 32: *Liebster Jesu, mein Verlangen*	203
BWV 36: *Schwingt freudig euch empor*	54
BWV 40: *Dazu ist erschienen der Sohn Gottes*	84
BWV 41: *Jesu, nun sei gepreiset*	148
BWV 57: *Selig ist der Mann*	97
BWV 58: *Ach Gott, wie manches Herzeleid*	173
BWV 61: *Nun komm, der Heiden Heiland*	42
BWV 62: *Nun komm, der Heiden Heiland*	49
BWV 63: *Christen, ätzet diesen Tag*	65
BWV 64: *Sehet, welch eine Liebe*	105
BWV 65: *Sie werden aus Saba alle kommen*	178
BWV 71: *Gott ist mein König*	280
BWV 72: *Alles nur nach Gottes Willen*	237
BWV 73: *Herr, wie du willst, so schick's mit mir*	226
BWV 81: *Jesus schläft, was soll ich hoffen?*	250
BWV 82: *Ich habe genug*	273
BWV 83: *Erfreute Zeit im neuen Bunde*	262
BWV 84: *Ich bin vergnügt mit meinem Glücke*	300
BWV 91: *Gelobet seist du, Jesu Christ*	72
BWV 92: *Ich hab in Gottes Herz und Sinn*	292
BWV 110: *Unser Mund sei voll Lachens*	78
BWV 111: *Was mein Gott will, das g'scheh allzeit*	232
BWV 121: *Christum wir sollen loben schon*	91
BWV 122: *Das neugeborne Kindelein*	134
BWV 123: *Liebster Immanuel, Herzog der Frommen*	185
BWV 124: *Meinen Jesum laß ich nicht*	198

BWV 125: *Mit Fried und Freud ich fahr dahin*	267
BWV 126: *Erhalt uns, Herr, bei deinem Wort*	311
BWV 127: *Herr Jesu Christ,*	
wahr' Mensch und Gott	334
BWV 132: *Bereitet die Wege, bereitet die Bahn!*	59
BWV 133: *Ich freue mich in dir*	111
BWV 144: *Nimm, was dein ist, und gehe hin*	287
BWV 151: *Süßer Trost, mein Jesus kömmt*	116
BWV 152: *Tritt auf die Glaubensbahn*	121
BWV 153: *Schau, lieber Gott, wie meine Feind*	166
BWV 154: *Mein liebster Jesus ist verloren*	191
BWV 155: *Mein Gott, wie lang' ach lange?*	209
BWV 156: *Ich steh mit einem Fuß im Grabe*	243
BWV 159: *Sehet, wir gehen hinauf gen Jerusalem*	340
BWV 171: *Gott, wie dein Name,*	
so ist auch dein Ruhm	160
BWV 181: *Leichtgesinnter Flattergeister*	317
BWV 182: *Himmelskönig sei willkommen*	347
BWV 190: *Singet dem Herrn ein neues Lied*	141

L - #0030 - 030325 - C0 - 229/152/25 - CC - DID4436256